New Directions in Economic Psychology

New Directions in Economic Psychology

Theory, Experiment and Application

edited by

Stephen E. G. Lea
Professor of Psychology,
University of Exeter

Paul Webley
Lecturer in Psychology,
University of Exeter

Brian M. Young
Lecturer in Psychology,
University of Exeter

Edward Elgar

Published by
Edward Elgar Publishing Limited
Gower House
Croft Road
Aldershot
Hants   GU11 3HR
England

Edward Elgar Publishing Company
Old Post Road
Brookfield
Vermont 05036
USA

A CIP catalogue record for this book is available from the British Library

Library of Congress Cataloguing in Publication Data
New directions in economic psychology: theory, experiment, and application/
  edited by Stephen E.G. Lea, Paul Webley, and Brian M. Young.
      p.   cm.
    Includes indexes.
    1. Economics–Psychological aspects. I. Lea, S. E. G., 1946–
II. Webley, Paul.   III. Young, Brian M.
HB74.P8N48   1991
330′.01′9–dc20

91–23879
CIP

ISBN 1 85278 462 8

Printed in Great Britain by
Billing & Sons Ltd, Worcester

Contents

Tables

Figures

1. Economic psychology: A new sense of direction

Stephen E. G. Lea, Paul Webley & Brian M. Young
University of Exeter

Economics and psychology share common intellectual roots. At least as they are practised in the English-speaking world, both have their origins in the philosophy of the 'British empiricist' school of the seventeenth to nineteenth centuries. But as they have developed in the nineteenth and twentieth centuries, they have drifted further and further apart.

In this chapter, we first argue that it is a difference in attitude to theory that has resulted in much of the mutual incomprehension between economists and psychologists. We then go on to show how the new generation of economic psychologists, which has grown up largely in Europe during the past two decades, has sought to overcome it. Finally, we show how a more empirical orientation has been developing in several different schools of economics recently; and how this is giving a new sense of direction to economic psychology.

THEORETICAL ECONOMICS AND EMPIRICAL PSYCHOLOGY

The separation between psychology and economics is in part inevitable. As each academic discipline accretes more knowledge and ideas about its own specific field, its practitioners are more and more able to devote their entire attention to their own specific interests; not just to their own discipline, but to their own specialism within that discipline. Links to neighbouring disciplines are necessarily weakened. But in some cases, there is a smooth transition between neighbouring disciplines. Between physiology and psychology, for example, or between economics and history, there is no very sharp boundary. Research in physiological psychology, or in economic history, grows up naturally between the two 'parent' disciplines, and does not have to belong very distinctly to either.

Between psychology and economics, however, there is a much more serious separation. The idea of an 'economic psychology' is quite old, dating back at least to the French social psychologist Gabriel Tarde (1902). (The phrase 'psychological economics' is even older, but it refers to a particular school of thought within economics, the late-nineteenth-century Austrian school, rather than to any seriously interdisciplinary effort.) But the concept of economic psychology did not take root very strongly, and many early-twentieth-century interactions between psychologists and economists were essentially unfruitful (see, for example, Florence, 1927). In the 1950s and 1960s, the only researcher widely known to be carrying on work in economic psychology was George Katona (for a summary of his main research see Katona, 1975, and, for a survey of his career, Wärneryd, 1982).

Why has there been this long separation? The subject matters of the two disciplines do not seem very far apart; both could fairly be described as sciences of human behaviour. The long predominance of the behaviourist paradigm in academic psychology, and in particular the influence of operant conditioning on general psychological thought, ought to have favoured increased interaction (Lea, 1978): modern economic theory has a strongly behaviourist stance, while the emphasis of operant psychology on the outcomes of behaviour and their incentive effect makes it a natural psychological foil for many kinds of economic analysis (for example, Alhadeff, 1982).

While there are many possible reasons for this separation between the two disciplines, recent trends in economic psychology suggest that one has been particularly important. Economics is dominated by a single theory; psychology is not.

Traditionally, economics and psychology have taken sharply different attitudes to empirical data. At the beginnings of economics and psychology as independent disciplines, the idea of deliberate empirical investigation in social science hardly existed. There is much empirical material in *The wealth of nations* (Smith, 1776/1908), for example, or in William James's (1891) early textbook of psychology; but in both cases it consists mainly of what every reader would know from his or her everyday experience, whether of the economic world or of mental life. The two disciplines developed in very different directions from this position. Economics became more and more theory-driven, with the role of any kind of data attenuating almost out of sight. In psychology, on the other hand, a very strong experimental tradition developed. New data were systematically sought through experiments, and theories rejected or revised in the light of them. The result has been that large-scale theory building has become practically impossible, and its role in modern psychology is really very slight.

The theory of rational choice is not, of course, accepted by every economist, nor is it a necessary part of every economic investigation. But it is part of the language and intellectual apparatus of everyone who has been educated as an economist, so that if we ask for 'the economic approach' to a particular theoretical question, there is no doubt about what we mean. Nor is there usually any difficulty in stating it, though the currently accepted economic theory of any particular economic phenomenon will naturally change over time.

In contrast, it is practically impossible to state the psychological position about any topic. In the first place, many different psychological positions are possible. Early texts in economic psychology (for example, Reynaud, 1974/81, Chap. 2) attempt to survey the implications for economic behaviour of various schools of psychology, such as psychoanalysis, behaviourism, and gestalt psychology. They do not agree, and this is likely to lead to frustrating experiences for the economist who wants to know what his or her psychological colleagues have to say about a particular issue.

But there is a second and more fundamental difficulty. Even a single school of psychology is unlikely to take a consistent view of a given economic phenomenon. As new experimental or observational data come to hand, so each theoretical school modifies its position. In an ideal world, these modifications would lead to greater unity, but in practice they have not yet done so. Theoretical standpoints are not irrelevant, even in empirical psychology, for they determine what data will be thought important and how they will be interpreted.

This difference in attitudes to theory and data has hindered the development of a truly interdisciplinary economic psychology in two ways. First, it has made it more difficult for there to be a smooth transition between economics and psychology. If an investigation is cast within the framework of the rational choice theory, it is likely to be seen as part of economics. If it is cast as an empirical investigation to determine what kind of theory might be appropriate, it is likely to be seen as part of psychology. There are exceptions, of course, but the difficulty is real. A second consequence is that discussion has focused on the issue of rationality, at the cost of other and perhaps more tractable questions.

Lea, Tarpy and Webley (1987, Chap. 5) argued that testing the assumption of rationality has become a paradigm for economic psychology. Such testing can take place at two levels: either the axioms of rationality may be attacked, or the deductions made from them for particular economic behaviours may be questioned.

The axioms of individual rational choice, as they appear in sophisticated treatments of demand theory (for example, Debreu, 1959; Simmons, 1974), appear to be clear statements about the behaviour of individuals; they appear to lie at the heart of economic theory; and, to most psychologists, they appear to be quite wrong. A few economists have also seen them as being open to empirical investigation (for example, Papandreou, 1957). The results of direct tests of the choice axioms are in fact quite inconclusive, but in any case, it has been strongly argued that they are beside the point (for example, Friedman, 1953). The axioms, Friedman argues, are abstractions. So long as the axioms make correct predictions at the economic level, their truth or falsity as descriptions of individual choice behaviour is irrelevant. The problem between economics and psychology, therefore, derives from differences in their ground rules of enquiry. In psychology, any statement claimed as fundamental must be subjected to empirical test, even if to do so, artificial situations must be constructed; in economics, interest focuses on constructing a coherent theoretical system which can be compared with the entire economic system.

MODERN ECONOMIC PSYCHOLOGY

Origins

Friedman's argument carries a good deal of weight. But it is less persuasive when we look, not at laboratory experiments on the axioms of choice, but at empirical studies of real economic behaviour. This has been the focus of the modern movement in economic psychology. The origins of this movement, which has been much stronger in Europe than in North America, are various, but two important influences can be detected, and oddly enough both are American. The first is the research of George Katona. Although Katona was a psychologist by training, circumstances (partly the accidents of wartime) led him to work on macroeconomic problems. But he retained a strongly data-driven approach. The second is the empirical work on consumer behaviour which in North America has tended to be identified as a separate branch of psychology (consumer psychology) or even as a separate discipline (consumer science). In either case it has a strong bias towards application in marketing contexts, with a very strong emphasis on empirical generalization rather than a priori theorizing.

These two influences have been synthesized within modern economic psychology. The resulting intellectual movement linked economists and psychologists who had in common an empirical approach to actual economic behaviour. In effect, they were concerned to look at some some of the consequences of the axioms of rational choice, rather than at the axioms themselves. This approach has been thriving for the past quarter-century, and is now becoming a fairly well organized sub-discipline. A number of books on economic psychology have appeared, both at the introductory level (for example, Maital, 1982; Furnham and Lewis, 1986) and more exhaustively (Lea *et al.*, 1987; Van Raaij, Van Veldhoven and Wärneryd, 1988). The *Journal of Economic Psychology* first appeared in 1981. Although quantitatively rather more psychologists than economists have been involved, some of the most significant contributions have come from economists (for example, Scitovsky, 1976, 1986; Earl, 1983).

Let us look at two case histories of this new, pragmatic approach. Neither of them is dominated by researchers who would think of themselves as economic psychologists, but both have been influential within economic psychology.

Risky choice

Edwards (1954) presented the ideas of decision theory to a psychological audience that was largely ignorant of them. That article covered a number of fields, but the one which bore most fruit was his discussion of the rational theory of risky choice, and this dominated his subsequent review of the area (Edwards, 1961). An extensive empirical literature developed, investigating how the simple expected value theory must be modified to account for individual choice behaviour in laboratory situations (for example, Davidson, Suppes and Siegel, 1957). There were some false trails in this research. Despite great mathematical sophistication (for example, Tversky, 1967), attempts to find consistent functional forms for utility or subjective probability functions failed. Enduring success, however, came when Tversky and Kahneman (1974) formulated their 'choice heuristics', followed up by 'prospect theory' (Kahneman and Tversky, 1979). Both these eschewed quantitative statements, but argued for consistent qualitative trends away from superficially rational decision making.

Saving

As a second example, consider the study of saving behaviour. Friedman (1957) developed the permanent income theory, to account for lifetime patterns of saving as a means of maximizing lifetime levels of consumption. The theory takes into account the factors which should sway a rational saver/consumer in deciding whether to spend money on consumption now, or save it to fund later consumption. But the theory is open to at least two crucial empirical objections. First, in order to make it fit the data on the use people make of 'windfall' income, Friedman had to suppose that there was a subjective rate of discounting future income on the order of 33 per cent per annum, almost ten times the rates of interest obtainable on bank deposits in the USA at the time. Secondly, it is inherent in the permanent income approach that consumers should aim to die more or less destitute, or at least that they should make less and less provision for the future as they grow older and face shrinking life expectancy. Studies of bequests (for example, Menchik and David, 1983) suggest that retired people in fact continue adding to savings until their death. Research to resolve these inconsistencies into a satisfactory behavioural theory of saving continues (for example, Cordes, 1990).

In addition, however, economic psychologists have added considerably to our knowledge of saving by considering the behaviour involved for its own sake, rather than for what it might tell us about rationality. Katona (1975) was particularly concerned about saving because of its macroeconomic effects. Ölander and Siepel (1970) summarize quite an impressive array of early data on saving behaviour, and this has been added to extensively in recent years (see Lea *et al.*, 1987, Chap. 8; Wärneryd, 1989).

Is rationality irrelevant?

At this point, the psychologist feels entitled to declare that the assumption of rational choice is an inadequate guide to behaviour, and that if economists ever wish to become respectable social scientists, they must learn to do without it. Lea *et al.* (1987) argued that this reaction was misplaced, and resulted from a misunderstanding of the role of the assumption of rationality in economic theory. The economist can and should deal with the bequest data by assigning a utility to accumulated wealth, independent of its use in future consumption (for example, Clower and Johnson 1968), and with the subjective discount rate by investigating why future consumption has such a relatively low utility. The psychologist who then cries fudge is again missing the point. The assumption of rationality is not itself a theory to be tested, because as such it has no empirical content. Any consistent behaviour whatsoever can be held to maximize utility. The interesting problem is to find out what contributes to utility. Substantive theories are constructed within the assumption of utility, and these theories are in fact modified response to data.

Interestingly, this 'declaration of peace' by Lea *et al.* has been largely rejected by economists, who have responded that the idea of rational utility maximization really does have empirical content. Some have argued that rationality is meaningful and true, and represents the uniquely valuable contribution of economics to the social sciences (for example, Pen, 1988). Others claim that rationality is meaningful and untrue, and economists actually need the aid of psychology to knock it from its inappropriate pedestal (for example, Wanner, 1989).

Whether or not we agree that rationality needs further investigation, however, the advantages of focusing on its consequences rather than its axioms are obvious. Research on risky choice and on intertemporal choice has yielded valuable information on significant economic behaviours, and economists and psychologists have been able to collaborate effectively and to use each others' ideas. A similar situation exists in many other branches of economic psychology, where economists and psychologists are working together on common empirical phenomena. Coexistence, if not peace, has been established, and economic psychology is flourishing.

A NEW SENSE OF DIRECTION

Lea *et al.* (1987, Chap. 20) argued for a 'new paradigm' in economic psychology, to replace what they saw as the undue emphasis on testing rationality. They argued that the way forward lay in empirical explorations of the constant interplay of two causal processes: the influence of individual economic agents (consumers, workers, and entrepreneurs) on the economy, and the influence of the economy as a whole on individuals. Van Raaij (1981) presented a more elaborate model which makes the same essential point while taking more account of the role of economic institutions. It will be some time, if ever, before the focus shifts right away from the rationality question, but independent developments seem to be producing the kind of shift in approach that Lea *et al.* and Van Raaij had in mind.

The key to these developments is a gradual change in the attitude of economists to empirical data. This change goes back a good deal further than the European-led resurgence of economic psychology, but it has only recently begun to bear fruit within the mainstream of economic thought. In a number of schools of economics, data have begun to be given the central attention usually reserved for theory. We shall look at three examples.

Econometrics

The oldest is the study of econometrics.   Supply and demand functions, Engel curves, and the other mathematical functions which constitute the language of price theory, were originally abstractions. Their properties could, perhaps, be assumed or deduced in broad qualitative terms, but they could not be measured directly.   But the attempt to measure them is quite old, and it has now developed into a most sophisticated statistical science.   Schultz (1938) published the first fairly comprehensive set of demand functions for a large group of consumer goods in the USA, and Stone's (1954b) study of UK household expenditure was even more extensive.   For technical reasons, these early studies had to deal with one commodity or commodity group at a time.   Demand for different commodities inevitably interact, however, and as computing resources increased, whole systems of demand could be analysed in a single operation. Early examples (for example, Stone, 1954a) were limited in scope and involved making fairly drastic simplifying assumptions about the nature of demand, but this is now less necessary.

The chief use of such demand system analysis has been in applied economics, particularly in attempts to predict the macroeconomic consequences of economic trends or government economic policies. They have not yet borne heavily on the construction of economic theory.   And the results of the recent, sophisticated analyses are in some ways less easy to grasp than those of earlier 'single equation' studies.   None the less, for some time now, our empirical, quantitative knowledge of many different national economies has been such that an elementary textbook of microeconomics can introduce demand theory using real supply and demand data for real commodities (for example, Suits, 1970), not the smoothly flowing curves for imaginary commodities of the past. This change in emphasis is crucial.

The theory of rational choice is vital to econometric research. Microeconomic demand theory determines what functions should be measured; often it is necessary to build theorems from demand theory into econometric models as assumptions, in order to make it possible to proceed to the statistical analysis. Econometrics, at least as it exists today, could not dethrone rational choice from its central position in economic theory.   But it can and does help displace it from its central place in economists' attention.

Socio-economics

The second development we want to emphasize is much more recent. A great stir has been created during the past few years by the publication of Amitai Etzioni's book *The moral dimension* (Etzioni, 1988). In that book, Etzioni brought to prominence the word and the idea of socio-economics, which he introduces more fully in Chapter 2 of the present volume.

Socio-economics involves, as its name implies, a consideration of the social dimension in economic affairs: both the social origin and the social effect of economic trends and policies. In many ways it is a marriage of sociology and economics. What is important for our present argument is that it puts social factors first, and brings with it from sociology an emphasis on empirical work. The brilliant constructions of economic theory may thus be swept aside if they conflict with sociological data or lead to socially undesirable results. Yet many of its practitioners are trained and respected as economists. The result, once again, is an infusion of an empirical spirit into economics, in a way that can only be helpful to economic psychology. In many ways, the relationship between psychology and sociology resembles that between micro- and macroeconomics, and psychology has its own aggregation problem in trying to bring its findings and predictions to bear at the sociological level. But in their relationships with economics, the two disciplines have common problems and can readily make common cause.

The stir created by socio-economics has been almost on the scale of a paradigm revolution (cf. Kuhn, 1970). As is common in such situations, much research that was ongoing at the time can now be recognized as fitting well within the new movement. Chapter 14 of the present volume, by James, Jordan and Redley is a good example of collaborative research between economists and sociologists; it does not place itself under the banner of socio-economics but would assuredly be most welcome there.

Experimental economics

Between these two in age lies a third development, and one that takes up most of Part II of this book: Experimental economics. '. . . Economists', stated a typical 1960s introductory textbook, 'like astronomers, are unable to experiment' (Fleming, 1969, p. 57), adding the cautious rider, 'at least at present'. Events since then have proved that Fleming's note of caution was wise. Not only is there now a lively school of experimental economics, but the use of experimental methods is increasingly accepted within the mainstream of economic thought (though this process does still have some way to go).

Hey's chapter introduces experimental economics in some detail, so there is no need for us to repeat the history here. It is interesting to note, however, that the experimental tradition in economics has grown up to a considerable extent independently of experimental social psychology. It has developed its own conventions and standards (cf. Smith, 1982), some of them arguably improvements on usual psychological practices. Experimental economists, for example, rarely ask their participants to enter fantasy worlds; rarely if ever deceive or mislead them about the purpose of an experiment; and try to make financial rewards large enough to be economically significant. There are important lessons here for those economic psychologists who were originally trained in psychology. More important, though, these conventions go a long way to make it easier for fellow economists to take experiments seriously. And to take experiments seriously is to recognize that it is empirical data that must determine the direction a scientific discipline takes.

CONCLUSION

Here, then, lies the new sense of direction that we see in present-day economic psychology. The earliest interactions between economics and psychology were governed by the strain between psychological data and the economic theory of rationality. The progress that has been made in European economic psychology in the past quarter-century has been the product of economists and psychologists being willing to work together on common problems, without really resolving the underlying difference of paradigm. But now we see an empirical spirit beginning to take a firm hold on economics itself, and the intellectual leadership in economic psychology passing to empirically-oriented economists. In this intellectual environment, new kinds of interdisciplinary work become possible. We cannot say in detail what they will be. But the purpose of this book is to provide some indications of what may lie ahead if we take this new direction.

REFERENCES

Alhadeff, D. A. (1982). *Microeconomics and human behavior.* Berkeley, CA: University of California Press.

Clower, R. W., & Johnson, M. B. (1968). Income, wealth and the theory of consumption. In N. Wolfe (Ed.), *Value, capital and growth* (pp. 45-96). Edinburgh: Edinburgh University Press.

Cordes, J. J. (1990). Socio-economic perspectives on household saving behavior. *Journal of Behavioral Economics*, **19**, 273-284.

Davidson, D., Suppes, P., & Siegel, S. (1957). *Decision making: An experimental approach.* Stanford, CA: Stanford University Press.

Debreu, G. (1959). *Theory of value.* New Haven: Yale University Press.

Earl, P. E. (1983). *The economic imagination.* Brighton: Wheatsheaf.

Edwards, W. (1954). The theory of decision making. *Psychological Bulletin,* **51,** 380-417.

Edwards, W. (1961). Behavioral decision theory. *Annual Review of Psychology,* **12,** 473-498.

Etzioni, A. (1988). *The moral dimension.* New York: Free Press.

Fleming (1969). *Introduction to economic analysis.* London: Allen & Unwin.

Florence, P. S. (1927). *Economics and human behaviour.* London: Kegan Paul, Trench, Trubner.

Friedman, M. (1953). *Essays in positive economics.* Chicago: University of Chicago Press.

Friedman, M. (1957). *A theory of the consumption function.* Princeton, NJ: Princeton University Press.

Furnham, A., & Lewis, A. (1986). *The economic mind.* Brighton: Wheatsheaf.

James, W. (1890). *Principles of psychology* (2 vols). New York: Holt.

Kahneman, D., & Tversky, A. (1979). Prospect theory: An analysis of decisions under risk. *Econometrica,* **47,** 263-291.

Katona, G. (1975). *Psychological economics.* New York: Elsevier.

Kuhn, T. S. (1970). *The logic of scientific revolutions* (2nd edn). Chicago: University of Chicago Press.

Lea, S. E. G. (1978). The psychology and economics of demand. *Psychological Bulletin,* **85,** 441-466.

Lea, S. E. G., Tarpy, R. M., & Webley, P. (1987). *The individual in the economy.* Cambridge: Cambridge University Press.

Maital, S. (1982). *Minds, markets and money.* New York: Basic Books.

Menchik, P. L., & David, M. (1983). Income distribution, lifetime savings, and bequests. *American Economic Review,* **73,** 672-690.

Ölander, F., & Siepel, C. M. (1970). *Psychological approaches to the study of saving.* Urbana, IL: University of Illinois.

Papandreou, A. G. (1957). A test of a stochastic theory of choice. *University of California Publications in Economics,* **16,** 1-18.

Pen, J. (1988). Boekbesprekingen – Reviews. [Review of *The individual in the economy. De Economist,* **136,** 403-405].

Reynaud, P.-L. (1981). *Economic psychology.* New York: Praeger. (Originally published, 1974.)

Schultz, H. (1938). *The theory and measurement of demand.* Chicago: Chicago University Press.

Scitovsky, T. (1976). *The joyless economy.* New York: Oxford University Press.

Scitovsky, T. (1986). *Human desire and economic satisfaction.* Brighton: Wheatsheaf.

Simmons, P. J. (1974). *Choice and demand.* London: Macmillan.

Smith, A. (1908). *An enquiry into the nature and causes of the wealth of nations.* London: Bell. (Originally published, 1776.)

Smith, V. L. (1982). Microeconomic systems as an experimental science. *American Economic Review,* **72,** 923-955.

Stone, J. R. N. (1954a). Linear expenditure systems and demand analysis: An application to the pattern of British demand. *Economic Journal,* **64,** 511-527.

Stone, J. R. N. (1954b). *The measurement of consumers' expenditure and behaviour in the United Kingdom 1920-1938* (Vol. 1). Cambridge: Cambridge University Press.

Suits, D. B. (1970). *Principles of economics.* London: Harper & Row.

Tarde, G. (1902). *La psychologie économique* (2 vols). Paris: Alcan.

Tversky, A. (1967). Additivity, utility and subjective probability. *Journal of Mathematical Psychology, 4*, 175-202.

Tversky, A., & Kahneman, D. (1974). Judgement under uncertainty: Heuristics and biases. *Science, 185*, 1124-1131.

Van Raaij, W. F. (1981). Economic psychology. *Journal of Economic Psychology, 1*, 1-24.

Van Raaij, W. F., Van Veldhoven, G. M. M., & Wärneryd, K.-E. (1988). *Handbook of economic psychology.* Dordrecht: Kluwer.

Wanner, E. (1989). Economic psychology or psychological economics? [Review of *The individual in the economy*]. *Contemporary Psychology, 34*, 990-992.

Wärneryd, K.-E. (1982). The life and work of George Katona. *Journal of Economic Psychology, 2*, 1-31.

Wärneryd, K.-E. (1989). On the psychology of saving: An essay on economic behavior. *Journal of Economic Psychology, 10*, 515-541.

2. Socio-economics: Select policy implications

Amitai Etzioni
The George Washington University

Socio-economics is a new paradigm that seeks to combine the kind of variables typically encompassed by neo-classical economics with those contained in other social sciences. It emerges out of work by many authors, for instance Albert Hirschman, Harvey Leibenstein, Herbert Simon and Amatalia Sen. It is not so much seeking to replace the kind of analysis associated with neo-classical economics (and found these days also in other branches of the social sciences, for example exchange sociology and Public Choice political science), but to encompass these works in a broader framework, one that systematically adds the study of institutions, values and emotions to that of markets, rationality and choice behaviour (for additional discussion, see Etzioni, 1988). While socio-economics is clearly less parsimonious than neo-classical analysis, it claims to be able to predict and explain better as well as to stand on firm ethical grounds, claims not evaluated here. Instead the discussion focuses on the kind of policy analysis, suggestions and insights the new paradigm leads to. In the process, these are compared with those provided by neo-classical analysis.

As socio-economics is a new discipline, often we need to indicate not only what it recommends, but also the lines of research needed to further support the suggested lines of policy analysis.

A quick example will serve to illustrate this approach. Neo-classical works in labour economics that summarize the state of the art, often discuss efforts to increase incentives for work performance. These books focus almost exclusively on monetary incentives such as differences between wages and salaries, pay-for-time vs. piece rates, and so on (see, for example, Bloom and Northrup, 1981; Reynolds, Masters and Moser, 1986). Socio-economics adds to such analyses

the concept of reference groups, that is, the observation that people
are also concerned with their relative (or nominal) wages and not only
with their absolute (or real) ones (Frank, 1985). The same may be
said about recognizing the *intrinsic* appeal of work (vs. leisure),
employees' desire for dignity and identity, the merits of employee
participation in decision making for certain categories of work, and
the significant role of corporate culture.

This chapter explores other major areas that seem to benefit from
incorporating studies of social factors. We shall discuss policy
implications, but not the theoretical, paradigmatic issues involved.
The chapter draws on the author's book *The Moral Dimension:
Toward a New Economics* (Etzioni, 1988).

POLICY IMPLICATIONS OF ALLOWING SHIFTING PREFERENCES

Many neo-classical analyses take preferences as given and stable
(Stigler and Becker, 1977), assuming that individuals have a
particular and constant set of 'tastes', 'values', or 'aspirations'.
Changes in behaviour are assumed to result from changes in
'constraints' or income, but not in preferences. Thus, for example, a
neo-classical analyst investigating the reasons that consumption of
alcohol in the USA has declined since 1980 will typically ask if the
price of alcohol has increased, whether the age of drinking has been
raised and so on, but not whether the desire to consume alcohol has
been reduced due to changes in the valuation of 'drinking'. The neo-
classical explanatory conceptions do not really accommodate the fact
that these changes are due largely to two social movements, the
health-and-fitness movement and a neo-temperance movement,
especially MADD and SADD (Mothers and Students Against Drunk
Driving).

The reasons that neo-classicists treat preferences as fixed should be
briefly explicated and arguments for disregarding these reasons
provided. Information about preference changes, neo-classicists
assert, is 'ephemeral', based on 'soft', nonbehavioural data such as
surveys of attitudes; further, preference changes involve non-
observable states of mind. Without asking if or how such data can be
used or made reliable, let us note that the *same* tools that are used to
study economic factors can be used to study non-economic variables,
as they are reflected in actual behaviour. For example, following
Lancaster (1966), one may disaggregate the attributes of a car to
determine the price of purchasers are willing to pay for each of the

attributes, such as speed, design and colour. The *same* disaggregation can be used to determine the amount people are willing to pay for a car to be American or non-Japanese (say, after World War II) and the change (presumably the decline) in this preference over the postwar years. The same goes for any other values, for example, a car that is 'beautifully' designed, environmentally sound, and so on.

Neo-classicists argue that incorporating preference changes in the explanation of behaviour precludes useful analysis, because whenever behaviour changes, presumably we shall state that preferences have changed. There is, however, a satisfactory rebuttal for this argument. If we have enough observations over time, we can test hypotheses about changes in constraints *and* in preferences (including value changes that often cause preference changes). For instance, tax compliance has been shown to be affected both by the level of taxation (basically, the higher the tax rates, the lower the level of compliance), and by whether or not taxes are viewed as fairly imposed (Lewis, 1982). Thus, if an increase in compliance follows a period in which tax rates have not been reduced, and if in that same period numerous loopholes were closed, then all things being equal, we would expect that the change is due to an enhanced sense of fairness.

The argument of some neo-classicists – that they need not study preference changes, or the value changes that drive them, because these phenomena belong to 'different' disciplines (namely psychology and sociology) – may indeed be correct. It is an argument that favours the development of a more encompassing paradigm, one that encompasses both social and economic factors: socio-economics.

A key policy implication of a paradigm encompassing the study of changes both in constraints and in preferences is that when we design public policies, we need not limit our efforts to providing information (action which relies on the assumption that people have fixed preferences, but need to understand better the costs and benefits of the choices they face). Rather, we may also seek to appeal to people's values and alter their preferences by, for example, drawing on public education campaigns and on community leaders. Several recent social movements have catalysed changes in the American public's values, changes that came about years or decades after relevant information was available. The civil rights movement of the 1960s brought both institutional reforms and a general change in the beliefs Americans held; blacks have come to be more widely viewed as full-fledged citizens, deserving social justice. The women's movement that followed the blacks' push for civil rights, also achieved significant changes in America's values. Large segments of American society now consider the old adage, 'a woman's place is in the home', not only outmoded but offensive. The recent shift in attitudes towards death further attests to changes in American values. Previously, a person was considered dead if their heart and breathing had stopped. Today, the idea of brain death has assumed primacy, largely because the health care community adopted the standard. Other significant changes occur mainly when the social web of emotive forces found in peer groups supports behavioural changes, as in the recent condemnation of smoking.

Recently, the distinction between informing individuals and seeking ways to appeal to values in other behaviour has been highlighted by the efforts to slow the spread of AIDS. In 1989 the Surgeon General sent a brochure to every home in the United States and pamphlets were handed out to drug addicts in the back streets, informing Americans about the danger of AIDS, and what is to be done. While this campaign demonstrates the government's concern and interest in changing American's behaviour to stem the tide of AIDS, it is difficult to imagine the psychological processes that would cause an addict to change his or her ways because of a piece of paper. Beyond this information campaign, finding means to involve such addicts in supportive social groups similar to Alcoholics Anonymous are needed. The nation's homosexuals, much more of a community than addicts, have been much more successful in changing their behaviour.

In response to the argument for appealing to values in order to modify preferences, neo-classicists raise an ethical objection. They state that individuals ought to determine their own conduct, that the government should not interfere, and that those who object to consumer sovereignty and seek to influence individual tastes are élitist snobs who wish to impose their 'tastes' on others. (Few neo-classicists have the courage of Mishan, 1969, chap. 9, to apply the same logic to commercial advertising.) Socio-economics takes a different normative stance, arguing that some 'tastes' clearly ought to be modified, for instance, those which cause harm to others (for example, smoking and reckless driving) and those which demonstrate open disregard for community needs (such as dumping toxic wastes into lakes). In yet other instances, it is proper to appeal to people's values, such as fairness.

Nor is government the only way of influencing tastes, or coercion the proper means; the community is often the most effective agent, and voluntary appeals are a main tool. Hence, community leadership and education by parents, neighbours, peers and churches should be included in policy design. For example, smoking is being significantly curtailed as its social valuation is changing. Peer pressure plays a key role in generating the emotive force needed to help smokers to mobilize themselves to overcome this addiction.

While socio-economists have identified many of the variables that affect preferences, there is no parsimonious conception of the factors that cause preference changes. Numerous factors are cited, but there is little consensus about the list. To illustrate in a very preliminary way the kind of propositions that are needed, it has long been held that social movements tend to have a set 'natural history' (Michels, 1915/49; Weber, 1922/48). They rise rapidly and then gradually decay, both through 'secularization' (loss of commitment) and through sectarianism (internal divisions and strife). They rarely last. Hence, value changes based only on a social movement, if not followed by institutionalization, will have much smaller and shorter term effects than is widely assumed at the height of popularity of the social movement.

If these propositions are correct, the longer-run effects of a social-religious movement such as fundamentalist Islam, widely assumed to be a major factor in the Middle East in the coming decades, are likely to be quite limited. The same pattern is visible in the United States, where one can already witness the cresting and the beginning decline of the neo-temperance movement and perhaps even the health-and-fitness movement. The 'couch potato' trend, a new movement of acquiescence that celebrates the comforts of home as an antidote to a perceived harshness in the economic environment, may be slowly ascending only to follow the same pattern of other social movements – a rapid rise and a gradual decline.

It is not argued here that these propositions about the patterns of social movements have been sufficiently validated or are close enough to the data to be relied upon in policy making. Rather, the propositions are used to illustrate the kind of parsimonious theory we need which would enhance the inclusion of the factors that shape preferences in socio-economic analyses, and are used for policy analysis.

EDUCATION: PERSONALITY DEVELOPMENT

The disregard of education (as distinct from teaching skills and transmitting knowledge, or training) leads many educational reformers in the USA to focus their agenda too narrowly. They leave out the need for basic psychological preparation, especially character formation, an essential prerequisite for acquiring basic skills, an essential in turn for being an effective employee.

Plans to reform schools tend to overlook the significance of the home and parenting for education. Many young Americans grow up in unstable families (Norton and Glick, 1986) which may not be viable from an educational viewpoint. Frequent divorces, frequent rotation of boyfriends, and parents coming home from work exhausted both physically and mentally, create in many homes (whether one or two parents are present) the potential for a tremendous parenting deficit. Character formation requires the kind of close, loving supervision that is more likely to occur in a stable home environment, if one or both parents invest time and energy in it.

As a result, personality traits essential for the acquisition of specific skills (mathematics, English, and vocational) often remain underdeveloped. Children come to school lacking self-discipline; they cannot defer gratification, concentrate, or mobilize attention to the tasks at hand. It is futile to pump into these youngsters more mathematics, foreign languages, long hours of science or liberal arts. Even so simple a skill as typing is a case in point. One can teach a person the mechanics in less than one hour (where to place the fingers, how to adjust the margins). The rest is simply a matter of patience, the ability to repeat the same drill often enough, long enough.

Many studies find that students cannot do mathematics or write English. They do not concern such advanced matters as whether students can craft a powerful essay or analyse a calculus problem; at issue is the ability to do arithmetic and write a clear memo. Again, close examination as to what is required points in the same direction. The elementary rules can be taught quickly. When you subtract A from B and get C, tally B and C to verify that they make A; a sentence ends with a period, and typically includes a finite verb; and so on. The rest is a matter of self-discipline, the ability to adhere to these rules and not to jump to conclusions or ramble on in a paper.

One of the best bodies of data is that collected on a nation-wide basis by James Coleman and his colleagues at the University of Chicago (Coleman, Hoffer and Kilgore, 1982). The data show that children who study well also have well-developed characters. The youngsters in 'high performance' schools had two main attributes: they did a great deal of homework and they identified with their teachers, teaching and school. Homework is the giveaway clue; those who can do a great deal of it, largely unsupervised, have acquired self-discipline. And students need to respect their teachers, and see their assignments as meaningful. Otherwise they do not internalize self-discipline, do not make it part of their own character.

Several other studies (Rutter *et al.*, 1979, especially) reach similar conclusions. Programmes such as the Conservation Corps, and some of the drug treatment programmes, take young people who often are disoriented, lacking in motivation and skills. They aim to develop, first and foremost, their self-discipline, psychic stamina, the ability to mobilize and make commitments. Once that is achieved, acquisition of specific skills and employment becomes relatively easy.

Beyond being a prerequisite for good study habits, self-discipline is essential for making an employee show up for work regularly, be responsible for the quality of his or her production or take the initiative, in short, for work ethics.

What socio-economic policy would enhance the development of character? It is important to start early. Companies might offer their employees (mothers and fathers) more leave in the first two years of the child's development. Parents ought to be advised that premature emphasis on cognitive achievements (learning to read, multiply, and so on) and neglect of human development, is self-defeating. One presupposes the other.

Recognizing that such a transformation in child-care policy is unlikely, and that many parents probably will continue to spend relatively little time developing their child's character, public policy requires that schools step in. Schools may have to start earlier, say at age four, and be open longer during the day and into the summer, to make up for some of the lost parenting.

Finally, resources must be shifted from the top-heavy end of the educational structure to the lower levels – early education. Currently we often prepare youngsters poorly in primary schools, mistrain them in high school, and then graduate them with poor working habits. For all too many of them, we then spend the first two years of college trying to correct what went wrong in the lower schools, teaching remedial English, catching up on mathematics, and above all, trying to instil better working habits. It is much more effective, both from a sheerly economic viewpoint and from a human one, to help young people learn things right the first time around.

TOWARD A SOCIO-ECONOMICS OF INCENTIVES

Policies are concerned more with hierarchies (for example, within corporations or the government) than with the market; markets are said to be best left to their own built-in self-regulating mechanisms. Here we consider the question of the most effective policies for compensating those subject to control and guidance by hierarchies. Neo-classical analysis favours paying for performance rather than for time units (as in payment by piece of work acccomplished instead of paying a regular wage or salary). The elementary reason is that when paying for time one does not know what level of performance, if any, one pays for (Baker *et al.*, 1988, p. 595). This is more than a mere theory; the widespread criticism of bureaucracies (of governments but also of large corporations, for example GM) is indicative (for example, Cyert and March, 1963).

But Baker *et al.* (1988) show that pay for performance is in fact rarely used. Two of the studies they cite illustrate the point. Medoff and Abram found that in two large corporations they studied, there was little financial reward for superior performance. In one corporation employees whose work was ranked 'not acceptable', the lowest ranking, were paid only 7.8 per cent less than the very best ('outstanding'). In another corporation, pay of those whose work was 'unacceptable' was only 6.2 per cent less than of those who topped six ranks, employees whose work was ranked as 'excellent'. There was also a strong tendency to rank most employees as high performers. For example, in one corporation 95 per cent of the employees' performance was ranked as 'good' or better. Similarly, citing six different studies of the relationship between pay and performance, Lawler found that

> evidence indicates that pay is not very closely related to performance in many organizations that claim to have merit increase salary systems. . . The studies suggest that many business organizations do not do a very good job of tying pay to performance. This conclusion is rather suprising in light of many companies' very frequent claims that their pay systems are based on merit. It is surprising that pay does not seem to be related to performance at the managerial level. (Lawler, 1971, p.158).

Socio-economics shows that the factor most important in explaining compensation is rank, not performance. While ranks are indirectly linked to performances, bonuses would be more effective (Baker, *et al.*, p. 601). However, employees seeking relief from anxiety, wishing power and visibility, are more motivated by ranks, which helps to explain why ranks and not bonuses are by far the most common and important mode of differential compensation. The same factors account for the observation that when one tries to shift to greater reliance on pay for performance, the result is a very sharp drop in productivity, attendance and other measures of performance. Psychologists have found that monetary rewards can be counterproductive in some laboratory situations. One explanation (Deci, 1972) 'argues that money actually lowers employee motivation, by reducing the "intrinsic rewards" that an employee receives from the job.' (Baker *et al.*, 1988, p. 596). Slater (1980) similarly concludes that '[u]sing money as a motivator leads to a progressive degradation in the quality of everything produced' (ibid). Kohn (1988) offers further explanation on the counter-productivity of monetary rewards, stating, 'First, rewards encourage people to focus narrowly on a task, to do it as quickly as possible, and to take few risks. . . Second, extrinsic rewards can erode intrinsic interest. . . [Finally], people come to see themselves as being controlled by a reward.'

Socio-economics does not conclude that competition policies cannot be modified to be somewhat more performance oriented; however, a major shift may neither by possible nor beneficial because of non-economic needs of the employees, including professionals and managers, not just blue collar workers. All of the studies cited here deal with these kinds of employees.

INSTITUTIONAL CHANGE

Neo-classical analyses tend to focus on transactions among individuals or small units (such as households and small firms), and their aggregation in anonymous markets, that is, markets that are assumed to have no collective controls. To the extent that institutions are studied at all within this paradigm, they are generally perceived as reflecting arrangements made voluntarily and knowingly by individuals, in line with their interests and goals. Traditionally, other social sciences tended to view institutions as reflecting historical (macro) processes, society-wide values, and power relations. Socio-economics seeks to encompass both the influence of individuals and that of society. It attempts to combine aggregative analysis with collective analysis by assuming that collective factors provide the context and are 'priors' within which individuals act, and which in turn are affected by them.

The significance of systematically including institutional analyses lies in the fact that the existence of institutions hinders or assists policy. So, even if one does not seek to modify the institutions, their effects on policy must be taken into account. For example, a multiyear economic policy formed within the United States (say, a corporate development plan) that ignored the well-established economic effects of the four-year political cycle driven by presidential elections, is less likely to succeed than an economic policy that takes the cycle into account. All other things being equal, the expansive policies of election years provide a much more hospitable economic environment for a new product, or newly expanded production capacities, than the first year of a new administration. 'Bitter medicine' is usually prescribed during this first year; hence, the period tends to be economically restrictive. The cycle, in turn, reflects the Constitution and not an aggregation of individual decisions. Similarly, one must expect little success for a policy that ignores differences among institutions. For example, shifting law enforcement functions from the FBI to local governments is unlikely to be successful given the widespread corruption institutionalized in many local police forces. The same must be said about a policy that shifts responsibilities from the Internal Revenue Service or the federal Social Security Administration to local tax collection or welfare agencies.

Beyond accounting for the established features of existing institutions and the powerful inertia and vested interests they tend to generate, one must also recognize that institutions can be changed and policy advanced via such changes. Thus, instead of, or in addition to, using educational campaigns to encourage many millions of Americans to increase their saving, one can enhance saving by changing the tax laws, under some conditions by reducing corporate outlay on dividends (that is, by increasing retained earnings) or, more effectively, by reducing government expenditures.

Segregating Social Security from the unified budget, and investing its surpluses into a portfolio of American corporate and government bonds will do as much or more for the American savings rate than will, say, doubling the size of funds individuals can salt away, tax deferred, in their Individual Retirement Accounts (IRAs). While a constitutional amendment to balance the budget may well create several new problems, it would modify significantly the institutional context of the struggle to reduce federal deficits.

Similarly, aside from working on individual incentive schemes, corporations often benefit when they also introduce institutional changes such as increased co-operation with labour unions (as in the case of General Motors and the United Auto Workers in recent years), quality circles, or participatory decision making. None of these is automatically sure to have the desired result; more research is needed about the conditions of success versus failure. One may argue whether individuals or institutions are more powerful; however, one conclusion is clear: policy analysis should consider both individual, aggregative and institutional factors.

ARE CRIMINALS JUST LIKE US?

Neo-classical economists analyse crime in terms of costs and benefits.

They argue that the probability of being arrested and convicted, the size of the penalty, and the size of the loot, that is, costs and 'benefits', correlate with the frequency of a large variety of crimes being committed, including murder and rape (Andreano and Siegfried 1980; Rottenberg 1979). The data are subject to considerable methodological controversies, but these need not concern us here. To the extent that these data have demonstrated that self-interest plays an important role in situations hitherto considered the domain of impulsive behaviour, neo-classical economists provide an important correction to the over-socialized view of crime, a view that focuses almost exclusively on the role of education, subculture, peer pressure and other such factors. However, to the extent that neo-classicists suggest that self-interest accounts for all or most of the variance, they vastly overstate their findings (Cook 1980), and their conclusions will tend to mislead policy makers. Thus, for instance, Rubin's statements (1980, p. 13) that 'the decision to become a criminal is in principle no different from the decision to become a bricklayer. . . the individual considers the net costs and benefits of each alternative and makes his decision on this basis', and 'tastes are constant and a change in [criminal] behaviour can be explained by changes in prices [such as penalty]', tend to mislead. They ignore the fact that despite whatever correlations are found between 'prices' and level of criminality, much of the variance (in crime rates) remains unexplained, most likely because moral and other social factors are at work. Second, such statements overlook the fact that the 'taste' for crime, like all others, is affected by normative and other social factors, for example, by the extent to which the relevant subculture disapproves of the particular kinds of crime involved (Grasmick and Green 1981; see also Casson, this volume).

Similarly, statements such as Murray's (1984, p. 168) that 'crime occurs when the prospective benefits sufficiently outweigh the prospective costs' are not only formulated in a way that makes falsification impossible (if no crime occurs under a given set of conditions, under which it is expected to occur, the benefits might be said to not 'sufficiently' outweigh the costs), but also tend to mislead policy makers into disregarding the role of education, subculture, leadership, and role-models. Of special interest in this context is Wilson's (1985) discussion of the role of various 'impulse control' movements and organizations in nineteenth-century America. Wilson points out that as industrialization advanced, youngsters who once left their homes only to work in other homes under the supervision of other farmers or artisans, then started to reside in boarding houses in the cities, without any family bonds or authority. The result was widespread disorderly conduct. This was followed by numerous efforts to advance control of impulse and build up inner control, self-discipline, and 'character'. These included Sunday schools, YMCAs, temperance movements, and various other religious and secular voluntary associations. Some had other goals, but impulse control was a by-product; others were aimed directly at instilling self-discipline.

The policy point is that one needs to work not merely on the cost-benefit, deterrence, incentive, and police side but also on the formation of preferences side, via moral education, peer culture, community values, and the mobilization of appropriate public opinion, factors that neo-classicists tend to ignore because they take preferences for granted, and their theories provide no analytical framework to conceptualize the ways in which preferences are formed and might be reformed. The trouble with theories that fit into a deontological paradigm is that they include numerous, complex, propositions that are difficult to quantify. They may have to be synthesized, made more parsimonious and more operational, before they can effectively play their role next to economic analysis.

Neo-classical analysis of crime is largely based upon work pioneered by Gary Becker (1968). Becker's economic approach to white-collar crime is summarized by Richard Posner (1980): 'the white-collar criminal . . . should be punished only by monetary penalties – by fines (where civil damages or penalties are inadequate or inappropriate) rather than by imprisonment or other 'afflictive' punishments (save as they may be necessary to coerce payment of the monetary penalty)'. Becker states that '[a]ccording to the economic approach, criminals, like everyone else, respond to incentives' (Becker, 1985a). By setting fines equal to the harm the corporate crime inflicts on society, companies will be deterred from certain crimes and society will be compensated for the harm imposed. Thus, Becker poses the question, 'If guilty companies pay for the harm to society, why should we want to discourage white-collar crime that raises a country's wealth?' (Becker, 1985b).

Posner furthers this economic analysis of crime by arguing that fines can be an equally effective deterrent and are socially preferable because they are cheaper to administer than costly jail terms. He arrives at this conclusion using a cost-benefit analysis which weighs the cost of collecting a fine and the cost of imprisonment. An important qualification is that the offender must be able to pay the fine, and that the fine must be set equal to the disutility imposed by a jail sentence.

A socio-economic analysis of criminal sentencing is offered by John C. Coffee. Coffee (1980) argues that fines are an inefficient way to deter white-collar crime. He criticizes Becker and Posner's optimal sanctions approach – which he calls the Free Market Model – finding it flawed upon investigating 'both traditional elements of economic analysis (such as uncertainty) and non-economic factors that are deeply embedded in the structure of our criminal justice system (such as the tendency toward nullification of extreme penalties) (p.422)'. Whereas neo-classicists see fines as the optimal form of punishment, Coffee shows that the threat of incarceration is a greater deterrent than a monetary penalty.

Coffee criticizes the Becker formula for determining an optimal fine as too elusive a formula to implement (there are too many unknowns left to be solved). Coffee suggests we try to achieve equivalence between penalties as opposed to determining precise monetary equivalents for a penalty. Also, socio-economists explain that there are symbols involved in criminal sentencing as well as 'cut and dried' costs. For example, Coffee criticizes Becker's model of punishment because it fines the rich and jails the poor. Values come into play as Coffee states that '[c]riminal justice reforms must take into account the problem of demoralization costs' (p.448). This represents an institutional bias, and 'some means of seeking equivalence is necessary'. Answering this point, Posner retreats to his logic that there is a quantifiable fine equivalent for every prison sentence and the offender should be imprisoned if the fine is not collected. He is left questioning how the rich are favoured under such a system.

A RAND study (Manning *et al.*, 1989) is sensitive to the need for a dual perspective. First it deals with external costs of drinking alcohol and smoking cigarettes (costs not reflected in the price, such as making others sick), by itself a broader perspective than many neo-classical studies use. Next, it uses the size of the excise taxes imposed, taxes that recoup some of the social costs not reflected in the pre-tax, market price. They concluded that taxes on alcohol are not high enough, while those on cigarettes are high enough – if economic efficiency is the criterion for determining taxation. Costs are regarded as recouped, however, only because the authors deduct 'contributions' smokers make to pension funds and to social securities (they die young and hence often do not collect; see also Koretz, 1989).

Most important, the RAND study does not stop at evaluation from an economic efficiency viewpoint. It openly and explicitly calls attention to factors that might lead to imposing higher taxes on cigarettes than economic efficiency might call for. These are:

(a) Signs that those who start smoking under-evaluate the risk involved. Higher taxes would act as a substitute for proper evaluations (cf. Bolle, 1990);

(b)   Smokers show a desire to quit and taxes would help accomplish
       their desire;

(c)   One might add that smoking often starts at a young age, before
       preferences are formed.   Hence it is proper, as part of the
       societal re-education effort, to use taxes to discourage formation
       of these preferences, even if one holds that it is wrong to affect
       people's preferences once they have formed them.

CONCLUSION

In this chapter, I have used as a test criterion the ability to generate
public policies that seem useful.   We examined an approach that
encompasses both economic variables (of the kind neo-classical
economists typically study) and other social, psychological and
political factors, and found that this combination, called 'socio-
economics', may yield more effective policies in several arenas.
While it seems worthwhile to move toward the broader perspective
afforded by socio-economics, it is also evident that additional work
must be done to develop fully what here has only been outlined.

REFERENCES

Andreano, R., & Siegfried, J. J. (eds) (1980). *The economics of crime.* New York:
      Wiley.
Baker, G. P., Jensen, M. C., & Murphy, K. J. (1988).   Compensation and
      incentives: Practice vs. theory. *Journal of Finance*, **43**, 593-616.
Becker, G. S. (1968). Crime and punishment: An economic approach. *Journal of
      Political Economics*, **76**, 169.
Becker, G. S. (1985a). The economic approach to fighting crime. *Business Week*
      (June 10th), p. 16.
Becker, G. S. (1985b). Tailoring punishment to white-collar crime.   *Business
      Week* (Oct. 28th), p. 20.
Bloom, G. F., & Northrup, H. R. (1981).   *Economics of Labour Relations.*
      Homewood, IL: Irwin.
Bolle, F. (1990).   Habit formation and long-term contracts.   In S. E. G. Lea,
      P. Webley, & B. M. Young (eds), *Applied economic psychology in the 1990s*
      (Vol. 2, pp. 643-661). Exeter: Washington Singer Press.
Coffee, J. C. (1980). Corporate crime and punishment: A non-Chicago view of the
      economics of criminal sanctions. *American Criminal Law Review*, **17**, 419-
      471.
Coleman, J. S., Hoffer, T., & Kilgore, S. (1982).   *High school achievement –
      Public, Catholic and private schools compared.* New York: Basic Books.
Cook, P. J. (1980).   Punishment and crime: A critique of current findings
      concerning the preventative effects of punishment. In R. Andreano & J. J.
      Siegfried (eds), *The economics of crime* (pp. 127-136). New York: Wiley.

Cyert, R. M. & March, J. G. (1963). *A behavioral theory of the firm.* Englewood Cliffs, N.J.: Prentice-Hall.

Deci, E. L. (1972). The effects of contingent and non-contingent rewards and controls on intrinsic motivation. *Organizational Behavior and Human Performance*, **8**, 217-229.

Etzioni, A. (1988). *The moral dimension: Toward a new economics.* New York: Free Press.

Frank, R. H. (1985). *Choosing the right pond: Human behavior and the quest for status.* Oxford: Oxford University Press.

Grasmick, H. G., & Green, D. E. (1981). Deterence and the morally committed. *Sociological Quarterly*, **22**(1), 1-14.

Kohn, A. (1988). Incentives can be bad for business. *Inc*, **10**(7), 93-94.

Koretz, G. (1989). Smokers may be keeping social security healthy . . . but pricier smokes may still make economic sense. *Business Week* (5th June), p. 27.

Lancaster, K. J. (1966). A new approach to consumer theory. *Journal of Political Economy*, 74, 132-157.

Lawler, E. E. (1971). *Pay and organizational effectiveness: A psychological view.* New York: McGraw-Hill.

Lewis, A. (1982). *The psychology of taxation.* New York: St. Martin's Press.

Manning, W. G., Newhouse, J. P., Sloss, E. M., & Wasserman, J. (1989). The taxes of sin: Do smokers and drinkers pay their way? *Journal of the American Medical Association*, 261, 1604-1609.

Michels, R. (1949). *Political parties* (Trans. E. Paul & C. Paul). Glencoe, IL: Free Press. (Originally published, 1915.)

Mishan, E. J. (1969). *Twenty-one popular economic fallacies.* Harmondsworth: Penguin.

Murray (1984). *Losing ground: American social policy 1950-1980.* New York: Basic Books.

Norton, A. J., & Glick, P. C. (1986). One parent families: A social and economic profile. *Family Relations*, **35**, 9-17.

Posner, R. (1980). Optimal sentences of white-collar criminals. *American Criminal Law Review*, **17**, 409-418.

Reynolds, L. G., Masters, S. H., & Moser, C. M. (1986). *Labor economics and labor relations* (9th edn). Englewood Cliffs, NJ: Prentice-Hall.

Rottenberg, S. (1979). *The economics of crime and punishment.* Washington, DC: American Enterprise Institute.

Rubin, P. H. (1980). The economics of crime. In R. Andreano & J. J. Siegfried (eds), *The economics of crime* (pp. 13-25). New York: Wiley.

Rutter, M. *et al.* (1979). *Fifteen thousand hours.* London: Open Books.

Slater, P. (1980). *Wealth addiction.* New York: Dutton.

Stigler, G. J., & Becker, G. S. (1977). De gustibus non est disputandum. *American Economic Review*, **67**, 76-90.

Weber, M. (1948). The social psychology of the world religions. In H. H. Gerth & C. W. Mills (eds), *From Max Weber.* London: Routledge and Kegan Paul. (Originally published, 1922.)

Wilson, J. Q. (1985). *Thinking about crime.* New York: Vintage Books.

3. Everyday conceptions of necessities and luxuries: Problems of cultural relativity and moral judgement

Sonia M. Livingstone
The London School of Economics

Peter K. Lunt
University College London

'I don't think that they are luxuries . . . [they are] gimmicks, I think. Things like high pressure hoses to clean your cars'

'They are luxuries because they are things you can do without. I mean a high pressure hose is just a luxury, better than a normal hose'

'I think of luxuries in a different way. A luxury is something extra, which gives my life something a bit more than just having necessities'

An account of consumption in modern Western society needs to address the definition of needs in relation to the diversity of available goods, variation in people's resources and changing consumption patterns. In everyday life, people must decide what they need and want to consume. Equally important, they must account for these decisions to themselves and others. How can they relate their socio-economic context to personal decisions concerning necessities and luxuries? How can they justify their decisions in the face of alternative approaches? How do their accounts relate to their understandings of broader social and economic issues? This chapter focuses on ordinary people's accounts of the distinction between needs and wants, necessity and luxury goods. We begin by considering the role this distinction plays in the economic, psychological and anthropological theories of consumption.

THEORETICAL PERSPECTIVES ON THE NECESSITY/LUXURY BOUNDARY

Most early analysis of consumer behaviour was conducted in terms of needs or wants (Baxter, 1988), indeed such analysis provided the underpinnings for utility theory in economics, which sees individuals' maximizing behaviours as motivated by needs and wants. Various hierarchies of wants were constructed, moving from the lower-order wants to higher-order wants (cf. Maslow's needs hierarchy, 1970). As one moves up this hierarchy, there is increasing variety of goods to satisfy the need (Baxter, 1988), and so from a psychological viewpoint, goods increasingly provide a means of social distinction. This has both economic and psychological consequences.

In economics, individual mechanisms of incentive value, reinforcement and utility are related to the perception of goods as necessities or luxuries, thereby generating discernable patterns of demand and resources at the macroeconomic level. Economists normally define necessities and luxuries in terms of the Engel curve. This links income level to the proportion of income occupied by particular goods: luxuries are defined as goods that occupy a small proportion of low incomes and an increasing proportion of larger incomes; necessities take up a decreasing proportion of income as income increases. Psychologically, this curve is problematic. Consider the colour television. This is a necessity according to the Engel curve, presumably because it is an expensive, indivisible object and the advantages of having more than one are rather slight. None the less, as income increases we can obtain more prestigious and technologically sophisticated versions of the product. So although the proportion of income spent on a colour television declines as income increases, it is still true that richer people own more luxurious versions than do poorer people, and that this difference has significance for the social identity and status of both rich and poor. Such goods become cultural markers which direct patterns of social interaction, and, incidentally, subsequent consumption patterns. The decision to buy is linked to the construction of a lifestyle which itself influences social identity through comparisons with other groups' consumption patterns. Social norms influence this decision to buy, and so consumption patterns reflect normative influences – and social representations of consumers, lifestyles, and goods – on personal decisions. In psychological theory it seems more plausible to link the necessity/luxury distinction to the use of goods as cultural markers rather than to the relation between income and demand.

On this view, a complex social understanding is required to make decisions concerning necessities and luxuries, and ultimately concerning lifestyles and social identities: 'One's view of satisfiers must be coloured, of course, by one's view of the nature of needs and wants' (Baxter, 1988, p. 39). Although Baxter is referring to economic theories of consumer behaviour, his remark also applies to lay theories. As any good may satisfy more than one want, and as one want may be satisfied by a variety of goods, people's choices gain meaning through their broader theories of needs and wants, and so these broader theories, as well as the decisions in which they result, merit investigation.

Lay theories of needs and wants form part of the subject matter of the anthropology of consumption, which provides an alternative to the Marxist economic approach. In the Marxist approach, 'the freedom promised by capitalism is an illusion, since it is wrested away by the capitalist from the people and becomes merely the freedom of the wage labourer to be exploited by the capitalist' (Miller, 1987, p. 181; see also Sahlins, 1976). Thus the freedom to satisfy needs and wants is denied to the individual, for the individual is seen as constructed through the aims and practices of advertisers and producers. Within the anthropological approach, Douglas and Isherwood (1978) have argued that the value of goods cannot be reduced to their utility or competitive display status but must be analysed in terms of their expressive, socio-cognitive and ritual functions: 'Instead of supposing that goods are primarily needed for subsistence plus competitive display, let us assume that they are needed for making visible and stable the categories of culture' (p. 59). This goes beyond both the economic theories of utility maximization and the psychological theories of social comparison to locate the meanings of goods, and hence of people's understandings of goods as necessities or luxuries, in a broader cultural context. Classifications of goods are thus related to classifications of people and hence to social structures. The way a culture separates necessities from luxuries reveals key cultural choices in the domains of morality, pleasure, desire, rights and responsibilities.

Douglas and Isherwood (1978) define necessities as high frequency goods in everyday use (for example, ordinary crockery) and luxuries as low frequency goods for high status use (for example, best china). This can be linked to social stratification by suggesting that objects that are luxuries among the poorer classes are necessities to the members of the richer classes. The definition of necessary goods is culturally relative. Different cultural standards have a moral component: 'A person's judgment about what is a necessity, while based in part on what is important to them personally, remains a judgment about what everyone in society today should be entitled to' (Mack and Lansley, 1985, p. 78). Such a judgement is a moral one, because it is a judgement about rights. Thus the notion of a minimum standard of living is a strong moral statement about what people should not fall below, and the broader debates about absolute or relative poverty (Townsend, 1979) and about universal or socially determined needs (Lederer, 1980) reflect moral debates in society about rights, standards, worth, duties, and so forth.

Douglas and Isherwood identify their approach as one which rejects the psychological, meaning individual differences or consumer irrationality. They identify three alternative perspectives on cultural analysis: phenomenology or the social construction of reality; structuralism or social processes of knowledge; and ethnomethodology or social accounting. Interestingly, these three perspectives are also currently influential within social psychology in research on discourse (van Dijk, 1987; Potter and Wetherell, 1987), rhetoric (Billig, 1987), ordinary explanations (Antaki, 1988; Lunt, 1988, 1989), and social representations (Farr and Moscovici, 1984). Social psychologists are concerned with ordinary understandings in relation to attitudes, values, moral judgements, attributions, motivations, decision-making, and so forth. As social psychologists, we may ask how people in everyday life draw the boundary between necessities and luxuries and what is the significance of this boundary for people's social and moral accounting? To be seen as a person of moral worth and social respect in society, people must coherently justify their actions both in public and private. As we shall see, they do not only justify, but also attempt to persuade, to offer their justifications as resources to others. How is this feat of sense-making achieved, and on what explanatory and rhetorical resources does it draw? Little or no research has yet been conducted on people's ordinary understanding of the necessity/luxury distinction in particular or of the meanings of goods more generally (although see Dittmar, 1989; Livingstone, 1990). We note here that in addition to throwing light on people's economic understandings, this research may also indicate possible explanatory variables for economic models of needs and wants, suggesting avenues for future research.

THE STUDY OF LAY ACCOUNTS OF NEEDS, NECESSITIES AND LUXURIES

The study was conducted using an open-ended questionnaire. Thirty people (identified here by numbers between 1 and 47), of both sexes, different ages, and a range of occupations and social classes were given the following instructions:

> We are interested in your opinions about *luxury* and *necessity*. Please use the space below to write down your thoughts on what people need in their lives and what counts as a luxury. Where is the dividing line between luxury and necessity? Please think about luxury and necessity both for *people in general* and *for yourself in particular*. For example, do you need things which others might consider a luxury, or do you consider a luxury things which others say they need? For example, have your ideas changed over your lifetime and why?

One way to analyse the resulting accounts is to identify lists of goods placed in each category. Table 1 provides a preliminary classification. Many 'necessities' were uncontentious. Most popular were goods satisfying basic, physical needs. Interestingly, the next most popular category was that of psychological needs. Little attention was paid to goods or facilities provided by society rather than possessed by the individual. Very few consumer durables were consensually seen as necessities. Many luxury items were similarly uncontentious, particularly objects owned for the status they confer rather than their usefulness. All who mentioned them agreed that alcohol and cigarettes were luxuries, and a few consumer durables were agreed to be luxuries also. However, the category of consumer durables proved to be the most contested, with respondents showing considerable disagreement over whether, for example, a car or a television was a luxury or a necessity. The necessity of leisure activities was also disputed.

Interesting though such lists of goods may be, they leave many questions unanswered. We need to know why certain goods count as necessities and others as luxuries, what underlying views of needs and wants these lists reflect, and what is the significance of this distinction to people. To address these questions, we conducted an interpretative analysis of the accounts people gave.

There were a number of common themes that emerged repeatedly from people's accounts which we take to be highly salient when drawing the boundary between luxury and necessity: the definition of basic needs; the relative importance of personal and social factors; historical and cultural relativity; and strategies for individual coping. The analysis will follow through these themes in turn.

Table 3.1 Classification of respondents' listings of necessities and luxuries (arranged by frequency of mention)

Category	Mentions	Examples
Uncontentious necessities		
Basic needs	61	Shelter, food, clothing, warmth, health, water, air
Psychological needs	29	Companionship, privacy, security, fulfilment
Social provision	8	Transport, employment, leisure facilities, nurseries
Consumer durables	3	Furniture, cooking utensils
Miscellaneous	16	Garden, bicycle, deodorant
Uncontentious luxuries		
Status objects	13	Expensive clothes, helicopter, boat
Disposables	12	Luxury foods, alcohol, cigarettes
Consumer durables	7	Microwave, tumble drier, dishwasher
Multiple objects	5	Second car, holiday home, several televisions
Miscellaneous	16	Swimming pool, pets, hairdresser, no worries

Contested goods (mentioned as both a necessity and a luxury)
Consumer durables:

car	17
washing machine	11
television	12
radio	6
record player	6
video recorder	6
fridge freezer	4
telephone	4
Leisure:	
entertainment	11
holidays	14

MODELS OF THE RELATION BETWEEN NEEDS/WANTS AND NECESSITIES/LUXURIES

One conceptual problem which people must resolve is the relation between accounts of the motivation to consume (needs and wants) and accounts of the nature of goods (necessities and luxuries). We observed three basic models of this relationship in the accounts analysed.

In the first and simplest model, needs are split into basic and higher needs and goods into necessities and luxuries. These are mapped on to each other so that luxuries serve higher needs and necessities serve basic needs.

> In general necessities are food, water, warmth, shelter. [39]

> The basic necessities are food, warmth and shelter. [17]

A variation on this model proposes that basic needs are to be met by material goods, but that higher needs are to be met by non-material things:

> Necessities are: healthy food, adequate housing, suitable clothes and/or the income to provide them. Also a feeling of 'belonging' or 'being loved' or being a useful member of society which is not dependent on income but may be provided by the job which also provides the income. [30]

> I believe that people in general have certain basic material needs – wholesome food, adequate housing, drinkable water, breathable air . . . They also have other non-material needs – love, a feeling of security in so far as society can provide this, meaningful work, social recognition quite independent of their bank balance. [15]

This implies that luxuries are a substitute for spiritual/religious/community based needs. This is a common cultural theme concerning the decline of the spiritual in the elaboration of material culture. These accounts indicate that in the hierarchy of needs only some needs are directly satisfied by material goods, but that people have been misled into buying goods to satisfy higher needs.

A further variant of Model I argues that the definition of basic and higher needs is social rather than biological. Thus some claim a universality for basic needs and others claim that basic needs are determined by culture and personal economic circumstances (cf. the psychological debate over needs, Lederer, 1980). The introduction of relativity into the necessity/luxury boundary leads into Model II.

For Model I, the debates in which people may engage involve identifying a good as satisfying a basic or a higher need. For adherents of Model II, people must also consider how these needs, basic or higher, are satisfied – by necessities or luxuries? Needs are seen as arrayed from basic to higher with an orthogonal distinction drawn between necessities and luxuries. Here then are four categories of goods, for luxuries may satisfy either higher or basic needs and it is considered necessary to satisfy some higher order needs in addition to satisfying basic needs. Thus, two new classes of objects emerge; luxuries which satisfy basic needs and necessities which satisfy higher needs.

I think that people (and myself) actually need very little but, in a 'real world' situation, what others have actually does affect what we need. If a large number of people have a private car, it isn't just the luxury of having this possession that matters, it actually means they can look farther afield for jobs . . . someone without a car will not be able to do these things and will be disadvantaged as a result. [29]

All people need more than necessities such as food, clothing, warmth, each person needs enough of their choice to satisfy their inner needs. [1]

In contrast to the first model, where luxuries simply satisfy higher needs and necessities satisfy basic needs, Model II introduces a debate about how to satisfy each category of need which requires a further level of accounting or justification on the part of the consumer.

The third model is a hybrid of the first two and identifies three classes of objects: necessities satisfying basic needs; necessities satisfying desires; and luxuries satisfying desires. In this model there is no class of luxuries which satisfy basic needs, for such items are deemed to be satisfying higher needs, thus retaining the notion that at the bottom end of the needs hierarchy there are basic needs that have a set of goods (necessities) with which they are satisfied. On this account, a luxury foodstuff, for example, would be deemed to be satisfying higher order needs rather than basic physiological needs and the classy colour television is not for ordinary entertainment but for self- aggrandizement.

Clearly there are certain commonly accepted 'necessities' in life such as food, clothing and shelter. There are also certain desirable things which could only be described as luxuries, such as fast cars, holidays in exotic places, daily champagne and caviar etc. The difficulty arises with the more mundane needs of life in the grey area . . . alcohol, tobacco, hairdo's etc. . . . for those to whom such things are important, their quality of life would be seriously diminished were they unable to afford those pleasures. [37]

One subject justifies adhering to Model III over Model I, retaining the luxury/higher need category, by pointing to the difficulty of adequately satisfying both higher and basic needs without resorting to luxuries or excess. Acknowledging the difficulties of satisfying one's higher needs in everyday life with the range of material goods available is seen to mitigate against the possession of luxury goods – they represent failed attempts to satisfy one's higher needs:

We all possess things which we don't really need. It is one of our basic human characteristics that we are forever demanding more of our environment. Satisfaction and contentment are very difficult states to achieve. [26]

Model I was endorsed by over half the sample. It can be seen as the most basic model, with some variations upon it (material versus nonmaterial satisfiers, and biological versus social needs), which straightforwardly maps categories of goods (necessities and luxuries) onto the distinctions embodied in a particular theory of human nature (basic needs and higher needs). The simplicity of this model reveals a harmonious and unified representation of the relationship between goods and human nature. Psychological theories, both scientific and lay, are given a specific role here, in terms of accounting for, and justifying, the distinction between basic and higher needs and their satisfiers. Herein lie the many debates concerning physiology versus desire, the material versus the spiritual, and the universal versus the cultural. The positions taken towards each of these problems by both ordinary people and psychologists result in different lay and scientific theories of consumption. Model II represents a fundamental elaboration of Model I, and was suggested by one third of the sample. It introduces further areas for public debate, specifically the various ways in which higher and basic needs can be satisfied. This too becomes an arena for accounting, justification and discussion. Finally, Model III, suggested by a small number of respondents, represents a compromise between Models I and II, accepting the elaboration of Model I only in the domain of the higher needs, and acknowledging the difficult nature of the problem which people face in resolving these complex issues in routine, daily practice.

THE ROLE OF PERSONAL AND SOCIAL FACTORS

Do people accept an account of the consumer (of themselves) as grounded in basic, universal, physiologically based needs with an overlay of wants which are open to psychological motivation and social influence? Or do they see consumption in modern society as inherently social, even in the consumption of objects that are ostensibly satisfying basic needs? Questions of classification of objects as luxuries and necessities fall back on more basic questions as to the universality of basic needs and the scope of influence of social and psychological factors. These questions, then, are grounded in people's broader belief systems, social representations and attitudes, and these in turn inform the positions they take on debates about consumption. Particularly important to these questions is the position people take on the problem of relativity (see next section).

First, though, let us relate the above three models of goods to scientific theories of needs and wants and their personal and social determinants. We can see a reflection of Maslow's needs hierarchy in the lay accounts. All of his needs, from basic physiological needs, through safety needs, to love, then esteem, and finally to the highest need of self-actualization are mentioned in the accounts. Despite their awareness that not all of these needs are satisfied for many people, the respondents none the less include all of these in the category of needs, accepting the argument that needs are defined by society rather than by physiology, although qualifying it by recognizing multiple competing standards from different cultures and times. People also accept Baxter's (1988) argument about the role of social and psychological determinants of needs and wants, in which the social environment is held to transform needs (also determined in part by the environment in addition to individual differences and physiology) into wants or desires for specific satisfiers available in the world of goods. The debate, as people appear to see it, is less about what people need – where this includes both physiological needs and self-actualization needs – but about how these needs are transformed into wants (here lies the role of culture, history and market forces), and about how these wants are to be satisfied (whether minimally or excessively, materially or spiritually, and so forth, with all the problems that this raises of rights, morality and equality).

HISTORICAL AND CULTURAL RELATIVITY

In past history and in the third world, people consider that there was/is primarily the problem of satisfying basic needs: there is little problem about the identification of luxuries, for most available commodities are necessities satisfying basic needs. The rarer the goods, the more they are luxuries. They consider that the development of mass consumption has led to an elaboration of the realm of luxury. Not only do we now, in the West, have more nice things but also the nice things themselves become necessities through processes of social influence (both mediated and peer influence). Conversely also, some basic things are taken into the realm of the luxurious: luxury foods, leisure, accommodation, even jobs.

So, basic to people's understanding of the distinction between luxury and necessity is an awareness of the changes that have occurred over their lifetime in relation to mass consumption and for which they are the recipients. Given the social construction of the desire for goods, relativity becomes a problem, and in their accounts people were acutely aware of the relativity of necessities and luxuries. This is one reason why they could not adopt the simple solution of explaining the differences between luxuries and necessities by just providing examples of each, for the same object may be a necessity under certain circumstances and a luxury under others.   People wanted to retain some notion of 'real needs', and to discuss the things that were commonly represented as necessities as social constructions. As well as being aware of and trying to make various resolutions of the problem of relativity, people were aware of a number of sources of relativity, individual, social, cultural and historical, as follows.

Individual sources of relativity

Upbringing

> Luxury and necessity in the minds of people largely depends on their child upbringing.

Personal circumstances

> Am disabled so have a car which I consider a necessity
> Video recorders are also luxuries but I have heard 'social workers' say that they are necessities for low income families 'to entertain the children'.

Individual differences

> Difficult to generalise about 'people'.

Personal preference

> Clearly there will be certain things which are near-necessities to one individual – alcohol, tobacco, hairdo's etc. which would be written off as mere luxuries by others without the inclination for such things. [37]

Social sources of relativity

Age differences

> Young friends seem to compensate for being out of work etc. by indulging in spending into debt. . . Older people seem to have learnt to manage better by having sorted out their priorities into 'needs' and 'wants'.

Income differences

> I have found that luxuries become necessities as my income has increased, and in general it seems to me that the poor man's luxury is inclined to become the rich man's necessity. [17]

Cultural comparisons
The third world

> Compared to the third world we have so many needs which are luxuries by comparison.

Survival versus civilised life

> One has to distinguish between the most basic level of human subsistence – the minimum necessary for human survival – and what may reasonably be deemed 'necessary' for civilized modern life.

Historical comparisons
Twenty years ago

> Twenty years ago what was considered a luxury is now considered a necessity.

Generation differences

> I firmly believe that people, mainly of the younger generation, want and expect everything that was a luxury years ago . . . Not necessarily having had to work for it. [16]

Historical relativity

> One might consider the evolution of the toilet which a hundred years ago would be an out-house in the garden is now firmly placed inside the house. I don't think anyone would now regard this setting as a luxury, but in Victorian times it would almost certainly be thought of as such. [26]

> Henry VIII was very rich but he didn't have a car or a TV or central heating so am I wealthier than the king of England? [29]

The above examples suggest that certain artifacts are fluid with regard to being classified as luxury or necessity depending on a variety of cultural, historical, economic and personal factors. Further, people appreciate that notions of luxury and necessity are subject to similar influences:

> When I was a child, necessities were provided by parents and for luxuries we were encouraged to save. [3]

> An individual's perceptions of luxury and necessity will vary according to his interests and character, as well as being reliant on his country's wealth. [31]

Here people are hinting at relativity not only in the necessity/luxury boundary but also in the broader social belief systems which underpin this boundary.

AN ILLUSTRATION

Either implicitly or explicitly, people do not feel they can answer the question of the distinction between necessities and luxuries without a broader consideration of socio-economic life. Thus they include an analysis of why people might classify goods in the way they do as part of their understanding of the distinction itself. In other words, as argued above, the basis of distinction between luxuries and necessities is complex and social. Some of the accounts made this explicit. Here we consider one account in some detail to exemplify this grounding of the economic understanding in a broader social belief system.

> People need as much comfort in their lives as is necessary to reduce the background stress of living to a tolerable (ignoble) level. The point where individuals draw the line, and their particular choice of comforts is due largely to peer group pressure which leads to in many cases people with lower incomes feeling that they need more of the latest brand-new and expensive hardware in their lives than is the case with people better placed to afford it. In fact all that we really need is food and shelter and all the rest may be held to be luxury. Then some will say we need food and shelter and provision for medical care. Then someone will say we need food, shelter, medicine and communication and things will be added to the list in greater numbers until the consensus view is reached that although a jacuzzi with variable bubble size and cocktail bar may be one of the bare essentials of a civilised life, having coloured disco lights in same would be utter and inexcusable decadence. For my own view, I do like a few gadgets, props and icons in my life, but I regard none of it as essential and seek to buy all durable items second-hand at a negotiated cash price. I do not oppose credit in principle – but administering my personal credit affairs would be an extra piece of work that I ain't prepared to do. [9]

This account makes no attempt to list goods which are luxuries and necessities. The account immediately suggests that necessary goods are those which compensate us for the stresses of modern living, for individuals take sustenance from different goods. The comforts they choose are partly determined socially, according to those chosen by their peer group. The account then introduces a cautionary tale in which people choose comforts beyond their means, because of the social influence of the better off. The author then suggest that social influence over the choice of goods has resulted in people losing touch with an analysis of their basic needs. People are seen not to make decisions based on an objective analysis of their needs but rather they are seen to accept socially-defined comforts as their goals. This process of social convention about the consumption of 'necessities' leads to an inflation of required goods. Here, interestingly, some goods are mentioned, to illustrate the over-layering of commodities as the range of appropriate goods expands. The inflation of expectations proceeds by the upgrading of consensus over what is an appropriate level of consumption – an essentially social process rather than one of individuals appraising their needs in isolation. The account then suggests that the only way around this is to detach oneself from the social influences by choosing second-hand goods over new ones. There is an interesting pairing here of second-hand with cash and new with credit – if we buy second-hand we avoid the credit system, and we step outside the social pressure for the new. A further strategy of resistance proposed is to personally resist the temptation to redefine luxuries as necessities.

This leads into a further aspect of the accounts offered, that of consequences for action and rhetorical advice concerning coping with consumption pressures.

STRATEGIES OF INDIVIDUAL COPING: THE RULES OF ECONOMIC RESISTANCE

When asked to draw a distinction between classes of goods, people express some of their views as advice. Accounts are motivated in part by the desire for control over the social environment. The accounts also have a strongly rhetorical flavour. People do not just propose various criteria for distinguishing necessities and luxuries. They also, perhaps inevitably, indulge in a variety of moral prescriptions and recommendations for living in and coping with material culture. The necessity/luxury distinction has implications for many consumer decisions – for example, we reward ourselves by purchasing luxuries, we economize by restricting purchases to necessities. The following strategies or rules of resistance were offered.

Make appropriate social comparisons
Do not think a good is a necessity for yourself just because someone else has it – they may have good reasons for having it. This rule stops people simply wanting what they see others possess. Before acquiring the good themselves they would have to ask whether the person who owned it had a need for it which they did not have or had greater resources than them.

I think a washing up machine (dishwasher) a luxury – but to others it is a necessity i.e. large families etc. [7]

I must compare myself to others actually living today and in my own country. However this makes it very easy to ignore people in other poorer countries whose situation seems very remote from our own. [29]

For a woman out at work a freezer is a necessity. [45]

Guiding principles

People offer abstract principles of consumption, which provide a framework for taking numerous specific decisions.

Credit is not taken lightly. [3]

Having sorted out (their) priorities into 'needs' and 'luxuries'. [4]

More important to spend money on either major house work or charities or holidays. [12]

Non-material needs – love, a feeling of security in so far as society can provide this, meaningful work, social recognition quite independent of their bank balance. [15]

[live] A fairly simple lifestyle. [15]

Ghandi once said 'there's enough in the world for everyone's need, but not for everyone's greed'. [22]

Learn to be content with the way things are: I've never known the life of Reilly but I've learned to be content with things as they are. [22]

Freedom from stress can be more important than luxuries. [39]

Coping actions

People suggest specific actions to aid coping.

Choosing luxuries for oneself and one's friends which are within one's resources. [1]

Use a credit card to your own advantage. [3]

Buy all durable items second hand at a negotiated cash price. [9]

Much of the time I buy things second hand. [12]

If I can afford a luxury I want I will have it, if I can't I won't. [36]

Cognitive coping

A variety of cognitive coping strategies are offered.

Define necessities very conservatively

> I consider anything I cannot afford as a luxury. [4]

> All that we really need is food and shelter and all the rest may be held to be luxury. [9]

> Really the basics of living as absolute necessity and anything else I would regard as a luxury. [35]

> I believe these (basic) necessities have not changed much over the years. [46]

Know which luxuries you want

> I don't think of holidays as a luxury mainly as I feel I need them so badly. [12]

> Personally my 'luxuries' are I suppose very limited – some books, wine, entertaining friends, a visit to friends. [15]

Have to justify spending

> I find it difficult to buy things for myself which I consider to be luxury items, to justify spending that sort of money when there is so much poverty in the world. [12]

Distance yourself from spenders

> I firmly believe that people, mainly of the younger generation, want and expect everything that was a luxury years ago . . . Not necessarily having had to work for it [16]

Adopt individualistic standards

> My ideas of needs and luxuries do not appear to have changed much, if at all. [21]

> Needs for myself include space, some solitude and being in contact with growing things. [42]

> Now I consider more abstract things important. [42]

Self control

The importance of having control over one's desires is often advocated.

Being able to say no to oneself or one's friends. [1]

The running of two cars is a luxury and with careful planning could be avoided. [38]

We used to have a car and it was greatly missed for a while, but we soon got used to being without. [45]

Warnings

People also offer warnings about what they see happening around them.

Consumption of material for reasons other than what is contained in them e.g. for perceived status value. [10]

For some people they will only 'feel okay' when they and their family consume more and more. [2]

These rules suggest a variety of views about the relationship between the individual and material culture. The point about specifying rules of personal behaviour is that a normal competent person should be able to carry them out. Therefore stating a rule refers to a theory of how the individual can affect the way that economic factors affect them: people offer an implicit theory of the role of human action in the economic process. Since the prescriptions must be realistic, they reveal an implicit theory of practice, of people's competence, and personal control. The last quotation emphasizes the dynamic nature of the consumption process, that pleasure in the act of consumption itself is the motivator which drives economic processes, and which therefore threatens to take society out of control.

ON THE PROCESS OF CLASSIFYING GOODS AS NECESSITIES AND LUXURIES

It could be argued that there is no problem in classifying goods into necessities and luxuries, for simply there exist three consensual categories of goods, necessities, luxuries, and things in between. We would argue strongly against this position for the following reasons. First, each individual has their own ideas about what counts as a necessity or a luxury, even though across individuals there is disagreement. To include most goods in a meaningless 'in-between' category is to lose a considerable domain of meaning for individuals. The distinction between necessities and luxuries is important to people, variously motivating them, directing their consumer decisions and providing an explanatory resource for accounting for one's behaviour to oneself and others, and so it demands further examination (Baxter, 1988). One may ask, as we have, which different positions exist, and what are the individual or group determinants of these positions—this being a question for future research.

When faced with the task of distinguishing luxury from necessity people do not necessarily offer an ostensive definition composed of categories of objects, nor do they offer the defining features of necessities or luxuries. People do not presume a consensual approach in which the only variation is that of lists with different items. Instead, they discuss how they would make the distinction. To classify a good as either necessity or luxury involves general principles of classification, functional assessments of goods, moral judgements of motivation or utility, advisory implications of classification, and pragmatic rules of classification in particular behavioural contexts. Classification is by no means merely descriptive, but also pragmatic, functional, contextual and rhetorical (Billig, 1987; Smith and Medin, 1981). In making the distinction between necessities and luxuries, people reveal lay theories of needs and wants, and of the relation between personal and social processes. These theories are complicated by a variety of relativities (historical, cultural, social and personal). The complications themselves result in a perceived need for rhetorical justification for the distinctions offered, where this justification is offered as advice. Drawing the boundary is not the end of the story, for advice on how to live with the distinction made has also to be offered. After all, the distinction between luxury and necessity is not an academic nicety but involves adopting positions on a variety of complex social issues. There is no choice here about adopting a position, though many choices lie behind the position adopted, for everyday life demands that people, in some way or other, come to a practical resolution of these consumption issues. This must be achieved in a manner consonant with their other social beliefs and everyday understanding.

The act of drawing boundaries reveals issues of cultural significance (Douglas and Isherwood, 1978). What does it mean that the criteria of necessities and luxuries are disputed, that the distinction is fuzzy, that the practice of separating these goods is difficult? Each model provides people with a justification for a range of actions which concern both consumption behaviours – spending, choosing, saving, economizing, getting into debt – and also social behaviours – perceiving and judging others, making attributions, giving advice. The different models adopted by people reveal a struggle to define the moral problems of consumption and materialism in different ways. Each model carries implications for the moral worth of the individuals who make particular decisions and for the perceived moral standing of contemporary Western culture in relation to other cultures and times. The debates between the models reveal the contested nature of these issues for people in everyday life.

Each of the three models endorsed the basic academic distinction between basic and higher needs (Baxter, 1988; Maslow, 1970), and some people agreed with the economic argument that luxuries were scarce goods and necessities were goods which were commonly available. In the main, however, people were concerned to draw this boundary not in terms of market constraints, supply, or economic pressures, but in terms of issues of lifestyle, social pressure, personality and cultural context. The focus, understandably, was on the problems and choices faced by the individual rather than the economy. The divergence from economic models was especially clear when we consider the earlier discussion of the Engel curve: the key difference between the lay models II and III lay in the question of whether there could be both adequate ways of satisfying basic needs, and prestigious or excessive ones. Model II, which was the more popular of the two, recognized that needs may be satisfied luxuriously.

The Marxist notion that industry constructs needs rather than satisfying pre-existing needs was not directly acknowledged in people's accounts. However, there was considerable resistance expressed towards consumerism and, implicitly, towards a capitalist ideology. This resistance took three forms. First, psychological, non-material needs were listed instead of material goods; this kind of resistance was reflected also in the spiritual/material distinction offered by some variants of Model I. Secondly, explicit strategies of resistance to consumerism were offered as an integral part of people's accounts. Finally, the debate over classifying goods as necessities or luxuries centred on consumer durables.

The anthropological approach to goods as revealing basic cultural categories was the approach least reflected in ordinary people's accounts. People mainly took goods on face value, rather than as symbols of underlying meanings. Generally, in contrast to current anthropological theory, goods were discussed in terms of utility and competitive display. However, even at this level, some acknowledgement of the deeper cultural meanings of goods can be found in the emphasis frequently placed on relativity in judgements of necessity and luxury, especially by supporters of Models II and III. Reactions to this relativity were mixed, for some felt it better to focus simply on one's own time and place, while others felt it a duty to recall competing frameworks within which to understand the role of goods in society. In general, it seems that ordinary people's accounts of the relation between necessities and luxuries reflect many of the ideas contained in academic theories. Like anthropological theories, they are concerned to go beyond the claims of economists, seeking the meaning of necessities and luxuries and recognizing the major cultural questions raised by the distinction.

ACKNOWLEDGEMENTS

The research described in this chapter was made possible by financial support from Nuffield College, Oxford. The authors wish to thank Fred van Raaij for comments on an earlier version.

REFERENCES

Antaki, C. (1988). (ed.). *The analysis of everyday explanations.* London: Sage.
Baxter, J. L. (1988). *Social and psychological foundations of economic analysis.* New York: Harvester-Wheatsheaf.
Billig, M. (1987). *Arguing and thinking: A rhetorical approach to social psychology.* Cambridge: Cambridge University Press.
van Dijk, T. A. (1987). *News as discourse.* Hillsdale, NJ: Erlbaum.
Dittmar, H. (1989). Gender identity-related meanings of personal possessions. *British Journal of Social Psychology, 28,* 159-171.
Douglas, M., and Isherwood, B. (1978). *The world of goods: Towards an anthropology of consumption.* Harmondsworth: Penguin.
Farr, R. M., and Moscovici, S. (eds) (1984). *Social Representations.* Cambridge: Cambridge University Press.
Lederer, K. (ed.) (1980). *Human needs: A contribution to the current debate.* Cambridge MA.: Oelgeschlager, Gunn and Hain.
Livingstone, S. M. (1990). Personal constructions of domestic technologies: gender relations and family dynamics. Paper presented to the International Communications Association Annual Conference, Dublin, June.
Lunt, P. K. (1988). The perceived causal structure of examination failure. *British Journal of Social Psychology, 27,* 171-179.
Lunt, P. K. (1989). The perceived causal structure of unemployment. In K. G. Grunert & F. Ölander, (eds), *Understanding economic behaviour* (pp. 107-120). Dordrecht: Kluwer.

Mack, J., & Lansley, S. (1985). *Poor Britain.* London: Allen and Unwin.

Maslow, A. H. (1970). *Motivation and personality* (2nd edn.). New York: Harper and Row.

Miller, D. (1987). *Material culture and mass consumption.* Oxford: Blackwell.

Potter, J., and Wetherell, M. (1987). *Discourse and social psychology: Beyond attitudes and behaviour.* London: Sage.

Sahlins, M. (1976). *Culture and practical reason.* Chicago: University of Chicago Press.

Smith, E. E., and Medin, D. L. (1981). *Categories and concepts.* London: Harvard University Press.

Townsend, P. (1979). *Poverty in the United Kingdom.* Harmondsworth: Penguin.

4. On the complementarity of economic applications of cognitive dissonance theory and personal construct psychology

Peter E. Earl
University of Tasmania

INTRODUCTION

Although Festinger's (1957) cognitive dissonance theory (hereafter CDT) and Kelly's (1955) personal construct psychology (hereafter PCP) have both been used to make sense of a variety of forms of economic behaviour, there has so far been little interest in their theoretical compatibility and the potential intellectual synergy between them. Pioneering uses of CDT by economists and decision theorists including Hirschman (1965), Steinbruner (1974), Akerlof and Dickens (1982), Maital (1982), Elster (1983) and Gilad *et al.* (1986) have made no mention of PCP, whilst those who have seen scope for using PCP in economics and marketing, including Gutman (1982), Loasby (1983), Earl (1983, 1984) and various contributors to Earl (1988), have either ignored contributions employing CDT, or have mentioned CDT only in passing.

Psychologists likewise have kept CDT and PCP in separate compartments. Of the three standard works reviewing PCP, namely, Bannister and Mair (1968), Bannister and Fransella (1980) and Adams-Webber (1979), only Bannister and Fransella make any mention of CDT and even they only mention it as an example of something presented as a 'theory' which they (1980, pp. 10–11) construe merely as a 'notion'. Kelly's work appeared whilst Festinger was completing his (1957) book, but neither he nor his associates displayed any awareness of PCP and its research methods in writing up their later empirical work (Festinger, 1964).

I believe that the impact of both lines of thinking could have been greater had efforts been made to integrate them. In this chapter I try to show how, through an exploration of the theoretical relationship between PCP and CDT, we may gain a better understanding of how patterns of choice emerge as time unfolds.

THE ECONOMICS OF REDUCING COGNITIVE DISSONANCE

Dissonance is defined in Festinger's work as the existence of non-fitting relations among cognitions. People experience cognitive dissonance because they are not in control of the information they receive and because many things tend to be a mixture of contradictions. Festinger (1957, p. 3) advanced two basic hypotheses:

1. The existence of dissonance, being psychologically uncomfortable, will motivate the person to try to reduce the dissonance and achieve consonance.
2. When dissonance is present, in addition to trying to reduce it the person will actively avoid situations and information which would increase the dissonance.

Festinger's (1957) book elaborated these hypotheses and many subsidiary ones, and a lesser known volume reporting experimental investigations of them appeared some years later (Festinger, 1964).

It is not surprising that attempts have been made to frame economic behaviour in terms of strategies aimed at reducing cognitive dissonance: many of Festinger's illustrative scenarios concern economic situations, including car ownership, employment choices, and decisions not to give up smoking. Even minor decisions, for example, whether to continue on a picnic expedition as gathering clouds start to raise questions about the likely weather at the destination, can be put in economic terms (what are the sunk costs of the preparations made so far?). But Festinger's scenarios also challenge core assumptions of orthodox economic theory, in at least three ways.

1. They portray decision-makers as prone to go to great lengths to avoid treating irrecoverable costs as having been mistakenly sunk, in situations where they encounter information that questions the wisdom of their decisions.
2. CDT also predicts that, rather than facing up to the fact that life is full of opportunity costs, choosers often try to gather information that will enable them to rationalize away sacrifices that they have

made as a result of committing themselves to particular courses of action. For example, after opting to buy a particular item, they may devote a great deal of attention to advertisements for it, all the while doing their best to ignore advertisements for and reviews of the alternatives that they rejected. This last position was modified by Festinger (1964, chapt. 4 and p.96) in the light of experimental work which showed that although people are prone to look at more advertisements for what they have just purchased, they nonetheless tend to look at some advertisements for rejected possibilities. Festinger recognised that confident people might actively expose themselves to dissonant material in order to demonstrate that they could counterargue. However, this bears as little resemblance to orthodox recognition of opportunity costs as the more usual processes of dissonance reduction.

3. Finally, CDT conflicts with the idea of given preferences, for it suggests that once people have made a commitment to a particular course of action, they will tend to re-evaluate the original alternatives, favouring the chosen scheme or disfavouring the rejected ones.

Economists have used CDT to make sense of a wide variety of behaviours that might otherwise prove puzzling. An early reference is Hirschman's (1965) paper on obstacles to economic development. Hirschman argued that the societies most likely to develop rapidly are those that are prone to let their motivation to solve their problems outrun their understanding of how to do so. Having plunged headlong into attempting to promote development they would ignore non-cognitive barriers such as poor natural resource endowments. Thus they might achieve more than better endowed societies that tend to avoid tackling problems unless easy solutions seem available.

Better known is Maital's (1982, pp. 142–3) use of CDT to explain why, despite believing that 'debt is wrong', American consumers were happily getting themselves deeper into debt with the aid of credit cards. Since credit cards can be used merely as means of payment rather than for their extended credit facilities, someone who has decided to purchase an item can implement her decision without having to admit to herself that she was getting into debt. She can tell herself that she will pay it off in full when her next statement arrives.

Financial speculation has also been investigated with the aid of CDT. Kaish (1986) has used the analogy of skaters on a frozen pond to explain how participants in a bull market may justify ignoring warnings that a crash is imminent because asset prices have become dangerously divorced from levels implied by underlying fundamentals. Someone having a great time skating may see others joining her on the pond and yet justify ignoring warnings about the danger of the ice cracking by reminding herself how cold it has been lately and how thick, therefore, the ice must be. (For a related discussion of the effects of dissonance reduction on financial behaviour, see Klausner, 1984, pp. 71–5).

Probably the most rigorous of economic applications of CDT to date is the work of Akerlof and Dickens (1982), which considers, amongst other things, the role for compulsory old age insurance (since people may feel uncomfortable contemplating themselves in retirement and therefore avoid considering things, such as life assurance schemes, that bring such thoughts to mind) and safety legislation (since people who view themselves as smart may choose to ignore the dangers of their well-paying but hazardous work environments).

Dissonance reducing behaviour can be incorporated into economic models whilst keeping the assumption that decision-makers choose by weighing up costs and benefits. All we need to note is that dissonant thoughts about the wisdom of a prior choice impose a mental cost and hence that a person may be prepared to incur other costs up to this level if this is the price that must be paid to avoid dissonance. Now, of course, one way to reduce dissonance is to discard some of one's beliefs and replace them with others that fit better with those that one retains. Unfortunately, this strategy is by no means guaranteed to be costless once one has 'made up one's mind'.

For example, if a commodity that I have chosen is turning out to be rather disappointing, I could escape the need to engage in dissonance reducing actions by simply telling myself that I had made a mistake, and cease to expect it to perform so well. But the admission that I can take poor decisions could generate another kind of dissonance, with its associated costs, by raising distressing questions about the viability of other expectations. To change my mind without worsening the dissonance problem, I may need to incur the mental costs of acquiring new perspectives and reframing thoughts about things in terms of these perspectives. These costs are additional to any pecuniary costs associated with liquidating prior commitments to commodities. The uncertain cost of finding a new way of looking at things may further encourage decison-makers to continue to struggle along with their existing, ill-matched beliefs. In short, if people are to be induced to revamp their expectations and change course, they must be aware of opportunities that offer compensation for both the mental and the commodity-related costs of change.

In Festinger's analysis, switches between different sets of ideas can be achieved without any bother prior to choice; it is as if, during the process of evaluating alternatives, the chooser's mindset takes the form of putty, capable of being moulded into a variety of shapes. This putty, or at least, part of it, becomes more akin to clay once the person's mind is made up: a commitment is made to a particular point of view, as well as to a particular course of action and its associated commodities. Only then does dissonance become a problem, for with her mind made up in a particular way, the decision-maker can no longer dismiss inconsistencies between her beliefs and/or actions by telling herself she is not committed to a particular way of looking at things.

Thus, suppose that, after making up her mind, a decision-maker encounters challenges to elements in the set of ideas to which she has committed herself, and judges that the alternative courses of action and beliefs associated with these alternatives do not offer advantages on a grand enough scale to make change attractive. Depending on the value that the decision-maker places on cognitive consistency, she will be prepared, up to a point, to incur costs of gathering information that neutralizes challenges to the mindset to which she has committed herself. She may also incur costs to avoid confronting such challenges in the first place, for example by imposing restrictions on the social circles in which she moves, or on the media she uses, or the information sources that she consults within a particular medium. In some situations these costs may seem considerable, even to a person whose willingness to tolerate cognitive dissonance is very limited. However, an upper limit to the costs that a person will incur to achieve cognitive consistency is always set by the expected costs of changing her way of looking at the world.

DISSONANCE REDUCTION FROM THE STANDPOINT OF PERSONAL CONSTRUCT PSYCHOLOGY

Personal construct psychology, pioneered by Kelly (1955), shares with CDT the idea that a concern with beliefs about the nature of things may underpin much of human action: in other words, that choices are often more concerned with the validity of images of the world than with attempts to obtain pleasure and avoid pain. PCP further proposes that we may usefully view people as if they are intent, like scientists, on predicting and controlling events. To inquiring people, choice is basically an experimental activity, not the solution of an optimization problem, and commodities are consumed as means of making discoveries and achieving control. Life becomes meaningless without hypotheses to test, without 'things to look forward to', without the opportunity to find what things 'are like'. Life becomes terrifying if one is at the mercy of events to such an extent than nothing seems under one's control.

Many of the kinds of behaviour identified by Festinger and his colleagues are not what one would initially expect of people seeking to enhance their abilities to predict and control events. Someone who becomes aware of non-fitting constructs in her view of the world has a problem stemming either from a mistake of logic or from an empirical anomaly. However, CDT suggests that instead of seeing dissonance as implying an opportunity for the reformulation of causal chains and the development of new hypotheses to test, people may go to extreme lengths to avoid refashioning some of their ideas. Moreover, instead of seeking to find the limitations of their hypotheses by testing them to destruction, people seem to seek to verify their hypotheses by rigging their data sets: gathering information from sources likely to be supportive, preferring to confront only those situations where they believe they will not encounter anomalies, and turning a blind eye when unavoidably placed in situations that have uncomfortable implications for their predictive systems.

This dissonance between the idea of man the dissonance reducer and man the scientist can be eliminated without ourselves adopting the sort of strategies just mentioned. First, we can note that CDT does stress that, in addition to the methods just described, people may actively search for new kinds of information and broader contexts, within which dissonances between cognitions may be resolved without denial of the evidence (Festinger, 1957, pp. 44-6). Suppose a person has been unable to find anything that fits all of her decision criteria. As she consumes the least unacceptable of the available options, she may actively look for ways of denying the importance of features she has chosen to forego. However, she may also try to see whether or not the strengths of her preferred option may enable her to reach, by another route, goals that initially seem blocked by its weaknesses.

Second, PCP overlaps with CDT via its conceptualization of anxiety and the effects that anxiety has on choice. Anxiety is defined in PCP in terms of an awareness that one lacks the experience or expertise required to form reliable hypotheses, or to live up to particular expectations (personal or social) in the context in question. Dilemmas can thus arise not merely because all possible courses of action involve ambiguities, but also where a strategy of trying to avoid some sources of anxiety by avoiding risks actually gives rise to other anxieties concerning the person's self- or social-image. For example, those who choose to act as 'stick in the muds' may find their own behaviour worrying if they have hitherto construed themselves as good at coping with novel situations. Moreover, their actions may lead to difficulties in a social setting where others were expecting more adventurous conduct.

Faced with such a dilemma, some people may feel that the best response to feelings of anxiety is to try to *prove themselves* by stepping boldly into unfamiliar territory: the uncertainty leaves open the possibility that they might be able to cope, even if it does not remove the possibility of failure. It also makes it possible for them to remove their misgivings by behaving in accordance with CDT. Other people may feel more comfortable with a risk-avoiding choice. Here, too, we would expect dissonance reduction strategies to be employed. For example, people who are worried because they find themselves behaving unadventurously may tell themselves (or their peers) that they are absolutely fascinated with the areas of the world to which they have chosen to confine themselves.

PCP predicts that one of two strategies will be adopted when all options involve great anxiety: (a) The decision maker may seek to avoid any irreversible commitment until the future becomes easier to anticipate, or (b) an impulsive decision may be taken as a means of reducing the number of worrying possibilities and thereby making the future easier to anticipate. Both of these strategies are also discussed by Festinger. He suggests that fear of dissonance may lead to a reluctance to make commitments (Festinger, 1957, p. 31), and notes (Festinger, 1964, p. 5) how Lewin (1951) 'believed that simply making a decision exerted a stabilizing effect on the situation. The person then tended to behave in line with the decision, even if this were difficult to do'. Later (pp. 154-5), whilst lamenting the lack of research on impulsive choices, Festinger comments that

> Perhaps such behavior is a means of avoiding a situation that promises to be a difficult one. If this were the case, one would expect such impulsive decisions more frequently if the decision is important and the person thinks the alternatives would prove very close together in attractiveness. Perhaps such impulsive decisons are made when the information gathering process seems endless. If this were the case, one would expect a greater frequency of impulsive decisions in instances where the person is faced with a large number of alternatives.

Third, PCP makes no presumption that people will run their lives according to methodologies that would win the approval of philosophers of science. People with no training in scientific method are likely to be using sets of key assumptions and rules about what should and should not be done or believed that they have developed for themselves in their light of their experiences in a social setting. These personally constructed ways of viewing the world give individuals their distinctive personalities. Most of the time, despite their homespun nature, these methodologies are good enough to keep their users out of major trouble. But sometimes they may prove to be grossly dysfunctional, as Nisbett and Ross (1980) have demonstrated. For example, smokers may take a particular observation, such as 'Churchill smoked and he lived past ninety!', and jump to misguided inferences about the risks of their habit.

Fourth, it is debatable whether the methodologies employed by scientists themselves preclude the sort of behaviour hypothesized by Festinger. Recent debates about the methods that economists use have included much criticism of the practice of 'data mining', particularly via adjustments of lead or lag times (Mayer, 1980; Cooley and LeRoy, 1981; Lovell, 1983; and Kuttner, 1985). For example, Cooley and LeRoy (1981, p. 836) considered the literature on the interest elasticity of demand for money and concluded that

> The preponderance of empirical studies of the demand for money which show significant negative interest elasticities reflect the unacknowledged prior beliefs of the researcher and not the information content of the data. . . . The data are such that a modestly energetic specification search will give almost whatever interest elasticity one wishes to extract, particularly if more than one interest rate is included and if the specification search involves extended tinkering with dynamic effects.

With computing becoming ever cheaper it is unlikely that economists will shake off the habit of trying to make data fit their theories, even if journals become more willing to publish papers embodying apparently disconfirmatory results. Worse still, as Kuttner (1985, p. 78) notes, 'Recent innovations, such as "vector auto regressions" and "multivariate auto-regressive moving average" models, in effect have the computer go on automatic pilot and search for correlations almost at random'.

Within debates about the scientific status of hypothesis testing activities of economists, Procrustean imagery has often been used, as with the comment by Mayer (1980, p. 175) that 'if you torture the data long enough, they will confess'. PCP likewise recognizes the possibility of Procrustean behaviour via its conceptualization of hostility as 'the continued effort to extort validational evidence in favour of a type of social prediction that has already proved itself a failure' (Kelly, 1955, p. 510). Man the scientist, just like man the dissonance reducer, is not someone who always willingly recognizes cognitive inconsistencies. If convenient evidence is hard to come by, then what evidence is available may be twisted with the aid of *ad hoc* arguments until it fits.

At the end of the previous section, dissonance reduction strategies were framed in cost/benefit terms. The same may be done in respect of Procrustean tendencies of scientists. Adam Smith provides a case study of this in his relatively unknown work on the history of astronomy (my discussion here draws on Skinner, 1979). Smith's study of the development of the Systems of Concentric, and Eccentric, Spheres and the two modern systems of Copernicus and Newton provides ample evidence of how astronomers resemble ordinary decision-makers when it comes to trying to avoid major changes of methodology. As Skinner (1979, pp. 113–14, italics in original) notes,

> The essence of Smith's argument would seem to be that each system at the time of its original appearance did satisfy the needs of the imagination, but that each was subject to a process of modification as new problems came to light; a process of modification which resulted in a growing degree of *complexity* which ultimately became unacceptable to the imagination, i.e. to the mind. This in turn paves the way for a new kind of response – the production not just of an account but of an *alternative* account (in this case of the heavens); a new thought system designed to explain the same problems as the first, at least in its most complex form, but cast in a more acceptable style – i.e. in a form which relied upon a smaller number of familiar or plausible principles, and which was for this reason more acceptable to the mind.

In short: when it becomes difficult to reduce dissonance by data mining, 'scientists' may try to reduce it by increasingly *ad hoc* modifications to their existing ways of looking at the world. The further accumulation of inconvenient information may mean that this Procrustean strategy begins to founder in the face of bounded rationality, so that ultimately it becomes worthwhile to incur the costs of designing more manageable systems.

IMPORTANCE OF BELIEFS AS A FUNCTION OF THEIR IMPLICATIONS

In considering which beliefs the person will opt to maintain when choices between rival sets have to be made, Festinger (1957, p. 16) recognizes that the pressure a person will feel to reduce a feeling of dissonance will vary according to the importance to that person of the belief that is being challenged. He also builds his theory around the idea that a person will find it easier to change some notions than others, writing that:

The maximum dissonance that can possibly exist between any two elements is equal to the total resistance to change of the less resistant element. The magnitude of dissonance cannot exceed this amount because, at this point of maximum possible dissonance, the less resistant element would change, thus eliminating the dissonance (Festinger, 1957, p. 28).

But Festinger's theory lacks any detailed analysis of why some of the beliefs to which a person has committed herself should be seen by the person as more important than others. The closest he comes is a comment that 'To the extent that the element is consonant with a large number of other elements and to the extent that changing it would replace these consonants by dissonances, the element will be resistant to change' (1957, p. 27). This suggestion has strong parallels with extensions of Kelly's work on PCP undertaken by Hinkle (1965).

The starting point for Hinkle's work was the 'organisation corollary' of Kelly's theory, which states that 'each person characteristically evolves, for his convenience in anticipating events, a construction system embracing ordinal relationships between constructs' (Kelly 1955, p. 56).

In other words, a person's expectations are not simply a collection of unorganized notions; rather, they are structured, with some beliefs being used as the basis for forming others. Here, the lay scientist's way of thinking is basically the same as that of, say, an economic scientist who uses core axioms (such as profit maximization and transitivity of preferences) to construct auxiliary hypotheses which are then tested. Without such a ranking of constructs a person would experience great difficulty in making up her mind about anything, for the validity of any belief is something that can only be judged from the standpoint of an existing way of looking at things.

Hinkle developed techniques for uncovering which of the constructs in a person's world-view are subordinate to which others, which ones are superordinate to which others, and which ones are unrelated. These enabled him to quantify, at the level of the individual, the 'implications' of a particular change: if a construct is superordinate to many others, then a change in it implies changes for those subordinate constructs. This could mean the latter constructs no longer match the unfolding pattern of events. The data obtained by Hinkle were not inconsistent with his hypothesis that, the more subordinate implications a construct carries in the mind of a particular person, the more that person will resist making a change in it. The greater the number of implications that a person has attached to a construct that is being challenged, the more, from the standpoint of CDT, we would expect that person to engage in dissonance-reducing behaviour in order to avoid changing the construct.

This sort of thinking and behaviour is most easily illustrated with reference to events such as bereavement, being unexpectedly left by one's spouse, and the loss of one's job. On these occasions people tend to find it very difficult indeed to believe what has happened and they grasp desperately at possibilities that onlookers may find hard to take seriously. No wonder, because these people are facing the destruction of a substantial part of their lives, of what they were looking forward to. No wonder, too, that orthodox economists cling desperately to their often wildly unrealistic core assumptions, without which many of their models would fall apart.

The same kind of phenomena can be seen working in other contexts on a smaller scale. For example, if my car starts to make a strange whirring noise, my tendency to engage in dissonance-reducing behaviour is likely to differ depending on whether the car is still under warranty and whether I am: (a) holidaying in mainland Australia and in danger of being stranded if I miss my place on the Melbourne-Tasmania ferry which is fully booked for the holiday season; (b) driving to the airport to catch a connection for an international flight; or (c) merely going shopping.

The comments about anxiety and impulsiveness should be recalled at this juncture, given that a challenge to a major construct is itself a cause for anxiety. It may be unwise to presume that all subjects rationalize threatening cognitions away by biasing their gathering and management of information. Some people may judge that the best view to take of a threat to their constructs is to assume it *will* come to fruition if they do not take steps to block it. Decision-makers who make such judgements may then try to deal with the threat by impulsive (they might say decisive) acts, which at unnecessary cost uphold their key constructs and let them preserve the subordinate expectations. And if someone is neither a rationalizer nor prone to act impulsively, we could instead expect more of a dependent response, such as a conspicuous display of panic aimed at attracting the attention of someone who can sort out the mess.

Differences in the mental strategies people use for coping with threatening cognitions are by no means the only differences in ways of thinking that will affect the importance people accord to particular pieces of information. It must be remembered that the structures of implicational linkages between constructs are ones that people set up for themselves. Some people may develop highly integrated ways of looking at a given situation; others may choose to avoid linkages. The former will be much more obsessively concerned with a threatening cognition about which the latter may take a pretty 'laid back' attitude (this theme is explored at length in Earl, 1986).

'SOUR GRAPES' FROM THE PERSPECTIVE OF PERSONAL CONSTRUCT THEORY

Hinkle is concerned with resistance to change of constructs. But if particular activities and commodities are seen as necessary for the upholding of constructs which the decision-maker is loath to change, then attachments to those material things would be expected. Similarly, differences in attachments to things should reflect differences in the number of constructs subordinate to them. Thus a theory of expectation formation and change gives us a theory of preferences. From this perspective it appears that CDT is needlessly restricting its domain by focusing on justification-oriented behaviour that occurs after a choice has been made. This is because there will be a clash of constructs whenever a person recognizes that she may not be able to obtain everything she expected. The need to engage in dissonance-reducing behaviour after a choice has been made will be less if, at the time of choosing, the decision-maker can select not just a course of action but also a set of justifications for the choice and the rejection of its rivals. This is very much the position that Elster (1983, chapter III) appears to take in his discussion of the 'sour grapes' phenomenon: he notes that 'The Festinger experiments mostly interpret dissonance reduction as a reaction to actual choices, whereas my main focus has been on the shaping of preferences by the feasible set' (Elster, 1983, p. 122).

Consider the predicament of someone who believes herself to be environmentally conscious and also believes that a safe car is a large luxurious one which is both comfortable and easily able to execute overtaking manoeuvres. She believes it is time to replace her existing large old car since it has been needing expensive repairs. Unfortunately, her budget limits her to choosing between a new, economical shopping car and a secondhand executive vehicle which is thirstier and which cannot use leadfree petrol. As a motorist, she must opt for the executive car, but as a conservationist she must buy the shopping car. What will she do? One outcome might be that the motorist in her wins, and in justifying her choice she says 'After all, the car already exists and will continue to guzzle leaded fuel whether I buy it or not'. Or the conservationist in her may win, and she points out that 'After all, most of my driving is around town, and often I have to fly on interstate trips, anyway'. This position may have the advantage that it invites less criticism from those she mixes with socially. A third possibility is that she avoids the dissonance between motoring and conservation by changing her belief about the size of her budget constraint: this belief is likely to be challenged when she discusses her requirements with car dealers, who may point out to her that she could afford more if she borrowed more but paid back the loan over a longer period. Fourth, the person may abandon her belief that she needs to replace her existing car and tell herself that although it uses leaded fuel, she will be more of a conservationist if she uses her money to pay for a stream of repairs rather than disposing of the old car and paying for something newer.

From the standpoint adopted in this chapter, it appears that the person's choice will depend on the relative importance she assigns to the competing beliefs that appear to be called into question by particular courses of action, and on the cost of explaining to herself, and to those who ask, how she got round the dilemma. (This latter cost can itself be seen in terms of the implications to the person of the sacrifices she has to make to justify her choice.) As Steinbruner (1974, chap. 4) stresses, uncertainty will make it cognitively easier for the decision-maker to believe, at the time of making up her mind, that the choice is one that does not entail dissonance. In the case in question, the decision-maker is unlikely to face 'hard' evidence about factors such as whether the gas-guzzling car would otherwise be purchased by someone who travelled very small annual mileages, the number of long distance trips in the future that it will make more sense to undertake by air, or the actual environmental implications of a strategy of patching up an old vehicle (is more pollution generated by the extra fuel consumption and remanufacture of worn components, or by the manufacturing of a new, fuel-efficient vehicle?). The complexity of the decision problem may also make it easier for a seemingly dissonance-free decision to be reached: the boundedly rational decision-maker may fail to see that dissonance would arise from exploring the deeper implications of some of the arguments used in justifying a particular choice. Later, of course, these inconvenient implications may surface and generate the sort of behaviour predicted by Festinger.

LINKAGES BETWEEN PAST AND PRESENT CHOICES

A major theme in the work of Akerlof and Dickens (1982) is that attempts to reduce dissonance in the past may affect preferences in the present. They give an example concerning attitudes towards the purchase of newly invented safety equipment. Well-paid workers may have resolved the conflict between (a) suggestions that their

work environment is dangerous, and (b) their views of themselves as
'smart guys', by turning a blind eye to the dangers and telling
themselves that their pay reflects their smartness, not the probability
of injury at work. Having convinced themselves their jobs are not
particularly dangerous, they will be less interested than new recruits
in buying the newly-available safety equipment. Before concluding
this chapter it seems worthwhile to outline some further implications
from CDT and PCP about the possibility of path-dependent choices.

First, in seeking to cope with the aftermath of previous choices,
people may develop new constructs to construe things in terms of.
When new decision points arise, the expansion in the repertoire of
constructs may affect the way in which schemes are ranked.

Second, attempts to reduce dissonance will affect the information
that people will gather about possibilities, even if these activities do
not lead to a change in their construct repertoire. This means that,
when the time comes to replace a product, consumers may be looking
at a field that has already been narrowed down in a biased way.

Third, through data-mining activities and wishful thinking, a
decision-maker may be able to continue believing that sunk costs need
not yet be written off, even though onlookers are claiming that a
venture should be abandoned because a mistake has been made (for
an extreme example, see Earl, 1984, pp. 95–7). As the decision-
maker persists in pouring more and more time and money into the
project, she is tightening up her future budget constraint and allowing
opportunities to slip by.

Finally, there may be a kind of thin end of the wedge effect where
a successful dissonance reduction strategy enables a person to dodge
an inconsistency between one of her actions and her normal moral
constructs. This is recognized by Etzioni (1986, pp. 179–80), who
stresses that moral dilemmas are often irreversible, discontinuous and
prone to involve threshold effects. Noting Maital's discussion of
CDT in relation to the use of credit cards, Etzioni comments that,
'Taking out the first loan, for people who feel being in debt is a moral
evil, is different from extending it or taking out a second one'.
Suppose people buy things whilst telling themselves they are using
their credit cards merely as debit cards. If they then fail to pay off
their outstanding balances in full when their statements arrive, they
can no longer construe themselves as the sort of people who do not
get into debt (though, so long as they meet their payments obligations,
they can still claim not to be living beyond their means). Having, so
to speak, lost their virginity as debtors and come to see that the
situation does not entail the nasty implications that they expected,
they may become avid users of finance. Taking on debt reduces the
inconsistency between their views about what they ought to be

purchasing, and their views of their own means for paying for such commodities right now. (Note how, for some, a euphemistic phrase such as 'using finance' may itself have nicer connotations than 'being in debt'.) The sources of finance that they now use may include hire purchase, overdrafts and personal loans that they used to shun because, unlike credit cards, such arrangements necessarily involved an admission that one was borrowing.

CONCLUSION

In a chapter on CDT and PCP, it was perhaps inevitable that material would be considered in a rather reflexive manner. I set out to explore the complementarity of cognitive dissonance theory and personal construct psychology and rapidly encountered dissonance between these two bodies of thought: on the surface, the kind of behaviour identified by Festinger did not seem to fit in well with views about how one would expect people modelled 'as if they are scientists' to go about their lives. As one who has found PCP a powerful way of making sense of economic behaviour, I was naturally concerned to eliminate this dissonance: not merely for my own peace of mind, but also because CDT leads me to suspect that the existence of this dissonance might be used by other economists as a basis for justifying adherence to an economic methodology that gets by without PCP. By showing that professional scientists also behave in the manner predicted by Festinger, and by using PCP to amplify Elster's suggestion that dissonance reducing processes are not merely a post-choice phenomenon, I hope that I will increase interest in CDT as well as PCP.

But there are some areas of the chapter that are likely to provoke mixed responses among economists, depending on the paradigms to which they normally adhere. The popular paper by Akerlof and Dickens (1982) probably achieved its appeal in no small part as a result of using CDT in conjunction with mainstream economists' assumptions about rational expectations and full information. Here, by contrast, I have not only emphasized how uncertainty and complexity may give rise to impulsive behaviour; I have also followed the methodology of PCP by recognizing the subjectivity of beliefs and the idiosyncratic ways in which individuals form judgements. This chapter could thus make mainstream economic theorists feel *less* comfortable with the idea of using these kinds of psychology. Subjectivists of the Austrian or Post-Keynesian schools, on the other hand, should find that it fits in very well with their views on rationality and the nature of decision-making.

REFERENCES

Adams-Webber, J. R. (1979). *Personal construct theory: Concepts and applications.* Chichester: Wiley.

Akerlof, G. A., & Dickens, W. T. (1982). The economic consequences of cognitive dissonance. *American Economic Review,* **72**, 307-319.

Bannister, D., & Fransella, F. (1980). *Inquiring man: The psychology of personal constructs* (2nd edn). Harmondsworth: Penguin.

Bannister, D., & Mair, J. M. M. (1968). *The evaluation of personal constructs.* New York: Academic Press.

Cooley, T. F., & LeRoy, S. F. (1981). Identification and estimation of money demand. *American Economic Review,* **71**, 825-844.

Earl, P. E. (1983). *The economic imagination: Towards a behavioural analysis of choice.* Brighton: Wheatsheaf.

Earl, P. E. (1984). *The corporate imagination: How big companies make mistakes.* Brighton: Wheatsheaf.

Earl, P. E. (1986). *Lifestyle economics: Consumer behaviour in a turbulent world.* Brighton: Wheatsheaf.

Earl, P. E. (ed.) (1988). *Psychological economics: Development, tensions, prospects.* Boston MA: Kluwer.

Elster, J. (1983). *Sour grapes: Studies in the subversion of rationality.* Cambridge: Cambridge University Press.

Etzioni, A. (1986). The case for a multiple-utility conception. *Economics and Philosophy,* **2**, 159-184.

Festinger, L. (1957). *A theory of cognitive dissonance.* Stanford, CA: Stanford University Press.

Festinger, L. (Ed.) (1964). *Conflict, decision, and dissonance.* Stanford, CA: Stanford University Press.

Gilad, B., Kaish, S., & Loeb, P. D. (1987). Cognitive dissonance and utility maximization: A general framework. *Journal of Economic Behavior and Organization,* **8**, 61-73.

Gutman, J. (1982). A means–end chain model based on consumer categorisation processes. *Journal of Marketing,* **46**, 60-72.

Hinkle, D. N. (1965). The change of personal constructs from the viewpoint of a theory of implications. Unpublished Ph.D. dissertation, Ohio State University.

Hirschman, A. O. (1965). Obstacles to development: a classification and a quasi-vanishing act. *Economic Development and Cultural Change,* **13**, 385-393.

Kaish, S. (1986). Behavioral economics in the theory of the business cycle. In B. Gilad & S. Kaish (eds), *Handbook of behavioral economics* (Vol. B, pp. 31-49). Greenwich, CT: JAI Press.

Kelly, G. A. (1955). *The psychology of personal constructs.* New York: Norton.

Klausner, M. (1984). Sociological theory and the behavior of financial markets. In P. A. Adler & P. Adler (eds) *The social dynamics of financial markets* (pp. 57-81). Greenwich, CT: JAI Press.

Kuttner, R. (1985). The poverty of economics. *Atlantic Monthly* (February), 74-84.

Lewin, K. (1951). *Field theory in social science.* New York: Harper.

Loasby, B. J. (1983). Knowledge, learning and enterprise. In J. Wiseman (ed.) *Beyond positive economics?* (pp. 104-121). London: Macmillan.

Lovell, M. C. (1983). Data mining. *Review of Economics and Statistics,* **65**, 1-12.

Maital, S. (1982). *Minds, markets and money: Psychological foundations of economic behavior.* New York: Basic Books.
Mayer, T. (1980). Economics as a hard science: Realistic goal or wishful thinking? *Economic Inquiry,* **18,** 165-178.
Nisbett, R. E., & Ross, L. (1980). *Human inference: Strategies and shortcomings of social judgement.* Englewood Cliffs, NJ: Prentice-Hall.
Skinner. A. S. (1979). Adam Smith: An aspect of modern economics? *Scottish Journal of Political Economy,* **26,** 109-126.
Steinbruner, J. D. (1974). *The cybernetic theory of decision.* Princeton, NJ: Princeton University Press.

5. Moral constraints on strategic behaviour

Mark Casson
University of Reading

INTRODUCTION

This chapter has a simple point to make. Overall economic performance depends on transaction costs, and these reflect the level of trust in the economy. The level of trust depends in turn on culture. An effective culture has a strong moral content. Morality can overcome incentive problems that formal procedures – based on monitoring compliance with contracts – cannot. A strong culture therefore reduces transaction costs and enhances performance – the success of an economy depends on the quality of its culture.

The point is not new. It has been made many times by sociologists, anthropologists, social psychologists and historians, not to mention politicians and preachers. What is new is that the argument has now been made rigorous.

It is most unfortunate, however, that the concept of culture is neglected by most economists, and even despised by many of them. It is regarded as an ambiguous and therefore unscientific concept. But by rejecting it, economists restrict the relevance of their theory. This chapter offers a simple but rigorous model of the economic effects of culture in an attempt to dispel this parochial professional view.

MICROFOUNDATIONS OF THE ECONOMY

Economic theory is essentially a theory of individual decision-making within an interdependent system. Culture can influence both the decision-maker's objectives and his perceptions of the constraints. As a result it can influence economic performance in many different ways (Brubaker, 1984; Hirsch, 1977; Weber, 1947). The particular emphasis of this chapter is on attitudes and beliefs relating to other people. It is concerned with the social rather than the natural environment. The division of labour, together with the spatial dispersion of the population, means that much economic activity is carried out by small groups of people. Some of these groups are fairly permanent – teams of workers in a factory, for example. Others are relatively transitory. Examples are traders attending a local market, and people assembling to share the benefits of a public good – listening to the news, attending a performance or ceremony, and so on. The spatial dimension of the economy means that people may also meet inadvertently – this can be a source of problems, for instance when routes to work or to market are congested.

Economic activity over time may, in fact, be conceptualized as a sequence of encounters between individuals (Wolinsky, 1987). Culture determines the social environment, and technology the material environment within which these encounters occur. Some of these encounters are one-off (opportunistic trades, for example) whilst others are recurrent (teamwork, for instance). Overall economic performance may then be related to the success with which the typical encounter fulfills its objectives.

Encounters which are intended to be beneficial can easily turn out to be harmful instead. A trading encounter can lead to harmful results if one of the parties lies about the quality of his supplies or subsequently reneges on some aspect of the agreement. If the encounter is designed to exchange goods on terms agreed at a previous meeting, and one party has already committed most of his costs, the other party may instigate an opportunistic renegotiation of price. Likewise, a production encounter may turn out disappointingly if one of the team members secretly slacks instead of working hard as the others do. More generally, the spatial extension of the economy means that there is a need for social order to make travel between encounters safe.

In conventional terminology, it may be said that any encounter between two people potentially affords mutual externality – each individual's actions impinge on the welfare of the other. These externalities can, in principle, be resolved through contractual arrangements. Since, however, some of the problems relate to behaviour before any contract has been agreed between the parties, the parties alone cannot resolve it. Even after the contract has been agreed, the victim may have difficulty enforcing a penalty against the offender (Sugden, 1986).

It is therefore normally necessary to invoke a third party with whom each of the parties has a prior contract of some kind. In the case of transactions it is the legal system which typically acts in this capacity. The victim is normally responsible for collecting evidence against the offender, but it is the judiciary that weighs the evidence and enforces the penalty. (Where contraventions of social order are concerned, however, the law itself normally collects the evidence and prosecutes independently of the wishes of the victim.) In practice, the costs of using the legal system are often prohibitive. There are substantial fixed costs in collecting evidence, holding hearings and determining a judgement, and this means that the legal resolution of minor disputes is inefficient. In practice, the success of encounters in which costs and benefits are small does not hinge on the rule of law but on the existence of goodwill between the parties involved.

In the absence of a viable legal framework, the crucial question for each individual is whether the other person can be trusted (Gambetta, 1988). Can you expect other people with whom no contract exists to forbear from taking advantage – as in a casual encounter when one person has a chance to steal from another? Can you expect people to forbear when negotiating a contract, by giving an honest description of their product and being willing to compromise over price? The conventional concept of economic man suggests that people cannot be trusted. More specifically, it suggests that other people will be honest or considerate only when it is expedient for them to be so. This in turn depends upon their preferences and constraints. The former are specific to the person and the latter to their situation. The key aspect of the constraints is the incentive structure. This includes the system of rewards and penalties associated with the current encounter, together with incentives generated by the effect of the outcome of the present encounter on any future encounters in which the parties may be involved.

Thus to know whether someone can be trusted a large amount of information is required upon their situation, and an extremely sophisticated model is needed to predict their most expedient strategy (Klein and Leffler, 1981). The conventional model of economic man therefore fails to provide the decision-maker with a simple method of prediction. Distrust based upon expediency is a major source of complexity. The difficulty of arriving at a rational solution may persuade the individual to avoid the encounter altogether. This reduces the volume of production and trade and, when other individuals follow suit, seriously impairs economic performance.

LEADERSHIP AND MORAL MANIPULATION

An alternative mechanism to self-interest is therefore required for successful co-ordination. Such an alternative exists, it may be claimed, because of people's capacity for moral commitment. Economic man offers a misleading caricature of human nature because he evaluates only means and does not consider the legitimacy of ends. In practice, individuals have sufficient imagination and empathy to consider the consequences of their actions for others, and to compensate for these by purely internal rewards and punishments. It is perhaps not too fanciful to say that these rewards and punishments are effected by adding to or subtracting from the individual's stock of self-esteem.

Individuals who are morally committed can recognize the potential for moral commitment in others. (A simple theory of human nature is, after all, that 'other people are like me'.) Trust in other people need not, therefore be based on a complicated calculation of how economic man would respond to a particular incentive structure, but rather on a simple judgement as to whether one is dealing with an 'ethical man' rather than an 'economic man'.

The same conclusion may be arrived at by a slightly different route. Given the prohibitive costs of monitoring small-scale encounters, an obviously superior system is one in which the individuals internalize the external consequences themselves. Each individual, in other words, forbears from actions damaging to the other party. Such activity automatically validates the trust the other party places in him, and helps to sustain mutual trust as a social equilibrium.

The superiority of the moral mechanism over the monitoring system is that it turns to advantage the natural information asymmetry which is the cause of the difficulty in monitoring. The information asymmetry is that people know their own plans and their own actions better than other people. Under the moral mechanism, people punish themselves for anti-social behaviour, rather than relying on a third party, such as the legal system, to do it for them. The moral mechanism turns people into self-monitoring agents and so avoids the costs of external monitoring.

A moral sense may be regarded as to some degree innate in most people but, whether one accepts this or not, it is clear that moral awareness can be manipulated – for example by parents, role models, priests and political leaders. It is assumed in this chapter that each individual is manipulated by a single leader, although it is clear that in practice multiple allegiance is possible. The leader simply personifies the source of moral manipulation. Even where moral influence is clearly dispersed – as with peer group influence exerted by the many different members of a group – the assumption of a single source of manipulation is retained for the sake of simplicity.

Economies which lack effective moral leadership are obliged to rely very heavily on formal monitoring mechanisms. Economies with strong leadership, by contrast have a choice of incentive mechanisms. They are not committed to formal monitoring in situations where information is costly to obtain and punishment difficult to enforce. The greater flexibility that effective leadership provides allows overall transaction costs to be reduced, and so overall performance to be improved.

Leadership is a consequence of the division of labour applied to social groups. Externally, the leader's role is to represent the group in its relations with other groups – for example, in a primitive group the leader may act as statesman, champion and warrior-general. Internally the leader is responsible for co-ordinating group activity. In a group with a formal monitoring system the leader's role is to supervise the system, which usually means acting as a sovereign in upholding the institutions of the law. In a group that does not rely on monitoring, the leader's role is that of a moralist and exemplar who engineers commitment in order to build up trust between the followers. Thus, just as the monitoring of contracts tends to be a specialized function, cultural engineering is specialized too. Unfortunately, leadership today often connotes a style of management which is designed merely to build up people's confidence in the leader himself. This style is particularly notable among military and political leaders, who wish to inspire blind faith in their personal judgement. Such leadership has justifiably acquired a bad reputation. There is, indeed, a strong Western tradition that leaders cannot be trusted. The trust which followers place in their leader gives the leader too much power. 'Power corrupts, and absolute power corrupts absolutely', it is claimed.

The leadership described in this chapter has a different orientation, however. The intention is to build up confidence in other people rather than in the leader himself. This in turn reflects the underlying strategy of engineering trust. There are two main aspects of this strategy, and the models in this chapter explain how these two aspects relate to each other. The first is to make each individual as trustworthy as possible, by building up moral commitment. The second is to make him or her optimistic about other people's honesty at the same time. Optimism serves two distinct purposes. To begin with, in many situations honesty is more advantageous if it is reciprocated. Second, there are other situations where people are so frightened of other people that they are unwilling to participate with them even on a trial basis. Unless people are sufficiently optimistic to give others a chance to prove themselves, they will never learn that they are really trustworthy.

PAIRWISE ENCOUNTERS

The rest of the chapter outlines a formal model which develops some of the implications of the general points made above. The focus is on a national leader who reduces transaction costs in a market economy. The model achieves simplicity by exploiting the fact than an encounter between two people maybe represented as a 2 x 2 non-cooperative game. Each individual has two strategies: he can choose to be honest or to cheat. Only mutual honesty achieves full co-ordination.

Suppose that everyone belongs to a large group of fixed size, n, within which pairwise encounters occur. The group is the basic economic unit in this analysis and the co-ordination of encounters governs group performance. In a material sense, everyone is identical – they experience the same material rewards from the same pairwise combination of strategies.

In the emotional dimension, however, people differ in their sensitivities. Sensitivity is measured by an indicator s which ranges from zero for a completely insensitive individual to unity for the most sensitive individual. The value of s determines whether a given intensity of moral manipulation by the leader – as measured by the intensity of his or her moral rhetoric – induces a small or large amount of guilt in response to cheating. Thus it is impossible to arouse feelings of guilt in a totally insensitive individual, but relatively easy in a more sensitive one.

The exercise of leadership through moral manipulation is costly. Many of the expenses incurred in government publicity, regulation of the media, resourcing moral instruction in schools and so on, can be interpreted as costs of manipulation. The intensity of manipulation, it is assumed, can be measured by a variable $\theta \geq 0$, so that costs of manipulation, c, can be expressed as an increasing function of θ. When the costs of manipulation are significant, moral rhetoric can only reduce the incidence of cheating – it is usually uneconomic to eliminate it altogether.

Each period each individual experiences one encounter with a randomly selected partner. This chapter concentrates on encounters over just a single period. At the beginning of the period there is no accumulated experience. In the absence of any announcement by the leader, everyone forms their own opinion of whether their partner is likely to be honest or not.

The material rewards generated by an encounter are indicated in Table 5.1. The rewards are those received by a typical follower in an encounter with a partner. Mutual honesty rewards each person with h ≥ 0. Encounters can, however, make people worse off rather than better off; with mutual cheating it would sometimes have been better that the encounter had never occurred at all. The *symmetric coordination gain* $a > 0$ measures the gain from mutual honesty compared to mutual cheating, and may well exceed the basic gain h.

The *incentive to cheat* when the other party is honest is b. Now if cheating merely redistributes rewards then what the cheater gains, the honest victim loses; thus the cheat who gains $h + b$ rather than h causes the honest victim to gain only $h - b$ instead of h, leaving the total gain to the pair of them unchanged at $2h$. This case in which cheating merely redistributes rewards is ruled out by assuming that the victim loses a further amount $d > 0$. This is the *asymmetric coordination gain* – it measures the gain to mutual honesty compared to one person taking the other for a sucker.

The structure of emotional rewards is illustrated in Table 5.2. The important point to note is that guilt is associated both with cheating an honest person and with cheating on a cheat. This may be justified on two grounds. The first is philosophical: guilt is related to moral intent, and the intent to cheat is formed before it is known whether the other party cheats as well. The second is more practical: confining guilt to cheating the innocent introduces non-linearities which complicate the analysis.

Combining the material and emotional rewards within the simplified follower's decision model outlined here gives the data set shown in Table 5.3. The follower associates a subjective probability p $(0 \leq p \leq 1)$ with the possibility that his partner cheats.

Table 5.1 Material rewards from an encounter

	Partner's strategy	
Follower's strategy	Honesty	Cheating
Honesty	h	$h - b - d$
Cheating	$h + b$	$h - a$

Table 5.2 Emotional rewards from an encounter

| | Partner's strategy | |
Follower's strategy	Honesty	Cheating
Honesty	0	0
Cheating	*g*	*g*

Table 5.3 Follower's data set for an encounter

| | Partner's strategy | |
Follower's strategy	Honesty	Cheating
Honesty	*h*	*h - b - d*
Cheating	*h + b - g*	*h - a - g*
Perceived probability	$1 - p$	p

The follower prefers honesty to cheating if the expected value of the benefit, as he perceives it, is non-negative:

$$(1 - p)(g - b) + p(g + a - b - d) \geq 0$$

that is,

$$g \geq b + kp \tag{1}$$

where

$$k = d - a \tag{2}$$

measures the excess of the incentive to cheat a cheat over the incentive to cheat an honest partner. The larger is *d*, the more you lose by being taken for a sucker compared to what you would gain by cheating someone honest. The smaller is *a*, the less you lose by cheating a cheat compared to reciprocating honesty to an honest party.

For an individual of sensitivity *s* ($0 \leq s \leq 1$) facing an intensity of manipulation θ, the guilt is

$$g = s\theta \tag{3}$$

whence, from (1) and (3), the critical level of sensitivity which induces honesty is

$$s^* = (b + kp)/\Theta \tag{4}$$

Consider now the distribution of sensitivity within the group. Since, according to (4), both sensitivity and the degree of optimism affect integrity, it is necessary to specify the bivariate distribution of both s and p. Let $F(s,p)$ represent the relevant cumulative distribution function; the value of F measures the proportion of the group comprising people with a sensitivity less than or equal to s who also hold a subjective probability less than or equal to p. The crime rate q corresponds to the proportion of the population which combines a probability p with a sensitivity $s < s^*$. Thus, in general, q depends on the parameters of F, the values b and k, and the intensity of manipulation, Θ. In the special case $k = 0$, discussed below, s^* is independent of p

$$s^* = b/\Theta \tag{5}$$

and so the crime rate is determined simply by the partial distribution of the crime rate across the population as a whole:

$$q = F(s^*, 1) \tag{6}$$

In other cases the derivation of q is more complex, as indicated later.

An altruistic leader pursuing materialistic objectives maximizes

$$u = v - c \tag{7}$$

where v is the expected value of the material reward of a representative follower and c is the cost of manipulation (note that this measure of reward ignores the guilt experienced by cheats). With a crime rate q the probability that both partners in an encounter are honest is $(1 - q)^2$ and in this case both receive a reward h. The probability that a cheat takes advantage of an honest victim is $2q(1 - q)$, and the reward, averaged over cheat and victim, is $h - (d/2)$. Finally, the probability that both cheat is q^2, and in this case each receives a reward $h - a$. Thus the expected value of the material reward is

$$v = (1 - q)^2 h + q(1 - q)(2h - d) + q^2(h - a)$$

$$= h - dq + kq^2$$

For $k = 0$, v is a linear function of q, but otherwise it is quadratic. To eliminate the non-linearity in order to permit a simple solution of the leader's optimization problem, a first-order approximation is taken about the mid-point of the unit interval over which q is defined. Using the first two terms of a Taylor's series expansion about $q = 1/2$ gives

$$v = v_0 - aq \tag{8}$$

where

$$v_0 = h - (k/4) \tag{9}$$

The cost of manipulation is

$$c = \begin{cases} 0 & \theta = 0 \\ c_f + c_v \theta & \theta > 0 \end{cases} \tag{10}$$

where $c_f \geq 0$ is the fixed cost of manipulation and $c_v > 0$ the marginal cost. Given the leader's knowledge of the follower's decision data, and the parameters of the distribution F, he can predict the crime rate as a function of the intensity of manipulation. The leader's utility can then be expressed as a function of θ and maximized accordingly.

OPTIMIZING LEADERSHIP IN A TRADING ECONOMY

The concept of an encounter is a quite general one, and embraces a number of interesting special cases. The next two sections focus on just one of these – namely trade. Trade involves two technically independent but contractually linked activities – namely the transfer of a good (or service) from one individual to another, and a matching transfer in the other direction. Trade therefore highlights the opportunities for default that arise for purely contractual reasons, quite independently of the technological externalities associated with team production.

Trade represents a Prisoner's Dilemma (PD) in which, in the absence of punishment, it always pays to cheat. If the other person is honest, then it pays to be aggressive and to take them for a sucker, whilst if the other person cheats it pays to be defensive – by cheating on them you avoid being taken for a sucker yourself. There are, however, two important differences from the usual formulation of a PD.

The first is that only the material rewards satisfy the PD. Once emotional rewards are introduced, the PD can be transformed into a game where cheating no longer pays. The second is that traders have limited information. Although their partner's material rewards are similar to their own, they do not know this. Each trader works with an oversimplified model of his environment in which he simply associates a subjective probability with the possibility that the partner cheats. It is only in recurrent trading that this probability is based on objective evidence. Although recurrent trading modifies behaviour, the principles that govern one-off trading still apply to recurrent trades (Casson, 1991). Thus the model of one-off trades is quite robust to changes of specification so far as its main predictions are concerned.

Consider a symmetric trading situation in which each party exchanges a single unit of a good he values at b for a single unit of a good he values at $a + b$ ($a, b > 0$). Supplies have to be despatched before purchases are received, and the individual does not know whether the purchases are on their way at the time he commits himself to despatch. Trade provides the cheat with an opportunity to take delivery of goods without making payment for them. This generates the structure of rewards shown in Table 5.4, which corresponds to Table 5.3 with $h = d = a$, which in turn means that $k = 0$.

Table 5.4 Partner's data set for an encounter

Follower's strategy	Partner's strategy	
	Honesty	Cheating
Honesty	a	$- b$
Cheating	$a + b - g$	$- g$
Perceived probability	$1 - p$	p

In the trade situation, therefore, the critical level of guilt needed to guarantee honest trade is independent of the perceived probability that the other party will cheat. This is because of the technical separability of the two parts of the exchange. The gain to cheating is that one party keeps the product that the other party is expecting to receive, and this product is of value b independently of whether the other part of the transaction is fulfilled.

The role of manipulation is to remove the PD by associating an emotional penalty with cheating. Since the material gain to cheating is b, and is the same for everyone, manipulation will have no effect until the intensity of guilt reaches b. Only then will the most sensitive decide not to cheat. As the intensity is increased beyond b, others will decide to be honest too, but given a suitable distribution F, the number crossing the threshold to honesty will decline steadily as those that remain as cheats are increasingly insensitive to guilt. Eventually some finite optimal intensity of manipulation is reached at which the marginal cost of greater intensity is just equal to the expected value of the marginal gain from greater honesty that will result. The only qualification is that the fixed cost of manipulation should not be so high that manipulation of any kind is uneconomic.

The best way to illustrate the optimization is to postulate a uniform bivariate distribution of sensitivity and probability.

$$F(s,p) = sp \qquad\qquad (0 \le s,p \le 1) \qquad\qquad (11)$$

Equation (11) implies that members of the group are uniformly distributed over the unit square in s,p space, with perceived probability being independent of the sensitivity of the individual concerned. The specification (11) is sufficient to guarantee that the numbers crossing the threshold to honesty decline continuously as manipulation increases.

Because $k = 0$ the derivation of the crime rate is very straightforward. Since (5) and (6) apply,

$$q = F(s^*, 1) = F(b/\theta, 1) = \begin{cases} 1 & \theta < b \\ b/\theta & \theta \ge b \end{cases} \qquad\qquad (12)$$

Substituting (8) – (10) and (12) into (7) and taking $\ge b$ gives

$$u = a - c_f - (ab/\theta) - c_v \theta \qquad\qquad (13)$$

The first order condition for an interior maximum

$$du/d\theta = (ab/\theta^2) - c_v = 0 \qquad\qquad (14)$$

gives

$$\theta^e = (ab/c_v)^{1/2} \tag{15.1}$$
$$q^e = (bc_v/a)^{1/2} \tag{15.2}$$
$$v^e = v_0 - (abc_v)^{1/2} \tag{15.3}$$
$$u^e = v_0 - 2(abc_v)^{1/2} - c_f \tag{15.4}$$

where the superscript e indicates an equilibrium (that is, maximizing) value. The second order condition for a maximum is

$$d^2u/d\theta^2 = -2ab/\theta^3 < 0 \tag{16}$$

and this condition is always satisfied since a, b and   are positive. The net benefit of manipulation compared with inaction is

$$\Delta u = u^e - u(0)$$

where

$$u(0) = v_0 - a$$

Manipulation is advantageous if $\Delta u > 0$, that is, if

$$c_f < a - 2(abc_v)^{1/2} \tag{17}$$

When interpreting the results (15), the obvious point to begin with is that the optimal intensity of manipulation is homogeneous of degree one in a and b; this means that as the value of the product traded increases, the intensity of manipulation increases in direct proportion. On the other hand, the crime rate is homogeneous of degree zero in a and b, so as the value of the product and the associated intensity of manipulation increase in line with each other, the crime rate remains unchanged.

When the cost of manipulation c_v is allowed to vary as well, the degree of homogeneity of the intensity of manipulation falls to one half; this implies that if the cost of manipulation increases in line with the value of the product then the intensity of manipulation will still rise to some extent, but even so the crime rate will increase as well. This is because the increase in the value of the product increases the material incentive to cheat, at a time when the rising cost of manipulation makes it difficult to achieve a corresponding increase in the emotional penalties involved.

The second point to note is that the crime rate is related to the ratio of the supplier's valuation of the product, b, to the gain from trade a. The crime rate is higher, the higher is the proportion of the buyers' valuation that is matched by the seller's valuation. This proportion is likely to be high for versatile goods such as land, but much lower for highly customized goods such as professional services, where the value to the customer is much greater than the opportunity cost of the professional's time. This suggests that moral manipulation will be more effective with customized goods such as professional services than with versatile goods such as land.

The third point concerns the effects of variations in the cost of manipulation c_v. When the traders come from very different ethnic or religious groups, or are highly dispersed over space, suitable moral rhetoric and effective communication may be difficult to achieve. Thus in international trade, for example, moral manipulation may be much less viable than in internal national trade.

COMPARISON WITH MONITORING

Suppose that a monitoring mechanism can be established at a fixed cost c'_f which is independent of the penalty imposed for cheating. It is assumed that monitoring is perfectly reliable; there is no risk of either failing to detect a cheat or wrongly accusing an honest person. Since the monitoring system is perfectly reliable, and the leader is fully trusted, the followers perceive no risk in placing themselves hostage to a penalty system. It follows that any penalty in excess of b will be sufficient to stop all followers from cheating. Thus the fixed cost c'_f may be identified as the total transaction cost associated with monitoring:

$$t' = c'_f \tag{18}$$

The transaction cost associated with manipulation has two components. The direct cost is the cost of manipulation, and the indirect cost is the loss of material co-ordination due to residual cheating. This second component reflects the fact that – unlike monitoring – manipulation does not completely eliminate cheating. Both cost components depend on the intensity of manipulation. The minimum transaction cost associated with manipulation is

$$t^e = v_0 - u^e = c_f + 2(abc_v)^{1/2} \tag{19}$$

The leader chooses manipulation if

$$t^e < t' \tag{20}$$

that is, if

$$c_f < c'_f - 2(abc_v)^{1/2} \tag{21}$$

The concept of transaction cost used here resembles quite closely the familiar concept derived from institutional economics. It reflects the costs of enforcing contracts between followers. The novelty is that moral manipulation is included within the transactions technologies, as well as monitoring. The predictions of the theory are much richer than those of ordinary transaction cost theory because they include the condition for choice of technique (inequality (21)) as well as the optimal manipulation functions (15).

Monitoring costs are likely to be high wherever default is concerned with the quality rather than the quantity of a good. When goods are easy to inspect, it is difficult to deceive the buyer about the quality, but in other cases poor quality may only come to light when the buyer attempts to utilize the good later on. Information asymmetries mean that the seller may have privileged information relating to the quality of the good, and he can use this to supply worthless 'duds' or 'lemons' instead of 'first quality' items (Akerlof, 1970).

In the context of the previous discussion, for example, the quality of specialist professional services is often difficult for the lay customer to judge. Monitoring costs are therefore high because another specialist may have to be called in to give a 'second opinion'. Moral manipulation is therefore particularly suitable in this case. Where international trade in relatively standardized products such as fabricated metals is concerned, however, monitoring costs are relatively low, while moral manipulation may be particularly difficult (for reasons of communication and cultural heterogeneity alluded to above). This is a case where monitoring is likely to be used instead.

ANNOUNCEMENT EFFECTS

An important aspect of leadership is the ability to influence not only the moral attitudes of followers but also their beliefs. In the preceding analysis the leader has operated only in the moral dimension. He has modified the distribution of the population in g,p space by operating only along the g axis.

In the special case $k = 0$ – as exemplified by the PD discussed in section 6 – the p dimension is, in fact, of no consequence, for the incentive to cheat is independent of whether other people are believed to be honest or not. When $k \neq 0$, however, manipulating beliefs can make an important contribution to economic performance. The larger the absolute value of k, the greater is the potential contribution.

Consider, therefore, a leader who can announce, before encounters commence, what he believes the crime rate will be. It is assumed that the followers trust his judgement sufficiently to take this as an accurate prediction. The same announcement is made to all members of the group, so that it has the characteristics of a public good. Since the subject of the announcement is the crime rate for the group, rather than for any specific individual, the leader is engineering the reputation of the group. It is, in fact, the reputation of the group with itself that is being affected.

In some cases an announcement is a complete substitute for manipulation, and in other cases only a partial one. Either way, the optimal announcement is the one that minimizes the resultant incentive to cheat. If $k > 0$, so that belief in the honesty of the other party stimulates honest behaviour, then the optimal announcement is that everyone is honest: $p = 0$. If, in addition, $b \leq 0$, then everyone will perceive honesty as optimal, and the announcement will be self-fulfilling without further manipulation. The case $b < 0$ is often encountered in teamwork, where it actually pays to be honest – but only if the other party is honest too. In the more familiar case $b > 0$ then some additional moral manipulation will be required, but the manipulation will be less than it would be for $p > 0$.

If, on the other hand, $k < 0$, so that belief in the honesty of the other party discourages honesty, then the optimal announcement is that everyone cheats: $p = 1$. If, in addition, $b + k \leq 0$, then everyone again perceives honesty as optimal – although for completely different reasons. This announcement strategy is somewhat bizarre because it works by being self-denying. It could not be used repeatedly on a group of intelligent followers. Because this chapter is concerned with one-off encounters, however, this is not a relevant objection at this stage. It is clear, though, that in the recurrent case announcements can deal with $k > 0$ more readily than with $k < 0$. The former requires a self-validating announcement of honesty whilst the latter depends on a self-denying announcement of cheating which will face insuperable credibility problems.

The details of the optimal announcement strategies are presented in Table 5.5. It is assumed that each announcement is coupled with an optimal degree of moral manipulation. The optimal manipulation is less when an announcement has been made than when it has not. The cases reported in lines 1 and 3 require no moral manipulation at all. Those in lines 2 and 4 require additional manipulation, and the results reported assume that this manipulation is cost effective. Indeed, it is a

Table 5.5 Announcement strategies and their value

Reference	k	$b, b+k$	Announced p-value	Optimal p	q	Gains to announcement compared to pure moral manipulation
1	$k > 0$	$b \leq 0$	0	0	0	$(2ac_v/k)^{1/2}(b+k) + c_f - c_a$
2	$k > 0$	$b > 0$	0	$(ab/c_v)^{1/2}$	$(bc_v/a)^{1/2}$	$2(ac_v)^{1/2}((b+(k/2))^{1/2}-b^{1/2})-c_a$
3	$k < 0$	$b+k \leq 0$	1	0	0	$(-2ac_v/k)^{1/2}b + c_f - c_a$
4	$k < 0$	$b+k > 0$	1	$(a(b+k)/c_v)^{1/2}$	$((b+k)c_v/a)^{1/2}$	$2(ac_v)^{1/2}((b+(k/2))^{1/2} - (b+k)^{1/2}) - c_a$

condition for the announcement to be economic in these cases that manipulation is economic too, because the announcement alone is insufficient to induce anyone to be honest.

The value of the announcement strategy is reported in the final column of the table. The value is higher the higher are the gains from coordination, the lower are the cost factors c_f and c_v (where they are relevant) and the lower is the fixed cost of the announcement, c_a. In each case the value of the announcement is greater the larger the absolute value of k. The results indicate that in the general case where the guilt requirement is probability-dependent, the leader's skill in publicising plausible predictions (as reflected in a low cost of announcement c_a) is an important influence on group performance.

COMPARATIVE STATICS

The model can be used to compare the behaviour of two different economies – such as the US and Japan – at a given point in time, or the performance of the same economy at different times – for example, the pre-Thatcher and post-Thatcher UK economy. Differentiating equations (15) shows that when $a, b, c_v > 0$,

$$\partial\theta^e/\partial a > 0 \qquad \partial\theta^e/\partial b > 0 \qquad \partial\theta^e/\partial c_v < 0 \qquad (22.1)$$

$$\partial q^e/\partial a < 0 \qquad \partial q^e/\partial b > 0 \qquad \partial q^e/\partial c_v > 0 \qquad (22.2)$$

$$\partial v^e/\partial a < 0 \qquad \partial v^e/\partial b < 0 \qquad \partial v^e/\partial c_v < 0 \qquad (22.3)$$

Focusing on the right hand column, it can be seen that an economy with a low cost of manipulation will be characterized by more intensive manipulation, less crime and improved performance. If it is assumed that the cost of manipulation is lower, say, in Japan than in the US, then the model predicts that Japanese leaders will invest heavily in manipulation in order to reduce cheating and raise performance above that of the US. Correspondingly, equation (17) implies that because of the higher cost of manipulation assumed above, the US is more likely to rely on monitoring instead. US reliance on formal monitoring procedures is corroborated by the extensive employment of lawyers and accountants in the US, and the cultural emphasis on legal process there. The model therefore provides a consistent cultural explanation for differences in economic performance between the US and Japan.

CONCLUSION

This chapter has presented a simple account of the ways in which culture can affect economic performance. It has developed a simple model which yields hypotheses of real explanatory power.

The basic idea of the model is to distinguish between material and emotional rewards. Emotional rewards can be influenced by moral considerations, but material rewards cannot. Morality, though ultimately a matter of individual conscience, has an important social dimension. The model postulates that each individual is affiliated to a social group. Within a group, the moral outlook represents value-laden information which has the property of a public good.

There is a division of labour between leader and follower within a group. Group performance depends on the efficiency of co-ordination, for which the leader carries overall responsibility. The model predicts the way in which leadership behaviour will respond to the natural economic incentives in the environment. It shows that optimal leadership will maximize economic performance, as measured, for example, by the gains from trade.

The basic model can be extended to include groups in which participation in encounters is voluntary, and in which encounters occur on a repeated basis (see Casson, 1991). This extension affords new insights, but does not substantially qualify any of the results presented here.

REFERENCES

Akerlof, G.A. (1970). The market for lemons: Quality, uncertainty and the market mechanism. *Quarterly Journal of Economics*, **84**, 488-500.

Brubaker, R. (1984). *The limits of rationality: An essay on the social and moral thought of Max Weber*. London: Allen and Unwin.

Casson, M.C. (1991). *Economics of business culture: Game theory, transaction costs and economic performance*. Oxford: Clarendon Press.

Gambetta, D. (ed) (1988). *Trust: Making and breaking cooperative relations*. Oxford: Blackwell.

Hirsch, F. (1977). *Social limits to growth*. London: Routledge and Kegan Paul.

Klein, B. & Leffler, K. (1981). The role of market forces in assuring contractual performance. *Journal of Political Economy*, **89**, 615-41.

Sugden, R. (1986). *The economics of rights, co-operation and welfare*. Oxford: Blackwell.

Weber, M. (1947). *The theory of social and economic organisation* (trans. A.M. Henderson & T. Parsons, ed. T. Parsons). New York: Oxford University Press.

Wolinsky, A. (1987). Information revelation in a market with pairwise meetings. *Warwick Economic Research Papers*, No. 284.

6. Experiments in economics – and psychology

John D. Hey
University of York

INTRODUCTION

One particular area of almost complete incomprehension between economists and psychologists is connected with the running of experiments – and most notably with the question of payments to subjects. On the one hand, psychologists generally appear to regard actual monetary payments to subjects as being relatively unimportant. A good recent example is provided by a plenary address by Tversky (Tversky and Kahneman, 1990) who reported an experiment involving varying amounts of hypothetical payments, ranging from a few cents to many thousands of dollars, which was validated (to Tversky's satisfaction) with real payments solely at the 'few cents' level. When questioned afterwards he was quite adamant that validation at the 'many thousands of dollars' level would not be worthwhile.

In contrast, economists generally quite clearly regard actual payments – particularly large amounts – as being very important. A good example is provided by Smith (Cox, Smith and Walker, 1990), who reported on an experiment conducted by him and his associates, in which subjects could earn hundreds of dollars for an hour's participation in an experiment.

Psychologists, who have been doing experiments for millennia (they would probably claim that the first psychological experiment was when God put Adam and Eve in the Garden of Eden) tend to regard experimental economists as Johnnies-come-lately who ignore all the good work done by psychologists, and who hope that the problems of experimental design will be solved simply by throwing large numbers of dollar bills around the laboratory. Economists, on

the other hand, view psychological experiments with deep suspicion –
viewing the typical subject in a psychological experiment as one who
is told that he will get a few dollars for doing a certain task, but who
knows that he will actually do something completely different – and
get 10,000 volts in his private parts as a reward.

Part of the reason for these differences is simply that economics
and psychology are different disciplines, and that economists and
psychologists are interested in different things.   For example,
economists, when carrying out an economics experiment are
interested in the economic decisions taken – and not in the subjects'
pulse rates or eye movements.

But more fundamentally it reflects the differing methodologies in
the two disciplines: The economists – at least the mainstream
economists – have a strong commitment to theory, and have a central
unifying theory as the central core of their discipline; in contrast, the
psychologists are more empirically oriented and lack a central
unifying theory. So for many economists, experiments are theory-
testing experiments – as in the natural sciences – rather than theory-
suggesting experiments – which is the more usual case in psychology.

THE ECONOMIC MAINSTREAM

Economists doing experiments have an additional problem that
psychologists doing experiments do not – that they are regarded with
some considerable suspicion by a majority of the mainstream in their
discipline. I speak from bitter experience gained from innumerable
seminars to die-hard mainstream economists. In order to explain what
I mean by this, I can most usefully start with a quotation which
exemplifies much of what the mainstream economist thinks about his
discipline. It is a quote from a major econometric text, *The Theory
and Practice of Econometrics*, by Judge, Griffiths, Hill and Lee
(1980):

> Economic theory, through a formal deductive system, provides the basis for
> experimental abstraction and the experimental design, but society in most cases
> carries out the experiment, possibly using its own design . . . The
> nonexperimental restriction . . . means that . . . one must . . . use non-sample
> information . . . Thus, much of econometrics is concerned with how to . . . use
> this non-sample information in conjunction with the sample observations. (p. 4)

Let me expand on this.   The conventional method used in
economics is to derive the economic theory under strict *ceteris
paribus* conditions.   The 'rules of the game' and the objective

functions of the various economic agents in the theory are well-defined and clearly specified; hence the solution is well-defined and clearly specified – under the *ceteris paribus* assumptions of course. Then (usually) the theory is subjected to test under conditions where the *ceteris* of the theory is quite clearly not *paribus*. In other words the data used to test a theory is not generated under the same conditions as those under which the theory itself is generated. This reflects the fact that the average economist thinks that the best way of collecting data is to lie in bed and hope that someone else will collect it for him. This point of view is reinforced by econometricians (see the quote from Judge *et al.* above) whose whole discipline is based on the presupposition that economics is a non-experimental science.

Naturally I shall argue against this presupposition later in this chapter but, for the time being, I want to explore a little further the implications of this conventional method. Since the theory is tested under different conditions from those under which the theory is specified, it follows that a conventional test of an economic theory is a combined test of:

(a) whether the theory is correct under the *ceteris paribus* conditions; and
(b) whether the theory survives the transition from the *ceteris paribus* world to the real world.

Unfortunately, this combined testing means that it is almost impossible to make any conclusive inferences from a (non-experimental) test of an economic theory. If the combined test is favourable does it mean that both (a) and (b) are correct or that both are incorrect (in such a way that the errors in each 'cancel out' the errors in the other)? If the combined test is unfavourable does it mean that (a) is correct and (b) incorrect or that (a) is incorrect and (b) correct or that both (a) and (b) are incorrect (in a non-cancelling out fashion)?

This difficulty seems to suggest clearly that one ought to do experiments so that one can test the theory under the *ceteris paribus* conditions of that theory. In this way one can isolate (a) from (b). Moreover, because of the way that economic theory is specified and derived, such an experimental testing procedure is almost always possible. Consider, for example, the following simple model (from Fudenberg, Gilbert, Stiglitz and Tirole, 1983), which is one of the new genre of Industrial Organization models beloved by economic theorists. It is a model of a Research and Development patent race and is typical of the genre.

There are two players/firms. They start level. The winning post is n steps away. Play takes place in rounds; each round the two players decide and announce simultaneously whether they will take zero, one or two steps towards the winning post that round. Going zero steps costs nothing; going one step costs an amount c_1 and going two steps costs an amount c_2. The player who crosses the winning line first gets the prize P; if the players cross the winning line together they each get half the prize. To make the problem an interesting one we impose the restrictions that c_2 is more than twice c_1 (so that it is more efficient to go one step at a time); that $c_2 n/2$ is greater than P (so that going two steps at a time all the time is not worthwhile); and that $c_1 n$ is less than P (so that there is some surplus to be gained by going one step at a time). The social optimum is for one firm to take one step at a time while the other goes to sleep on the start line; the social product is P and the cost is $c_1 n$ – giving a social surplus of $P-c_1 n$ which can be divided between the two firms in some appropriate fashion.

However, the social optimum is not the Nash equilibrium of the game. This latter is actually rather complicated. It involves the players invoking mixed strategies some of the time and pure strategies some other of the time. To simplify matters only part of the Nash equilibrium strategy will be described, this part applies if the number of steps (remaining) to the winning line is sufficiently small in relation to the prize (relative to c_1 and c_2). The Nash equilibrium in these circumstances is as follows: (1) if one player is two or more steps ahead of the other, then that player should take one step at at time thereafter while the other player should drop out; (2) if one player is one step ahead of the other, then that player should play a mixed strategy over one or two steps (with respective probabilities p and $1-p$) while the other player should play a mixed strategy over zero and two steps (with respective probabilities q and $1-q$); and (3) if the two players are level then both should go two steps; the probabilities p and q depend on the parameters of the problem.

It should be noted that there is no exogenous uncertainty in this game; all the uncertainty is endogenous. It should also be noted that the whole game (its rules and objectives) is well-defined and clearly specified. It is therefore straightforward to reproduce in the laboratory. This I am doing; the software is written and I am shortly to pilot the experiment. The subjects are told the rules of the game and then play several of these patent races against differing opponents – being paid at the end of the experiment the sum of their surpluses on the various races. The whole experiment is computerized and can accommodate up to 16 participants – each playing either against some other participant or against the computer (which can be programmed to play the Nash equilibrium strategy or some other strategy).

The results from running this experiment will enable me to test whether human beings actually do play the Nash equilibrium strategy (either when playing other human beings or when playing the computer programmed to play the Nash equilibrium strategy); or whether they play some other strategy; and if they do not play the Nash equilibrium strategy, I might be able to infer what strategy they are playing. (This turns the experiment into a theory-suggesting experiment – which can then be used to motivate a further theory-testing experiment).

Let me anticipate my results: With some confidence I can predict that human beings do not play the Nash equilibrium strategy (though they might approach it as they gather experience). Let me also anticipate the response of mainstream economists to such results (or indeed to the experiment itself). The response will probably take one of three forms (or a confused mixture of the three):

1. 'What you are doing is misdirected. The theory that you are testing is based on Game Theory – so why do you not simply test that?'
2. 'What you are doing is worthless. We know that the theory is right.'
3. 'What you are doing is pointless. The real world is much more complicated.'

Let me expand on these. The misdirection argument (1) is used by those people who follow what I call the stripped-down approach. They would argue that all models of strategic interaction used in economics (including the game-theoretic 'new IO') are based on game theory; hence, in order to test these economic models of strategic interaction, one simply needs to test the basic game theory on which they are based. The 'ultra-stripped-down' school would take this argument to the limit, arguing that one should eliminate all 'irrelevant' aspects of any game and test the most stripped-down formulation of which one can conceive. For example, at least until recently, the most stripped-down model of a static (one-off) game was thought to be the classic Prisoner's Dilemma; accordingly, this has been subject to a large amount of experimental investigation (see Roth, 1988). However, the trend towards minimalization has gone yet further, particularly in the field known as Co-ordination Games, with even more stripped-down models subjected to experimental scrutiny. Let me parody one such model. There are two players. Each, independently of but simultaneously with the other, selects and announces a point in a square. If both players select the same point then they both get a prize – otherwise not. Note that there are an infinite number of Nash equilibrium strategies in this game – none of

which dominate any other. Under experimental scrutiny it is
discovered that players tend to choose one of the four corners, and
that top-left is more frequently chosen than any of the other three
corners. So one learns from this that convention is important, and that
convention might be determined by social custom (rather than by
economic reasoning). This, to my mind, may be interesting and
useful – but it does not help the cause of economics (at least as I
understand it).

The same stripped-down argument operates in non-strategic
models of behaviour under risk and uncertainty. Here the argument
can be spelt out more clearly; it is based on the conventional wisdom
of behaviour under risk and uncertainty – Subjective Expected Utility
Theory (SEUT). As is well-known, SEUT is first derived in a static
world without learning; some half-dozen axioms are needed – some
more crucially than others (the Independence Axiom which allows the
inferred utility function to be independent of the context, and a similar
axiom which allows inferred probabilities to be independent of their
context). Then SEUT is extended, first to a dynamic world (by
showing first that all models of dynamic behaviour under risk and
uncertainty can be reduced to a static model of strategy choice, and
second that one does not actually need to do the reduction since
backward induction does the same job); and then to an adaptive (a
learning) world by showing that Bayes Theorem is the natural
appendage to SEUT in such a world. The stripped-down school then
asserts that if SEUT is valid in the static fixed world then it must also
be valid in the dynamic adaptive world – since the same basic axioms
underpin SEUT in the two worlds. Thus, in order to test the validity
of SEUT (in all and any worlds) one merely needs to test the basic
axioms (in a static fixed world). And indeed there has been a great
deal of very interesting experimental work focusing on these basic
axioms. But here again the stripped-down school are in the
ascendancy – since experimental testing is increasingly being focused
on one axiom at a time. The logic is the same – if we can get a set of
axioms that work in a simple setting then any theory built on these
axioms and then extended to more complicated settings will also
work. This is the essence of the stripped-down argument; it argues
against the type of experiment I have just described because it is
insufficiently stripped-down.

But at least this school approves of experimental investigation.
Arguments (2) and (3) do not. Argument (2) is frequently invoked by
those economists who implicitly regard theory as tautological. Such
economists can simply not conceive of economic theory being wrong
in this sense. Either the agents would employ experts to take the
correct decision for them (these economists seem to forget the fact

that sometimes the economists who publish models of economic behaviour in academic journals have often taken months to solve the mathematics of the decision problem apparently solved instantaneously by the agents whose behaviour is being modelled; these economists also seem to forget that some academic journals solely publish mathematically complex papers whose sole *raison d'être* is the complexity of the mathematical model presented and solved). Or the agents who do not behave in accordance with the theory would soon die out (this is the evolutionary school of economic thought); clearly the economists who argue in this way have forgotten their own grandparents, parents, wives and children.

But perhaps the oddest thing about the economists who put forward the 'worthless' argument (2) above is what their argument implies about conventional empirical testing of economic theory. If the theory is (tautologically) correct as they assert, then empirical testing must relate solely to the question ((b) above) of whether the theory survives the transition from the *ceteris paribus* world to the real world. So now the issues relate not to what is in the theory, but rather what is not in the theory. A good theory is one that includes the relevant bits and excludes the irrelevant bits; a good theorist is one who can identify what parts of the real world are crucial to a problem (and hence should be included in the theory) and what bits are relatively unimportant (and hence can safely be excluded). The implication, of course, is that a good theorist should be able to identify which real worlds a theory can relate to and which real worlds a theory can not relate to. But economic theorists seldom do this.

Argument (3) is also very strange: If the experiment is too simple as a description of the real world, then *a fortiori* the theory which that experiment is a replication of, is too simple as a description of the real world. So what then is the status of the theory?

Economists who seriously worry about this latter argument try and produce more complicated theories; this is the modern trend. Nevertheless, they still produce well-defined theories with well-defined rules of the game and well-defined objective functions – ripe for experimental investigation. So they cannot evade this experimental objection.

EXPERIMENTS IN ECONOMICS IN GENERAL

Partly as a consequence of these and other objections, experimental work in economics has to date primarily been confined to two broad areas, which can be categorized as (1) Testing Fundamentals and (2) Investigating Situations where Theory Sheds Little Light. Category (1) mainly consists of Theory-testing experiments, while category (2) mainly consists of Theory-suggesting experiments.

Let me be more specific. In category (1), I include (a) testing theories of individual decision-making under risk and uncertainty, and (b) testing strategic (game) theories. Here the recent tendency has been towards testing more and more stripped-down versions of the basic theory. Thus, for example, under (a) there have been recent experimental investigations specifically of the Betweenness Axiom ('if an individual is indifferent between risky prospect A and risky prospect B, then he or she is also indifferent between A and B and any mixture of A and B [that is, a risky prospect that gives A with probability p and B with probability $1-p$]'), of the Independence Axiom ('if an individual is indifferent between risky prospect A and risky prospect B then he or she should also be indifferent between the risky prospect A', which gives A with probability p and C with probability $1-p$, and the risky prospect B', which gives B with probability p and C with probability $1-p$ [where C is any risky prospect]') and the Reduction of Compound Probabilities Axiom ('the individual treats a multi-stage gamble as the same as the single-stage gamble to which it reduces using the conventional probability calculus'). Such experimental investigations are particularly useful as they enable the isolation of certain key features of decision making under risk and uncertainty; they illustrate the very essence of experimental work – the ability to control for certain key aspects of the environment.

In category (2), I include all the experimental work on those bits of economics where economic theory has not been particularly illuminating. Elsewhere (Hey, 1991) I have categorized such experiments under two broad headings: (a) those that relate to the investigation of the attainment of unique equilibria that economic theory has shown to exist, and (b) those that relate to the investigation of the identification of the specific equilibria that are attained in situations where theory merely concludes that multiple equilibria exist. The work under (a) has been motivated by important pieces of economic theory – of an essentially static nature – that prove the existence of equilibrium, but which, of necessity, have nothing to say about the attainment of such an equilibrium – this latter requiring a dynamic theory (which generally is too complicated for the theorist to provide). A good example is provided by the theory of equilibrium in a perfectly competitive market. This shows that, under certain conditions, an equilibrium exists in the following sense: If all agents in the market are price-takers, then an equilibrium price exists such that, at that price, the sum of the demands for the good exactly equals the sum of the supplies of the good. The theory, however, says nothing about the attainment of the equilibrium price; indeed it cannot, because all the agents in the theory are price-takers so there is no-one whose job it is to set the price. Unfortunately, the whole theory rests crucially on the assumption of price-taking behaviour so that if any one of the agents is endowed with the price-making role, the whole theory collapses. Despite much theoretical work, the difficulty remains largely unresolved. Here, experimental methods have been employed to investigate what happens in practice under different 'rules of the game' concerning the setting of prices. Much to the theorists' relief it has been repeatedly found that convergence to the competitive equilibrium is usually achieved – and often surprisingly quickly, irrespective of the number of agents in the experiment.

The work under (b) has been motivated by those theories which indicate a large number of theoretical equilibria which cannot be discriminated between on purely theoretical grounds. A good example is the infinitely repeated Prisoner's Dilemma in which there are an infinite number of Nash equilibria. Here, experimental work has been carried out to try to discover which equilibria, if any, are likely to be attained in practice.

Note, however, that the experiments under both (a) and (b) are primarily not Theory-testing experiments, but rather Theory-suggesting experiments. As such, they are generally frowned upon by the majority of the mainstream of the economics profession. In a sense, the majority is correct in this attitude as it is difficult to conclude anything concrete from what appear to be purely descriptive experiments; yet they are incorrect in that they forget that before one can test a theory one needs to have it suggested first.

EXPERIMENTS IN ECONOMICS AT EXEC

EXEC, the Centre for Experimental Economics at the University of York in the United Kingdom, has been involved in experimental work covered by the two categories mentioned above. Indeed, Loomes in particular has been extremely active in experimental investigations of the key axioms underlying models of decision-making under risk and uncertainty (for example, Loomes, 1990; Loomes, Starmer and Sugden, 1988). However, in addition, work has been ongoing at EXEC in areas 'in between' those categorized under (1) and (2) above. A summary list will indicate the major recent and ongoing concerns of EXEC:

(a) Competitive Firm
(b) Consumption/Saving
(c) Demand for Money
(d) Duopoly/Oligopoly
(e) Dynamic Behaviour under Uncertainty
(f) Expectations
(g) Fundamentals of Behaviour under Uncertainty
(h) Public Goods and Bads
(i) R and D (and Patent Races)
(j) Search.

In many of these cases our strategy has been to take a model 'off the shelf' of the economic theorists' store of models and to subject the model to direct experimental testing. Thus, for example under (c), Ansic has taken three models from the Demand for Money literature (related to, respectively, the transactions demand, the precautionary demand and the speculative demand) and tested them experimentally (for example, Ansic, 1990a; Ansic, 1990b; Ansic and Loomes, 1990). So, for example, the Miller–Orr model of the transactions demand for money (in a stochastic world) is subjected to test by precisely reproducing it in the laboratory; subjects are motivated exactly as in the Miller–Orr model by paying them their realized profits (interest receipts less transactions payments), and the problem they are given to tackle is precisely the Miller–Orr model. This example illustrates neatly why economists are interested in paying subjects real money – it enables them to carry out a genuine theory-testing experiment. This also helps to explain why psychologists are not so concerned with paying real money.

It should be noted that (with the exception of those experiments under (g)) most of the experiments listed above implicitly deny the validity of the 'stripped-down' school of thought. For many of these experiments are tests of economic theories built on the foundation of SEUT or of Game Theory, yet they are not tests of the most stripped-down version of SEUT or Game Theory. This is because I, and some of my colleagues, believe strongly that the stripped-down school have got the argument wrong. In sharp contradistinction we believe that we need to investigate complex theories of economic behaviour because we feel that it is in the handling of complexity that economic theory fails. My own gut feeling (which is, at this stage, pure intuition with no strong empirical justification) is that economic agents, if given the chance, will solve most simple problems in a manner akin to the optimal solution. However, as problems get more complicated, then the agents' ability to solve the problem in a manner close to the optimal declines. So we need to carry out experimental investigations of theories of varying degrees of complexity and study how human beings respond.

This is the broad thrust of my own recent research. I am particularly interested in dynamic decision problems under risk and uncertainty. I have already carried out search experiments, consumption/savings experiments and I am now looking at experiments on the dynamic competitive firm. In the near future I shall carry out a very large-scale repeated experiment of a more abstract dynamic decision problem. To give some insight into what this work is about, let me briefly summarize my most recent experiment of this genre, on the dynamic competitive firm (Hey, 1990a, 1990b).

THE DYNAMIC COMPETITIVE FIRM UNDER PRICE UNCERTAINTY

Let me first set the scene. Consider the perfectly competitive firm operating in a discrete period, finite horizon world, facing uncertainty about the price of its (single) output; it must choose its production in a particular period before it knows what the price of its output will be that period. To make life a bit simpler assume that the firm knows the distribution of the output price (and that this distribution is the same each period). To help the firm avoid some of the effects of the uncertainty (and to introduce a genuinely dynamic element into the decision process) we introduce inventories; thus the firm can store any amount of its output that it does not wish to sell; it is allowed to take the sales decision in any period after it is told the price for its output that is to prevail that period. To keep life simple, let the storage cost be a constant unit cost. The cost of production is specified by a known cost function.

Once the various parameters (the price distribution, the cost function, the unit storage cost and the length of the time horizon) are specified this becomes a straightforward, well-defined economic problem with a well-defined solution – for any given objective function. Let us try to fix this by paying the subjects their accumulated profits and by assuming for the time being that our subjects are risk-neutral.

Under these assumptions, the objective of the firm/subject is to devise a strategy which will maximize its/his/her expected profits over the finite horizon. The appropriate optimizing strategy can be derived using conventional (backward induction) techniques. An intuitive sketch may illuminate what is to follow.

John D. Hey

Begin in the final period, with the final decision – that is the final period's sales decision. With non-negative prices this decision is trivial – it is optimal to sell everything. Now consider the final period's production decision. Given that this is the final period, this problem reduces to the static problem – the solution of which is to produce where marginal cost equals expected price.

Now move back to the penultimate period and consider first the sales decision in that period. The firm knows the price in the penultimate period and knows that for any unit not sold it will have to pay the unit storage cost; it would then expect to get the expected price from the sale of that unit next period. The optimal sales rule is thus clear: Sell (everything) if the price now is greater than the expected price next period less the unit storage cost; store (everything) otherwise. This gives a reservation sales strategy with reservation price equal to the expected price minus the unit storage cost. This in turn implies an optimal production rule in the penultimate period: Produce where marginal cost equals the expected price on sales. Note that this latter (through the operation of the reservation sales strategy) is larger than the unconditional expected price.

The optimal strategy unfolds backwards. In the general period t the rule is simple: Sell (everything) if the price in t is larger than the reservation price in t, R^*t; otherwise sell nothing; produce where marginal cost equals expected price on sales (as viewed from that period). Note that this latter decreases with t: as time passes the expected price on sales must decline – as time is running out. Thus optimal output declines with t. Likewise, the optimal reservation price on sales, R^*t, declines with t. These two features are crucial characteristics of the optimal dynamic strategy. In contrast, one can examine what one might term the myopic strategy. In this, the firm proceeds period by period – so each period output is where marginal cost equals (the unconditional) expected price and all the output is sold, irrespective of the price.

This experiment was carried out with 96 subjects, who each performed the experiment (on an individual basis) twice, with several days intervening between the two repetitions. For 64 of the subjects, who were organized on a group basis, a group discussion also intervened; for the other 32 subjects no such group discussion was organized (though they might well have discussed it amongst themselves nevertheless). The intention was to examine whether there was a group effect on behaviour. No such effect was observed.

My main interest was in how well the subjects were able to cope with the dynamics of the problem and in how behaviour improved with practice. The experiment revealed quite clearly that behaviour on the first repetition was far from optimal though it improved considerably on the second repetition. Looking at the detail of the experimental results it becomes clear that some subjects were better at approaching the dynamic optimum than others, and that certain features of the dynamic optimum were easier to 'discover' than others. Indeed, it seems that one can 'rank' the steps from the myopic to the dynamically optimal as follows:

1. the use of a reservation price rule on the sales strategy;
2. the use of a declining output strategy;
3. the use of a declining reservation price on the sales strategy.

Many subjects used (1) on the first repetition and most used (1) on the second. Virtually no-one used (2) on the first repetition but many used (2) on the second. No-one appeared to be using (3) on the first, but some used (3) on the second. So subjects were trying, with varying degrees of success, to take on board the dynamic elements of the problem.

CONCLUSIONS

The results of the experiment suggest to me the following tentative conclusions:

1. that the carrying-out of such a non-stripped down experiment provides us with useful material additional to that provided by stripped-down experiments;
2. such experiments emphasize that not all human beings are always able to solve all problems optimally and instantaneously and, moreover, they shed light on how human beings simplify complicated problems;
3. such experiments shed light on which parts of difficult problems are relatively difficult to solve and which are relatively easy to solve.

Of course, my division of the 'difference' between the myopic strategy and the dynamically optimal strategy into the three steps (1) to (3) above is easy with the benefit of the hindsight provided by the experiment. What would be useful to know would be how one might derive a general theory which will enable us to make such divisions in other contexts. Hopefully, further experiments of this type will help us to do this.

In the meantime, I fear, experimental economists will still have to bear the (ignorant?) criticisms of their mainstream colleagues, though it would be nice to think that this chapter might help experimentalists in the disciplines of economics and psychology to view each other's work with rather more understanding.

REFERENCES

Ansic, D. (1990a). A multiperiod two-asset investment model – a laboratory experiment. Discussion Paper, EXEC, University of York.

Ansic, D. (1990b). An experimental investigation of the Miller–Orr transactions demand for cash model. Discussion Paper, EXEC, University of York.

Ansic, D. & Loomes, G. (1990). The Bond Model: A laboratory experiment into the demand for money. Discussion paper, EXEC, University of York.

Cox, J. C., Smith, V. L., & Walker, J. M. (1990). Reward saliency, dominance, and decision cost in experimental economics. Plenary Address to the Fifth International Conference on the Foundations and Applications of Utility, Risk and Decision Theories, Duke University, Durham, North Carolina, June 9–13 1990.

Fudenberg, D., Gilbert, R., Stiglitz, J., & Tirole, J. (1983). Preemption, leapfrogging and competition in patent races. *European Economic Review, 22*, 3-31.

Hey, J. D. (1990a). A pilot experimental study of the dynamic competitive firm under spot price uncertainty. *Journal of Behavioral Economics, 19*, 1-22.

Hey, J. D. (1990b). Dynamic decision making under uncertainty: An experimental study of the dynamic competitive firm. Discussion paper, EXEC, University of York.

Hey, J. D. (1991). *Experiments in economics.* Oxford: Blackwell.

Judge, G. G., Griffiths, W. E., Hill, R. C., & Lee, T. C. (1980). *The theory and practice of econometrics.* London: Wiley.

Loomes, G. (1990). Preference reversal: Explanations, evidence and implications. *Annals of Operations Research, 23*, 65-90.

Loomes, G., Starmer, C., & Sugden, R. (1988). Preference reversal: Information processing effect or rational non-transitive choice? *Economic Journal, 99*, 140-151.

Roth, A. E. (1988). Laboratory experimentation in economics: A methodological overview. *Economic Journal, 98*, 974-1031.

Tversky, A. & Kahneman, D. (1990). Cumulative prospect theory: An analysis of attitudes towards uncertainty and value. Plenary address to the Fifth International Conference on the Foundations and Applications of Utility, Risk and Decision Theories, Duke University, Durham, North Carolina, June 9–13 1990.

7. An endowment effect in market experiments?

Reinhard Tietz
University of Frankfurt

INTRODUCTION

The phenomenon of evaluation disparities, that is where there are high selling prices and low buying prices, is discussed in the literature from various aspects. The phenomenon may be explained by the prospect theory of Kahneman and Tversky (1979, 1982). The evaluation is made from the reference point of status quo and the value function is concave for gains and convex for losses. 'Loss aversion' leads to 'status quo bias'. Underweighting the opportunity costs relative to the out-of-pocket costs is called the 'endowment effect' by Thaler (1980). Knetsch and Sinden (1984, 1987) used predefined money amounts to determine experimentally the proportions of accepted and refused contracts; thus, they isolated the higher 'minimum compensation necessary to accept the loss of an asset' and the lower 'maximum willingness to pay to maintain it'. Coursey, Hovis and Schulze (1987) showed that the disparity between the willingness to accept (WTA) and the willingness to pay (WTP), as measured by the bids made in auctions, is reduced by experience through repetitions (cf. also Knetsch and Sinden, 1987, and Knez, Smith and Williams, 1985). The evaluation disparity can be interpreted as a 'reluctance to trade', since the volume traded on a market is lower than one can expect under the hypothesis of equal distributions of WTA and WTP (Kahneman, 1988).

The evaluation disparity is of general importance for many fields of microeconomic theory and their applications. If the endowment effect influences the utility function, the utility function would depend on the status quo, and would change after each transaction which varies the composition of assets. The indifference curve would have to be modified to an indifference area. The evaluation disparity would have an effect similar to that of the transaction costs. Although the phenomenon has been observed in many investigations, its causes are not yet fully clear.

We will report on a series of market experiments performed over many years mainly for the purpose of teaching economics. Before drawing conclusions we will investigate the following questions:

1. Is the evaluation disparity revealed only in offers and bids or does the role position also influence expectations about the market price?
2. Will the bids and the expectations be seen as parts of an aspiration grid?
3. Is the reluctance to trade different across market sides and is it stable?
4. Under which conditions does the disparity vanish?

EXPERIMENTAL PROCEDURE

The market experiment BÖMA (BÖrsenMArkt) is a double sealed bid auction for a homogeneous good, organized like a real commodity exchange. The commodities traded usually are apples, oranges, or tangerines. The classroom experiment can be performed with any number of participants. In the standard version S of BÖMA about half of the participants take the role of sellers and the other half the role of buyers. As a gift from the experimenter, each seller receives the ownership of one unit of the fruit, but not yet the possession, and that unit can be offered for sale. A buyer can purchase at most one unit.

The participants have to write down in a contract form their expectation about the resulting uniform market price and their bidding price for one unit. The bidding price is a limit order for one unit. The seller's bid, the offer, is the lowest price for which he is willing to sell the one unit of the good (minimum selling price); the buyer's bid is the highest price for which he is willing to buy one unit of the good (maximum buying price).

The experimenter, acting as a stock broker, sorts the collected contracts according to the bids. The resulting demand and supply functions are written on the blackboard in table form. The broker determines the uniform market price p^* at the point of intersection of both functions. In case of ambiguity as a consequence of the discrete step functions a bid of a seller is selected as the market price. Other special rules concern repartition or the obligation of the broker to balance, up to a certain amount, excess demand or supply from his own resources (self-dealing for a settlement of balance). In such cases we use in the following the mean between the volumes offered and demanded at the market price as volume traded (x^*).

After the determination of the market price, trades are consummated through the broker. Buyers with bids higher than or equal to the market price get one unit of the good and have to pay the market price. Sellers with bids less than or equal to the market price are paid the market price and sellers with higher bids get one unit of the good.

BIDDING BEHAVIOUR AND THE EVALUATION DISPARITY

Table 7.1 gives the results of 18 experiments performed with students of economic disciplines at different places (D = Technische Universität Dresden, in DDR-Mark; F = Universität Frankfurt; K = Fachhochschule Köln; T = Universität Tübingen; W = Technische Universität Wien, ÖS transformed to DM at an exchange rate of 7:1). The commodities traded were apples (A), oranges (O) or tangerines (T). To make the results independent of incomplete or extreme answers (some of them are obviously not serious), we consider for the statistical analysis here only answers of such subjects who bid or expect prices under DM 5.00 and expect a positive market price. In this way we disregard the decisions of 18 sellers and 10 buyers; this weakens the disparity effect, since making high offers implies no disadvantage and therefore occurs more frequently than high bids of the demanders. The corrected numbers of participants for both roles are given under S (supply side) and D (demand side) in columns 6 and 7; corrected figures are put in parentheses. x^* gives the volume exchanged on the market (mean of demand and supply) at the uniform market price p^* (cols. 8 and 9). The total volume traded is at 302 units, only about one third of the initial endowment of 844. All prices are given in 'pfennig' (1/100 DM).

The average bids of the supply (p_S) and demand (p_D) sides and their differences ($\delta p = p_S - p_D$) are given in columns 10 to 12. In all experiments except number 17 the differences are positive. The 17th experiment was performed with young graduates from China. Problems of understanding or the different cultural and political background may have influenced the result; our elimination of a

Table 7.1 Average bids in the market experiments

exp.	date	pl.	com.	n	S	D	x*	p*	pS	pD	δp	δpr	pSM	pDM	δpM	δpMr	MRRp	MW:α<
(1)	(2)	(3)	(4)	(5)	(6)	(7)	(8)	(9)	(10)	(11)	(12)	(13)	(14)	(15)	(16)	(17)	(18)	(19)
1	11.4.74	F	A	79	41	38	7.5	30.0	65.3	19.7	45.6	1.073	60.0	15.5	44.5	1.179	2.388	0.0001
2	4.12.75	F	O	121	(61)	(57)	15.0	37.0	53.5	31.1	22.4	0.530	49.0	30.0	19.0	0.481	1.864	0.0001
3	17.5.79	F	O	38	(18)	19	9.5	50.0	69.4	60.7	8.7	0.134	52.0	50.0	2.0	0.039	1.242	n.s.
4	25.1.80	K	O	58	29	29	13.5	30.0	53.2	25.0	28.2	0.721	50.0	25.0	25.0	0.667	2.300	0.0001
5	12.11.80	F	O	18	10	(7)	3.5	49.0	54.7	37.9	16.8	0.363	60.0	40.0	20.0	0.400	1.628	0.1
6	26.6.81	K	A	51	25	26	4.0	40.0	68.0	30.3	37.7	0.767	65.0	30.0	35.0	0.737	2.667	0.0001
7	2.11.82		O	33	16	17	6.0	60.0	75.9	58.4	17.5	0.261	75.0	60.0	15.0	0.222	1.581	0.02
8	14.12.83	W	A	55	(27)	27	9.0	62.0	89.7	53.9	35.8	0.499	85.7	54.3	31.4	0.449	1.973	0.0001
9	8.11.84	F	A	41	20	21	8.0	40.0	51.1	43.1	8.0	0.170	50.0	35.0	15.0	0.353	1.482	0.02
10	14.6.85	K	A	29	(13)	(14)	4.5	50.0	88.1	40.3	47.8	0.745	90.0	40.0	50.0	0.769	2.193	0.001
11	7.11.85	F	A	297	(142)	150	41.0	48.0	69.7	36.2	33.5	0.633	60.0	35.0	25.0	0.526	1.831	0.0001
12	12.12.86	K	A	20	10	10	5.0	40.0	67.9	49.9	18.0	0.306	44.5	37.5	7.0	0.171	1.143	n.s.
13	30.4.87	F	A	234	(89)	(138)	48.5	50.0	79.2	44.7	34.5	0.557	60.0	40.0	20.0	0.400	1.541	0.0001
14	11.12.87	K	T	105	50	55	18.0	40.0	56.6	35.1	21.5	0.469	50.0	30.0	20.0	0.500	1.609	0.0001
15	3.11.88	F	A	265	(105)	159	41.5	50.0	68.7	44.5	24.2	0.428	65.0	42.0	23.0	0.430	1.675	0.0001
16	24.11.88	T	A	309	(131)	(172)	54.0	40.0	68.1	31.7	36.4	0.729	50.0	30.0	20.0	0.500	1.706	0.0001
17	3.3.89	K	T	31	(15)	15	8.0	30.0	43.0	71.7	-28.7	-0.500	30.0	60.0	-30.0	-0.667	0.970	n.s.
18	18.4.90	D	O	41	24	17	9.0	69.0	87.6	79.3	8.3	0.099	77.5	70.0	7.5	0.102	1.186	n.s.
Σ/μ				1825	826	971	302	45.56	67.21	44.08	23.12	0.443	59.65	40.24	19.41	0.403	1.721	
σ								10.93	13.11	15.42	17.27	0.337	14.65	13.52	16.85	0.366	0.443	
weighted mean									67.94	39.50	28.45	0.529	58.39	36.60	21.80	0.459		
ditto exp. 2-18				1746	785	933			68.08	40.30	27.78	0.513	58.31	37.46	20.85	0.435		

Notes:

Σ = sum; μ = mean; σ = standard deviation; weighted means are computed with the number of participants

(1) exp. experiment-number   (10) pS average price supply side

(2) date   (11) pD average price demand side

(3) pl. place   (12) δp (pS average price supply side) - (pD average price demand side)

(4) com. commodity (A = apples,   (13) δpr δp/(the mean of pS and pD)

    O = oranges, T = tangerines)   (14) pSM median of prices supply side

(5) n number of participants   (15) pDM median of prices demand side

(6) S number of sellers (corrected)   (16) δpM (pSM median of prices supply side)

    - (pDM median of prices demand side)

(7) D number of buyers (corrected)   (17) δpMr δpM/(the mean of the medians pSM and pDM)

(8) x* volume traded   (18) MRRp mean rank relation of prices

(9) p* market price   (19) MW:α< significance level of the Mann-Whitney U test (one tailed)

seller's offer of DM 5.00 and the fact that three buyers bid about DM 2.00 for a tangerine may also have had some influence.   The nonparametric Mann-Whitney U test is not significant for this negative result (col. 19).

If each experiment is regarded as an independent observation, the result that the supply side makes higher bids on average than the demand side is highly significant according to the binomial test ($\alpha < .001$).   Although the traded fruits were different and the experiments were carried out at different places over more than 15 years, the means of the bids do not vary too much to allow a direct comparison of the unweighted means of the 18 experiments.   The mean of $p_S = 67.2$ is about 23.1 higher than the mean of $p_D = 44.1$. The one-tailed nonparametric Wilcoxon matched-pairs signed-rank test as well as the corresponding parametric t-test are significant at the .001-level.

To make the difference $\delta p = p_S - p_D$ independent of the general level of the bids, we normalized δp by the unweighted mean of p_S and p_D (δp_r, col. 13).   In the average of the 18 experiments this proportion amounts to .443, with a standard deviation of .337.   Since the coefficients of variation of columns 12 and 13, as well as of columns 16 and 17, are very similar, we may consider the original values only. A greater effect is derived by computing the means weighted with the relevant number of participants (cols. 10–11, 14–15); this reduces especially p_D and thus increases the difference between the means to 28.5 and their normalized relation to .529.

Since the distributions of the bids are not symmetric, the medians may be a more adequate measure.   The medians in most cases are distinctly smaller than the means, especially on the supply side, where very high bids are without any risk.   The medians (cols. 14 to 17) also reflect better the preference for prominent numbers.   The disparity effect can also be measured by the relation of the mean ranks of supply offers over the demand bids from ranks computed across all offers and bids within an experiment (*MRRp*, col. 18).   This relation is higher than 1.5 in 13 of 18 experiments.   In the average, the mean ranks of the supply bids are 72.1 per cent higher than those of the demand bids.   The Mann-Whitney U test (col. 19) shows that the evaluation disparities for all 10 experiments with more than 50 participants are significant at a level of $\alpha < .0001$.   Thus, by various measures it is evident that the supply bids are higher than the demand bids.

The evaluation disparity may be a sign of profit-seeking behaviour. However, this argument is not a very consistent one since the subjects know that, individually, they have no influence on the market price *de facto*.   The argument that a single seller would expect that the other sellers would ask for higher prices also, and thus the market price would rise neglects the fact that corresponding argumentation and behaviour on the demand side would counterbalance these expectations. Only a low volume traded will result.

Aside from the general evaluation disparity there are behavioural differences between the two roles. To illustrate these differences, we computed separate regressions of the supply and demand functions $p_S(x)$ and $p_D(x)$ for the ten large experiments (*LE*) with more than 50 participants. Table 7.2 gives the regression coefficients of the linear functions. The demand functions always have an absolutely smaller slope than the corresponding supply function (binomial test: $\alpha < .001$). The smaller slope is only partly due to the fact that there are about 22 per cent more buyers than sellers. The statement remains valid after multiplying the coefficients b_{1D} by D/S, a normalization which inflates the demand coefficients to the same number of participants as the supply side (cf. b_{1Dn}, col. 9). Figure 7.1 illustrates the average supply and demand functions computed as the weighted means of the individual coefficients. The supply function is steeper (+1.547) than the demand function (-0.650 or –0.791, respectively), and covers a wider range also. Whereas the lower limit of zero is natural and identical for both market sides, bidding high prices is risky for the demanders only and possibly profitable for the suppliers.

THE EXPECTATION BIAS

In addition to offers and bids, participants were asked for their expectations about the resulting uniform market price. As Table 7.3 shows, there are corresponding effects, but to a reduced extent. Here the average relation of the price difference to the price mean is only 11.3 per cent for the means ($\delta\pi_r$, col. 7) and 10.8 per cent for the medians ($\delta\pi_{Mr}$, col. 11). Similarly as with the bids, the computation of weighted means enlarges the effect to about 15 per cent via a higher reduction of the demand-side expectations. The mean rank relation of the expectations MRR_π amounts to only 1.264 (col. 12), and the Mann-Whitney U test is highly significant for four experiments only (8 times: $\alpha < .1$, col. 13). In experiment 12 and again in experiment 17 the differences show reversed signs. The binomial tests over the 17 experiments show significantly that the means and the medians of the expected prices on the supply side are more frequently higher than on the demand side ($\alpha < .002$).

Answering our first question, we can state that the evaluation disparity occurs not only between offers and bids, but also between

Table 7.2 Regression coefficients of supply and demand functions
$p_S(x)=b_{0S} + b_{1S}*x; \; p_D(x) = b_{0D} + b_{1D}*x.$
Experiments with more than 50 participants only (LE).

	exp.	date	S	D	b_{0S}	b_{1S}	b_{0D}	b_{1D}	b_{1Dn}
No.	(1)	(2)	(3)	(4)	(5)	(6)	(7)	(8)	(9)
1	1	74.04	41	38	1.78	3.025*	39.28*	-1.002*	-0.929
2	2	75.12	61	57	13.96~	1.275*	52.67*	-0.743*	-0.694
3	4	80.01	29	29	18.43*	2.318*	45.69*	-1.377*	-1.377
4	6	81.06	25	26	29.85*	2.935*	45.26*	-1.110*	-1.154
5	8	83.12	27	27	30.72*	4.216*	80.49*	-1.902*	-1.902
6	11	85.11	142	150	6.88	0.879*	68.11*	-0.422*	-0.446
7	13	87.04	89	138	-4.20	1.853*	87.17*	-0.612*	-0.949
8	14	87.12	50	55	7.99*	1.906*	69.07*	-1.215*	-1.337
9	15	88.11	105	159	24.75*	0.829*	80.89*	-0.455*	-0.689
10	16	88.12	131	172	-9.72	1.179*	64.94*	-0.384*	-0.504
μ			70.0	85.1	12.04	2.042	63.36	-0.922	-0.998
σ			41.7	58.3	13.26	1.038	16.00	0.467	0.429
weighted mean					7.66	1.547	69.62	-0.650	-0.791

Notes:
* significant at $\alpha < .001$; ~ significant at $\alpha < .01$
(1) exp. experiment no.
(2) date date (year.month)
(3) S number of sellers (corrected)
(4) D number of buyers (corrected)
(5) b_{0S} constant term of the supply function ($p_S = b_{0S} + b_{1S}*x$)
(6) b_{1S} slope of the supply function
(7) b_{0D} constant term of the demand function ($p_D = b_{0D} + b_{1D}*x$)
(8) b_{1D} slope of the demand function
(9) b_{1Dn} slope of demand function normalized by D/S

the expectations of both market sides. The role and the preference direction influence not only the bids but also the expectations about which market price will result as a fair compromise between both market sides. 'The wish is the father of the thought.' How the decisions of all other participants on both market sides are evaluated, depends on the role. The 'expectation bias' favours one's own preferences. The expectations are not neutral estimates of a fair value of the commodity.The bids and the expectations are highly correlated. Regarding only the nine large experiments (LE), the correlation coefficients are significant at $\alpha < .001$ in all nine on the supply side and in seven on the demand side. The weighted means of the correlations are $r = .675$ on the supply side and $r = .534$ on the

Table 7.3 Expectations about the market price

exp.	S	D	Π_S	Π_D	$\delta\Pi$	$\delta\Pi_r$	Π_{SM}	Π_{DM}	$\delta\Pi_M$	$\delta\Pi_{Mr}$	MRR_Π	MW:$\alpha\leq$
(1)	(2)	(3)	(4)	(5)	(6)	(7)	(8)	(9)	(10)	(11)	(12)	(13)
2	61	57	55.1	39.5	15.6	0.330	50.0	40.0	10.0	0.222	1.505	0.0001
3	18	19	72.1	68.0	4.1	0.059	50.0	50.0	0.0	0.000	1.065	n.s.
4	29	29	47.8	29.3	18.5	0.480	40.0	24.0	16.0	0.500	1.798	0.0001
5	10	7	52.1	42.9	9.2	0.194	50.0	50.0	0.0	0.000	1.179	n.s.
6	25	26	61.1	40.7	20.4	0.401	55.0	40.0	15.0	0.316	2.001	0.0001
7	16	17	70.0	68.5	1.5	0.022	65.0	50.0	15.0	0.261	1.145	n.s.
8	27	27	79.1	72.9	6.2	0.082	64.2	60.0	4.2	0.068	1.225	0.1
9	20	21	53.7	49.9	3.8	0.073	47.5	40.0	7.5	0.171	1.188	n.s.
10	13	14	77.2	66.4	10.8	0.150	80.0	65.0	15.0	0.207	1.283	n.s.
11	142	150	63.1	50.8	12.3	0.216	60.0	50.0	10.0	0.182	1.300	0.0001
12	10	10	61.0	69.6	-8.6	-0.132	47.5	57.5	-10.0	-0.190	0.953	n.s.
13	89	138	63.0	59.3	3.7	0.061	55.0	50.0	5.0	0.095	1.085	n.s.
14	50	55	51.1	47.3	3.8	0.077	50.0	40.0	10.0	0.222	1.252	0.05
15	105	159	61.8	57.0	4.8	0.081	60.0	50.0	10.0	0.182	1.187	0.01
16	131	172	54.8	42.7	12.1	0.248	45.0	40.0	5.0	0.118	1.165	0.02
17	15	15	39.4	70.9	-31.5	-0.571	26.0	55.0	-29.0	-0.716	0.950	n.s.
18	24	17	84.0	72.2	11.8	0.151	79.5	65.0	14.5	0.201	1.201	n.s.
Σ/μ	785	933	61.55	55.76	5.79	0.113	54.40	48.62	5.78	0.108	1.264	
σ			11.56	13.47	11.53	0.224	12.91	10.22	10.95	0.251	0.266	
weighted mean			60.43	52.16	8.27	0.147	54.31	46.59	7.72	0.153		

(1) exp. experiment-number
(2) s number of sellers (corrected)
(3) D number of buyers (corrected)
(4) Π_S expected market price supply side
(5) Π_D expected market price demand side
(6) $\delta\Pi$ $\Pi_S - \Pi_D$
(7) $\delta\Pi_r$ $\delta\Pi$ / (the mean of Π_S and Π_D)

(8) Π_{SM} median of expected market price supply side
(9) Π_{DM} median of expected market price demand side
(10) $\delta\Pi_M$ $\Pi_{SM} - \Pi_{DM}$
(11) $\delta\Pi_{Mr}$ $\delta\Pi_M$ / (the mean of Π_{SM} and Π_{DM})
(12) MRR_Π mean rank relation expectations
(13) MW:$\alpha\leq$ significance level of the Mann-Whitney U test, one tailed (n.s.: not significant at $\alpha = 0.1$)

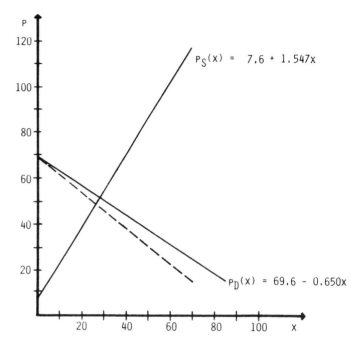

Figure 7.1 Average demand and supply function

Notes: Weighted coefficients of 10 experiments with more than 50 participants.

Demand function normalized to the same number of participants (70) as the supply side: $p_D(x) = 69.6 - .791 x$.

demand side.

To answer our second question, the occurrence of the bias in bids and expectations as well as the high correlations allow us to interpret both variables as a part of an aspiration grid. The expectation corresponds to the third highest aspiration level called 'regarded as attainable' in a bargaining context (Tietz, 1972). The bids are comparable to the 'planned bargaining result', the goal. Whether the goal is seen as attainable or not depends on the constellation of both aspiration levels. In the averages the expectations are not compatible, but in only two experiments (4 and 5) the market price falls between the average expectations of the two sides (cf. Table 7.1, col. 9 and Table 7.3, cols. 4 and 5). Normally, the market price is even lower than buyers' expectations (Wilcoxon test: $\alpha < .0005$). This may be a consequence of the small slope of the demand function and the high reluctance to trade on the demand side.

The establishing of aspiration levels is based on subjective considerations with the status quo as the starting point. The evaluation disparity and the expectation bias may be influenced by the asymmetry assumption of the aspiration level approach; there it is assumed that the same absolute distance is felt as a larger utility gap from below an aspiration level, in the case of failure, than from above, in the case of success (Starbuck, 1963).

RELUCTANCE AND WILLINGNESS TO TRADE

The expectations allow a division of each market side into two subgroups, namely those participants who plan or expect to make a transaction on the market, and those who do not. A seller whose offer price is equal to or lower than his expected market price ($p_S \leq \pi_S$) is regarded as willing to trade (*WT*). A seller with a bid higher than his expected price ($p_S > \pi_S$) is not willing to trade and does not expect to sell his unit of the good; he shows reluctance to trade (*RT*). The demand side may be divided in an analogous way (*WT*: $p_D \geq \pi_D$; *RT*: $p_D < \pi_D$).

Using these definitions globally, the evaluation disparity may be partitioned as shown in Figure 7.2. (The computations are based on experiments 2 to 18, cf. Table 7.1, last row). The total difference between the (weighted) average of the means (medians, respectively) of 27.78 (20.85) Pfennig may be divided into the expectation bias, which is 29.8% (37.0%), and two parts due to a global reluctance to trade. Of the latter, the supply side amounts to 27.5% (19.2%), and the demand side to the larger contribution of 42.7% (43.8%). Still, one third of the evaluation disparity is due to a role-dependent expectation bias. The corresponding order $p_D < \pi_D < \pi_S < p_S$ is fulfilled in 11 experiments only; this, as well as the higher gap on the demand side, calls for a more detailed analysis of the reluctance and the willingness to trade.

For each experiment we can measure the willingness and the reluctance to trade by the corresponding proportions. In Table 7.4 columns 4 to 5 and 7 to 8 give the absolute proportions, and columns 6 and 9, the relative proportions (in per cent) of subjects who are, by our definition, willing to trade. The supply side has an average willingness to trade of 48.5% (381/785), whereas on the demand side only 23% (215/933) of the subjects are willing to trade. The complement, the reluctance-to-trade quota, is higher for the demand side than for the supply side in 14 experiments (binomial test: $\alpha <$ .01). Two of the three exceptions, namely game 17 and 18, have an extremely high willingness to trade on the demand side ($WT_{Dr} >$ 76%); this may be due to the novel situation for the participating students with a differing political background.

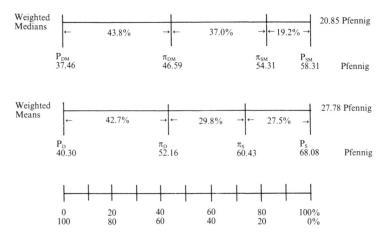

Figure 7.2 The partition of the evaluation disparity (Experiments 2-18)

For the reluctance quota the chi-square test does not indicate significant differences between the experiments for the supply side (chi-square = 19.3, df = 16, $\alpha > .25$), whereas the chi-square for the demand side amounts to 76.5 ($\alpha < .001$). If experiments 17 and 18 are disregarded the latter is reduced to chi-square = 21.0 (df = 14) and is not significant at the .1 level.   Games 2 to 16 do not differ significantly in the reluctance quota; the average reluctance quota for these games amounts to 51.1 per cent on the supply side and to 71.1 per cent on the demand sides with standard deviations of 12.1 per cent and 10.5 per cent, respectively. The third question may be answered by the observation that the reluctance quota is relatively stable with students from West Germany and Austria. The demand side has a significantly higher reluctance quota. Individually this is true in 14 out of 17 experiments (binomial test: $\alpha < .01$).

For each type of behaviour (WT and RT) the absolute differences between expectations and bids are similar on both market sides. The mean differences are $p_{DWT} - \pi_{DWT} = 11.63$, $\pi_{SWT} - p_{SWT} = 11.09$, $p_{DRT} - \pi_{DRT} = 20.81$, and $\pi_{SRT} - p_{SRT} = 23.64$. The coefficients of variation lie between .10 and .16 (cf. σ and μ in Table 7.4). This is illustrated (for the weighted means) by Figure 7.3, with price and reluctance-to-trade quota as co-ordinates. There is one line for each of the four variables p_D, π_D, π_S, and p_S. Each is drawn from the mean price at RT = 0% to the mean price at RT = 100%. The four lines form two Xs. The points labelled 'MEAN' are the global weighted means computed for all participants. It can be seen that the global mean for demand appears at a reluctance quota of 77.0 per cent and for supply at 51.5 per cent. The evaluation disparities at RT = 100% are high for the bids and low for the expectations. In the willing-to-trade case (RT = 0%), the disparity is enlarged for the expectations and reversed to a negative difference for the bids. The global orders of the pure cases are not fulfilled in all experiments. The middle relations $\pi_{DRT} < \pi_{SRT}$ (cols. 15 and 16) as well as $p_{DWT} > p_{SWT}$ (cols. 10 and 13) hold in 9 of 17 experiments only.

Since there are no significant differences between the standard deviations of corresponding bids and expectations for the 17 experiments (Wilcoxon test: $\alpha > .20$), the variances of both types of variables may be regarded as similar. The absolute changes of the expectations between the RT- and WT-cases in Figure 7.3 are smaller than those of the bids; this indicates that the expectations may be seen as a point of orientation for a subjectively 'fair' market price. The individual bids vary between the reluctance and the willingness case to a larger extent than the expectations. They are influenced by the individual preference for the good, as well as by the expectations.

Regarding only the nine large experiments (LE), the weighted averages of the nine correlation coefficients between p and π on the supply side are .910 in the WT-case and .744 in the RT-case; the corresponding values on the demand side are somewhat lower with .738 and .683, respectively (cf. Table 7.5, cols. 14 to 17, last row). The higher degree of market orientation of the supply side is revealed again. The WT-case shows higher correlations than the RT-case.

Table 7.5 shows the corresponding separate regression coefficients. All the 18 slope-coefficients on the supply side a_{1Sj} are significant at the .001-level (cols. 7 and 9); the same is true on the demand side in only 13 of 18 cases (cols. 11 and 13). Since only nine of 36 coefficients a_0 are significant with $\alpha < .01$, homogeneous regression lines may be assumed (binomial test: $\alpha < .002$). In the weighted average the regressions of p on π lie nearer to the 45-degree line ($p = \pi$) in the WT-case than in the RT-case, as Figure 7.4 shows. Individually, in 12 of 18 regressions the slopes in the WT-cases are nearer to 1 than those in the RT-cases.

The two extremes have a correspondence in the constellation of the grids of potential aspiration levels in bilateral bargaining. The RT-case, with its unattainable goals, corresponds to a bargaining situation we call 'normal in planning', a tough situation in which an agreement needs large concessions normally on both sides. The WT-case, in which the goals are seen as attainable, is more comparable to the situation we call 'inverse in planning', in which an agreement can be found easily (Tietz and Weber, 1972).

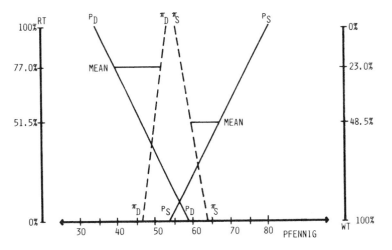

Figure 7.3 Willing- and reluctant-to-trade cases
Notes: WT = willing-to-trade quota,
          RT = reluctant-to-trade quota

EXPERIMENTAL MODIFICATIONS

To answer the fourth question, about the conditions under which the evaluation disparity vanishes, we consider modified experiments. We repeated experiment 18 in Dresden a second time with exchanged roles (SX-version). The 24 subjects who were sellers in the first round took the roles of buyers in the second round and vice versa. The evaluation disparity in the first round (col. 12 of Table 7.1) was $\delta p = 8.3$ Pfennig and increased to 14.1 in the second round. The corresponding expectation bias was reduced from $\delta \pi = 11.8$ (col. 6 of Table 7.3) to 5.9 Pfennig. The disparity of the medians $\delta_{pM} = 7.5$ (col. 16 of Table 7.1) remained unchanged for the bids, and decreased from $\delta_{\pi M} = 14.5$ (col. 10 of Table 7.3) to 5.0 for the expectations. The mean rank relation increased for the bids from $MRR_p = 1.186$ to 1.320, whereas the expectations showed from $MRR_\pi = 1.201$ in the

Table 7.4 Willingness and reluctance to trade (*proportions, bids, and expectations*)

exp.	S	D	WTS	RTS	WTSr	WTD	RTD	WTDr	pDWT	pDWT	bSWT	pSWT	pDRT	pDRT	bSRT	pSRT
(1)	(2)	(3)	(4)	(5)	(6)	(7)	(8)	(9)	(10)	(11)	(12)	(13)	(14)	(15)	(16)	(17)
2	61	57	38	23	62.30	13	44	22.81	40.2	36.2	57.9	46.7	28.5	40.5	50.6	64.7
3	18	19	11	7	61.11	7	12	36.84	108.0	79.1	87.3	74.5	33.2	61.5	48.1	61.3
4	29	29	14	15	48.28	10	19	34.48	25.9	22.2	58.6	54.1	24.6	33.0	37.8	52.3
5	10	7	5	5	50.00	2	5	28.57	55.0	37.5	65.8	55.2	31.0	45.0	38.4	54.2
6	25	26	9	16	36.00	4	22	15.38	27.0	25.8	65.8	60.0	30.9	43.6	58.5	72.5
7	16	17	7	9	43.75	6	11	35.29	73.3	51.7	82.1	65.0	50.2	77.7	60.6	84.4
8	27	27	9	18	33.33	10	17	37.04	56.9	46.0	108.3	99.7	52.1	88.6	64.5	84.7
9	20	21	9	11	45.00	6	15	28.57	75.5	70.2	57.6	32.0	30.1	41.8	50.5	66.6
10	13	14	4	9	30.77	1	13	7.14	80.0	70.0	90.0	70.0	37.2	66.2	71.4	96.1
11	142	150	71	71	50.00	24	126	16.00	55.2	42.4	62.0	50.5	32.6	52.4	64.1	89.0
12	10	10	8	2	80.00	0	10	0.00	0.0	0.0	53.8	44.9	49.9	69.9	90.0	160.0
13	89	138	42	47	47.19	26	112	18.84	68.5	53.2	66.0	54.7	39.1	60.7	60.4	101.1
14	50	55	27	23	54.00	11	44	20.00	60.9	42.8	51.0	41.9	28.6	48.5	51.2	73.9
15	105	159	54	51	51.43	32	127	20.13	63.6	52.1	65.9	57.3	39.7	58.2	57.4	80.8
16	131	172	52	79	39.69	38	134	22.09	46.2	34.7	58.2	51.0	27.6	45.0	52.6	79.3
17	15	15	6	9	40.00	12	3	80.00	67.5	57.1	57.5	52.8	88.3	126.3	27.4	36.4
18	24	17	15	9	62.50	13	4	76.47	79.2	64.2	93.5	82.2	79.8	98.3	68.2	96.4
Σ/μ	785	933	381	404	49.14	215	718	29.39	57.82	46.19	69.48	58.38	41.38	62.19	55.98	79.63
σ			20.3	22.9	12.03	10.7	47.3	20.39	24.31	19.16	15.99	15.70	17.59	23.52	14.03	26.22
weighted mean					48.54			23.04	59.09	46.81	64.68	54.48	34.67	53.77	56.41	80.91

(1) exp. experiment-number
(2) S number of sellers (corrected)
(3) D number of buyers (corrected)
(4) WTS willing to trade supply side (pS≤pS)
(5) RTS reluctance to trade supply side (pS>pS)
(6) WTSr relative willingness to trade supply (%)
(7) WTD willing to trade demand side (pD≥pD)

(10) pDWT pD with WT (pD≥pD)
(11) bDWT pD with WT
(12) bSWT ps with WT (ps≤ps)
(13) pSWT ps with WT
(14) pDRT pD with RT (pD<pD)
(15) pDRT pD with RT
(16) bsRT bs with RT (ps>ps)

Table 7.5 Regressions p(π) separately for willingness and reluctance to trade

$p_{ij}(\pi_{ij}) = a_{0ij} + a_{1ij}*\pi_{ij}$ with $i = \{S, D\}$, $j = \{WT, RT\}$. Large experiments (LE) with $n > 50$ only.

	game	WT_S	RT_S	WT_D	RT_D	a0SWT	a1SWT	a0SRT	a1SRT	a0DWT	a1DWT	a0DRT	a1DRT	rSWT	rSRT	rDWT	rDRT
No.	(1)	(2)	(3)	(4)	(5)	(6)	(7)	(8)	(9)	(10)	(11)	(12)	(13)	(14)	(15)	(16)	(17)
1	2	38	23	13	44	9.42*	0.644*	-2.06	1.320*	-1.82	1.161*	18.86*	0.237	0.951*	0.979*	0.974*	0.302
2	4	14	15	10	19	-4.54	1.000*	5.03	1.251*	0.56	1.141*	2.53	0.668*	0.974*	0.878*	0.945*	0.920*
3	6	9	16	4	22	2.17	0.879*	6.35	1.131*	-4.00	1.204~	-6.17	0.710*	0.984*	0.827*	0.986	0.774*
4	8	9	18	10	17	-9.19	1.006*	2.67	1.272*	2.48	1.184~	40.40*	0.131	0.981*	0.836*	0.910*	0.524
5	11	71	71	24	126	16.92*	0.541*	11.20	1.213*	19.57	0.840~	7.93	0.621*	0.784~	0.814*	0.585~	0.694*
6	13	42	47	26	112	12.69~	0.637*	-31.89	2.203*	41.93	0.500	5.96	0.546*	0.872*	0.713*	0.240	0.737*
7	14	27	23	11	44	-0.60	0.832*	24.59~	0.963*	-19.32	1.874*	9.05~	0.403*	0.919*	0.787*	0.862*	0.736*
8	15	54	51	32	127	0.23	0.866*	27.41	0.930*	-13.33	1.477*	12.09*	0.473*	0.957*	0.493*	0.863*	0.720*
9	16	52	79	38	134	2.15	0.839*	15.95	1.204*	-0.29	1.341*	6.61~	0.466*	0.986*	0.719*	0.826*	0.672*
Σ/μ		316	343	168	645	3.25	0.805	6.58	1.276	2.86	1.191	10.81	0.473	0.934	0.783	0.799	0.675
σ						7.86	0.155	16.46	0.351	17.14	0.361	12.25	0.182	0.064	0.128	0.228	0.164
weighted mean						6.56	0.739	7.86	1.296	5.36	1.162	9.17	0.497	0.910	0.744	0.738	0.683

* significant at α < .001; ~ significant at α < .01

(1) game   game number
(2) WTS   willingness to trade supply side
(3) RTS   reluctance to trade supply side
(4) WTD   willingness to trade demand side
(5) RTD   reluctance to trade demand side
(6) a0SWT   constant term (a0) of regression p(p), supply side, willingness to trade
(7) a1SWT   slope (a1) of regression p(p) SWT
(8) a0SRT   a0, supply, reluctant to trade
(9) a1SRT   a1, supply, reluctant to trade

(10) a0DWT   demand side corresponding to supply side
(11) a1DWT
(12) a0DRT
(13) a1DRT
(14) rSWT   correlation between pS and pS in the WT-case
(15) rSRT   correlation between pS and pS in the RT-case
(16) rDWT   correlation between pD and pD in the WT-case
(17) rDRT   correlation between pD and pD in the RT-case

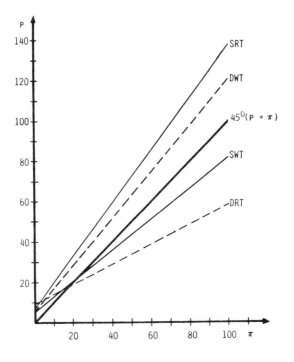

Figure 7.4 Weighted average regressions p(π) separately for WT- and RT-cases

first round to MRR_π = 1.219 no substantial change. Only the expectations show a reduction of disparity, whereas the disparity of the bids even increases in the second round as far as measured in the means. This may be due to the fact that reluctance to trade increased, on the supply side from 37.5 per cent to 52.9 per cent and on the demand side from 23.5 per cent to 29.2 per cent. Since for the bids in the second round the evaluation disparity is only slightly significant (Mann-Whitney U test: $\alpha < .1$) and the disparity in the medians remained unchanged, one should not conclude that experience enlarges the evaluation disparity generally. At least, a reduction was not observed. A repeated decision in the opposite role seems to improve the consistency of the expectations indicated by a reduction of the expectation bias.

Table 7.6 Results under random assignment of roles
Z-version, two experiments (n = 20 and n = 26), weighted means

n S/D	bids p total 46	RT 13/16	WT 33/30	expectations π total 46	RT 13/16	WT 33/30
supply side (p_S, π_S)	64.2	80.2	57.9	66.0	66.9	65.6
demand side (p_D, π_D)	60.6	55.6	63.3	59.5	66.0	56.0
evaluation disparity (δp, δ_π)	3.6	24.6	-5.4	6.5	.9	9.6
relative eval. disp. (δp_r, $\delta \pi_r$)	.058	.363	-.089	.104	.014	.158
mean rank relation (MRR_p, MRR_π)	1.002			1.229		
Wilcoxon tests on disparity	n.s.			$\alpha < .01$		

WT-quota supply side (WT_{Sr})	71.7%	
WT-quota demand side (WT_{Dr})	65.2%	

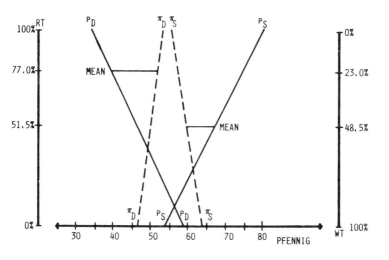

Figure 7.5 Random assignment of roles (Z-version)

The price expected in the second round depends on whether the expected price in the first round was higher or lower than the market price. There was a counter-movement in the expectations. Those who expected a price less than the market price in the first round (69 Pfennig) raised their expectations, and those who expected a higher price lowered their expectations. This direction of expectation-change is true for 36 out of 41 subjects (binomial test: $\alpha < .00001$). A saturation effect, revealed in falling price expectations, was counteracted by rising price expectations of those who expected a price below the market price before. The shorter supply side in the second round (17 instead of 24) then led to a higher market price of 80 Pfennig. Another experiment, performed this summer and not reported on in detail here, gave quite different results; experience led to a reduction of evaluation disparity of both bids and expectations, though in the presence of increasing willingness to trade. Additional experiments with repetitions are needed to clarify the influence of experience.

To test for vanishing evaluation disparity, our fourth question, we performed two experiments in a version Z, where the roles were assigned randomly with equal probabilities after each subject had completed two conditional contract forms, one for the case that he would be a seller and on the reverse side one for the case that he would be a buyer. Table 7.6 gives the main results of these experiments.

In both experiments there are no significant evaluation disparities of the bids. The relative evaluation disparity $\delta p_r = .058$ is low as well as the mean rank relation $MRR_p = 1.002$. It is astonishing that the expectation biases are significant at the .01 level in both experiments, particularly since it was common knowledge that the roles would be assigned with equal probability. The absolute and the relative evaluation disparity $\delta_\pi = 6.5$ and $\delta\pi_r = 0.104$, respectively, as well as the mean rank relation $MRR_\pi = 1.229$ are distinctly higher than the corresponding values for p. The high willingness to trade, especially on the demand side, can explain these results.

Figure 7.5 represents the willing- and reluctant-to-trade cases for the Z-version. It looks like a compressed image of the S-version in Figure 7.3. The most significant change occurred for p_{DRT} from 34.7 (col.14 of Table 7.4) to 55.6 (Table 7.6 and Figure 7.5). The high willingness to trade moves the means into the WT-area where the expectations lie outside the bids. For the 20 (of 46) subjects in the two experiments who have $p_S < p_D$, a negative evaluation disparity, the WT-quotas of both market sides are extremely high on 90 per cent. We can answer our fourth question in the sense that the evaluation disparity vanishes under random assignment of roles. The endowment effect is not valid for anticipated or unassigned property rights. Additional experiments with this version are needed to show whether these results are typical under random role assignment.

The task of considering the two opposing positions reduces the role dependent evaluation disparity as well as the expectation bias. The willingness to trade, like the wish to climb on the bandwagon, is increased by a thorough and more rational analysis of the decision situation. The questions asked for and the consideration made before the decisions may improve bounded rational behaviour. Thus, the experimental design of the planning phase prior to the decision may have an important framing effect.

The evaluation disparity does not vanish if subjects have the possibility to act as 'traders' (*T*), that is to buy or to sell at the market depending only on their own bids and the resulting market price (H-version). In this H-version the traders also get, like the suppliers, one unit of the fruit as a gift at the beginning of the experiment. They had to write on their contract forms their expectation, a selling price and a buying price. Figure 7.6 shows the results of five experiments performed with 55 suppliers, 55 demanders, and 54 traders between 1977 and 1984. The values are given in Pfennig. At the top are shown the relatively low bids and offers of the traders (p_{DT} and p_{ST}, respectively). The evaluation disparity amounts δp = 17.3 Pfennig. For comparisons, we compute the 'demand's reluctance quota' here as the ratio of demand side reluctance ($RTD = \pi_T - p_{DT}$) to the sum of demand and supply side reluctance ($RTD + RTS$). This quota $(11.6/(11.6 + 5.7) = 67.1\%)$ is similar to that of the S-version of 60.8 per cent analogously computed from the means of experiments 2 to 18, which are shown at the bottom of Figure 7.6. The similarity also of the absolute values in Pfennig makes traders' behaviour look like a combination of the behaviour of the suppliers and demanders in the standard version. The typical trader shows a reluctance to trade in both directions, with the higher reluctance at the demand side. He is willing to buy an additional unit only at a distinctly lower price than expected and he is willing to sell his unit only at a higher price than expected. The saturation effect is able to give a rational explanation of this behaviour. Additional units have lower 'marginal utility' than the unit of the good in possession. The same consideration cannot be made for the pure roles of suppliers and demanders as investigated in the standard version.

In the middle of Figure 7.6 the bids of normal suppliers and demanders in the H-version are shown. The evaluation disparity δp = 27.0 Pfennig is similar to that of the S-version, but the expectation bias, 17.3 Pfennig, is distinctly higher, and is identical to the evaluation disparity of traders. One may assume that participants in pure roles misinterpret the situation in presence of traders, seeing the

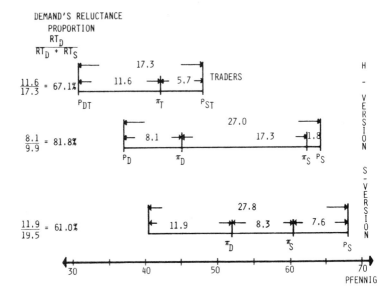

Figure 7.6 Behaviour of traders compared with pure roles
Notes: H-version: 5 experiments 1977-1984; S = 55, D = 55,
T = 54. S-version: experiments 2-18

one market as split into two separate markets, like retail and wholesale markets. They allow a 'trade margin' for the traders by the space in the expected prices. This may be the reason for the small difference $p_S - \pi_S = 1.8$ Pfennig and the high reluctance proportion, 81.8 per cent.

CONCLUSIONS

The evaluation disparity between (minimum) selling prices and (maximum) buying prices occurs in many market experiments and seems to be a framing effect in the sense of Kahneman and Tversky (1982). Its occurrence depends on whether a favorable interpretation of the decision situation is subjectively reflected in the bids and expectations, established in aspiration levels, and internalized. A corresponding expectation bias contributes about one third to the evaluation disparity. Thus, the whole disparity in the bids cannot be accounted for by value differences.   An overestimation of the attainability shifts the whole aspiration grid in the own preference direction.

Expectations allow us to distinguish between subjects who are willing to trade and those who are reluctant to trade. Reluctance to trade is normally higher on the demand side. Exceptions to this rule are found with participants from socialist countries and with a random assignment of the roles; under these conditions the evaluation disparity is low or vanishes.

The evaluation disparity cannot be explained by collector's or sentimental values, since the subjects get only the ownership, not the physical possession of the good, before their decision.   Although transaction costs may have an effect similar to the evaluation disparity, they cannot explain the expectation bias and may have only a small influence on the evaluation disparity.   Transaction costs are low and nearly similar for all market participants.   All the suppliers and the buyers have to come to the broker for the transaction.   The remaining asymmetry on the demand side, that only a portion of the demanders have to come to the broker afterwards, can be eliminated by an initial monetary endowment to the demanders.   That varying initial monetary endowments do not reduce the disparity in a lottery context is shown by Knetsch and Sinden (1984).   In the preliminary experiment with such transfer payments to demanders, the evaluation disparity as well as the expectation bias are still slightly significant. Additional corresponding experiments in preparation will clarify whether the evaluation disparity can be interpreted as an endowment effect, since both sides get an initial endowment there.   Such modified experiments will also eliminate the feeling of being disadvantaged on the demand side, and will control for budget constraints as possible influences.

The argument of profit seeking was shown to be inconsistent or at least based on incomplete, bounded rational considerations.   The occurrence of the expectation bias is an additional argument for the incompleteness of these thoughts.   That a random assignment of the roles reduces the evaluation disparity shows that more thorough considerations lead to more consistent expectations and decisions. The task of making potential decisions for alternative situations produces a cognitive dissonance (Festinger, 1957) if the scenarios used as decision bases are not consistent.   We assume that the random procedure induces such a cognitive dissonance at first, and this calls for its reduction by an intensification of considerations.   Feedbacks in the cybernetic process of decision making ultimately lead to reasonable decisions (Tietz, 1982). More subjective feelings are replaced by more objective criteria, and aspiration levels become more realistic. Additional methods which intensify the planning phase have to be tested.

We think that the disparity of bids and expectations is a result of fragmentary rationality. The overestimation of the power and the influence of one's own position is a consequence of the fact that thinking about the decision situation starts at the status quo. It is a characteristic of bounded rational behaviour that the decision process is terminated when a satisfying solution is found. If the outcome is not satisfying, inconsistencies are seen, or cognitive dissonances are felt, then additional and possibly recursive considerations are made which also take the positions of others into account. The disparities vanish if the decision process lasts long enough. Whether the initial endowment as status quo still has a substantial influence on the result depends on the intensity and the duration of this process. In this way, we may speak of an 'endowment effect' in bounded rational decision making.

REFERENCES

Coursey, D. L., Hovis, J. L., & Schulze, W. D. (1987). The disparity between willingness to accept and willingness to pay measures of value. *Quarterly Journal of Economics*, **102**, 679-690.

Festinger, L. (1957). *A theory of cognitive dissonance.* Stanford: Stanford University Press.

Kahneman, D. & Tversky, A. (1982). Risiko nach Maß - Psychologie der Entscheidungspräferenzen. *Spektrum der Wissenschaft*, 89-98. [Translated from Scientific American (1982)].

Kahneman, D. (1988). Experimental economics: A psychological perspective. In Reinhard Tietz, Wulf Albers, & Reinhard Selten (eds), *Bounded rational behavior in experimental games and markets.* New York: pp.11-18.

Knetsch, J. L. & Sinden, J. A. (1984). Willingness to pay and compensation demanded: Experimental evidence of an unexpected disparity in measures of value. *Quarterly Journal of Economics*, **99**, 507-521.

Knetsch, J. L. & Sinden, J. A. (1987). The persistence of evaluation disparities. *Quarterly Journal of Economics*, **102**, 691-695.

Knez, P., Smith, V. L., & Williams, A. W. (1985). Individual rationality, market rationality, and value estimation. *American Economic Review*, **75**, Papers and Proceedings, pp.397-402.

Starbuck, W. H. (1963). Level of aspiration theory and economic behavior. *Behavioral Science*, **8**, 128-136.

Thaler, R. (1980). Toward a positive theory of consumer choice. *Journal of Behavior and Organization*, **1**, 39-60.

Tietz, R. (1972). The macroeconomic experimental game KRESKO: Experimental design and the influence of economic knowledge on decision behavior. In Heinz Sauermann (ed.), *Contributions to experimental economics, Vol. III.* pp.267-288. Tübingen.

Tietz, R. (1982). Verhandlungsprozesse als Bausteine ökonomischer Systeme. In Rolf Pfeiffer & Helmut Lindner (eds.), *Systemtheorie und Kybernetik in Wirtschaft und Verwaltung.* pp.389-400. Berlin.

Tietz, R. & Weber, H-J. (1972). On the nature of the bargaining process in the KRESKO-Game. In Heinz Sauermann (ed.), *Contributions to Experimental Economics, Vol. III.* pp.305-334. Tübingen.

8. Receiving a gift: Evaluating who gives what when

Rik G.M. Pieters
Erasmus University, Rotterdam

Henry S.J. Robben
Tilburg University

INTRODUCTION

Despite the obvious impact that gift-giving has on the economy (see, for example, Belshaw, 1965; Belk, 1979), relatively little is known about the exact reasons why people give each other gifts, and about the criteria that people use when evaluating the gifts they receive from others. Moreover, the available research has almost exclusively focused on the donor and his or her perceptions, evaluations and behaviours. The recipient has received considerably less attention. A likely explanation is the strong marketing orientation of consumer research leading to an emphasis on the purchase of products and a de-emphasis on the use and disposition of products. Since the donor is usually the buyer of the gift and since the donor is not the recipient, the giving instead of the receiving of gifts has been highlighted.

Gift-transfer is an interactive process, with numerous occasions for feedback and reciprocation from the recipient to the donor (Banks 1979; Sherry 1983). Eventually, donors will become recipients, and the other way around. This does not imply that in the giving and receiving of gifts the same processes and factors are involved. The factors influencing the evaluation of gifts as a donor may differ from those influencing the evaluation of gifts as a recipient. For instance, money as a gift may be less acceptable to the donor than to the recipient. If the reader has ever been in a situation where he or she was disappointed with a gift that was chosen after intensive search by the donor, the need to analyse factors influencing the evaluation of gifts by recipients is self-evident.

GIFT-TRANSFER

The two central elements in gift-transfer are communication and transaction. Gifts communicate how valuable the relationship between donor and recipient is. Gifts are non-verbal signs that communicate what the donor wants from or likes in the recipient. Belk (1979) explains that gifts from parents to children socialize the children in certain roles: dolls to girls, cars to boys. In general, all gifts have such socialization properties to a certain extent. Gifts communicate what a recipient is, or how the donor would like to see the recipient. Imagine receiving spirits from all guests, each year on your birthday. Gifts are social and economic objects of exchange. Gifts are given by persons to other persons, by organizations to organizations, from organizations to persons, and vice versa. Gifts are means to start, reinforce, change or end relationships. Several factors influencing the gift-giving process have been investigated.

Involvement

Psychological involvement is the extent to which a stimulus (issue, object, person, situation) is personally relevant or important. Shopping for a gift tends to be a relatively highly involving activity due to the social and, sometimes, financial risk (Belk, 1982; Vincent and Zikmund, 1976). When involvement is high, consumers are motivated to invest more of their behavioural resources in the activity (Petty and Cacioppo, 1986). For instance, the quality of a product tends to be more important, and the price less important, when it is bought as a gift rather than for personal use (Shapiro, 1970). Grønhaug (1972) found that compared to recent buyers of tableware for personal use, those giving tableware as a gift reported considering more alternative choices, shopping at more dealers, seeking more advice from others and reading dealers' brochures more thoroughly. Consumers report that they spend more time and money selecting a gift, and that they visit more shops than when selecting the same products for personal use (Clarke and Belk, 1979). When involvement is high, but, for some reason, the ability to invest behavioural resources is low, consumers tend to use simple heuristics in choosing gifts. Ryans (1977) found that gift buyers of small appliances reported a greater use of high status stores than self-use buyers of the same product. Involvement will be returned to when the reception of gifts is discussed.

Occasions

Gifts are given at many occasions, for example, at personal life-cycle moments, like birthdays and weddings, at achievement occasions, like graduations, at special 'gift-transfer' days, like Christmas, and at many other occasions, or just to express love, friendship and the like. The occasions at which gifts are transferred affect the appropriate attributes in gifts. DeVere, Scott, and Shulby (1983) found that gifts for a birthday should reflect innovativeness, imaginativeness, novelty, and spontaneity. For a wedding, somewhat expensive durable goods (with a warranty) are often valued. Scammon, Shaw, and Bamossy (1982) showed that buying cut flowers for personal use represents a different situation from buying the flowers for gift use. For personal use, cut flowers are bought largely unplanned, while minimizing costs. For gift use, cut flowers are bought 'planned for special occasions'.

Type of gifts, and social relationships

Webley, Lea, and Portalska (1983) investigated whether it is appropriate for students to give money as a gift to their mothers. The students strongly preferred giving a real present over money. Would-be recipients rated money as a gift as unacceptable. Hussein (1985) found that only one out of 20 mothers in Cyprus preferred money as a gift from their children on Mother's Day. In a second study with young Turkish Cypriot adults, Hussein found that all subjects in the 'giving' and 'receiving' conditions expressed their preference for a selected gift rather than money. Relative status and intimacy in relationships are expected to influence the (un)acceptability of money as a gift. Webley and Wilson (1989) found that money appeared unacceptable as a gift, independent of the relationship between donor and recipient. Overall, their subjects reported spending more on intimates than on superficial friends (£8 versus £4.50). The intimacy of the relationship influenced the amount of money spent on a gift; nearly £10 on an intimate friend, and just over £3 on a superficial friend. Almost identical amounts of money were given to intimates and acquaintances (about £6). Burgoyne and Routh (1989) had 92 undergraduates keep an extended diary on gifts given and received at Christmas. Multidimensional scaling analyses revealed two dimensions of particular interest: status and intimacy. Gifts communicate the current level of intimacy between donor and recipient, while simultaneously taking into account any differences in status. The precise value of money, its universalistic exchangeability and commercial connotations may make it an inappropriate commodity to present as a gift, in particular in intimate relationships.

'Real' gifts are expected to communicate these delicate matters of intimacy and status better. Money gifts can be made by superiors to their employees, or by older relatives to younger ones.

RECEIVING A GIFT

What do recipients value in a gift? Which factors are important when evaluating a gift that one has received? Research reveals that recipients often tend to search for attributes in the gift that express the psychological involvement of the donor with the recipient (at this occasion). Since behavioural costs invested by the donor in the gift are an indicator of psychological involvement (see above), gifts that express the investment of behavioural costs, that is, a sacrifice, by the donor are valued highly by the recipient. In experiments on gift evaluation by recipients, Robben (1984) found that perceptions of high behavioural costs dominated the preference for a gift completely. That is, the amount of time the donor spent on selecting the gift, the physical trouble taken, and the psychological appropriateness of the gift were positively related to the expressed preference for receiving the gift. Psychological appropriateness was the only significant factor in deciding on which gift to give; cost factors probably do not matter that much, as long as the gift is something the recipient values very clearly. The attributed reasons for giving the gift, and the value of the gift affect the evaluation of the recipient as well. Tesser *et al.* (1968) conducted an experiment in which they presented subjects with vignettes, describing a benefactor who provides a hypothetical benefit to a recipient, in this case the subjects. The design included three independent variables – intentionality of the donor, economic costs of the benefit to the donor, and the subjective value of the benefit to the donor; each factor with three levels. All three factors influenced the felt gratitude of the recipients significantly. Felt gratitude increased when the gift was seen purely as to please the recipient, with high economic costs to the donor, and when it had a high subjective value to the donor.

Gifts represent a bundle of characteristics. For one thing, there are the intrinsic product attributes that make up the VCR, the fountain pen, or the hand-made vase. Next, there are the extrinsic or not directly observable attributes. The recipient infers these characteristics from his knowledge of the gift occasion and the relationship with the donor. This leads to highly complex, and often very subtle situations in which the value and 'meaning' of gifts is determined by the recipients. For instance, at weddings in the

Netherlands it is quite common to present the groom with an envelope with money (you may kiss the bride however). A vase or a money gift are equally suitable in this situation. At Sinterklaas, on 5 December, surprise presents are what really count; money is, in general, out of the question. Similarly, knowledge of donor characteristics influences the evaluation of gifts as well.

GOAL OF THE STUDY

The present study is conducted to shed more light on the factors influencing the evaluation of gifts by the recipients. Relevant factors suggested by prior research are analysed jointly.

Behavioural costs, sex and age

Prior research indicates that the higher the perceived behavioural costs, effort and time, invested in the gift by the donor, the more it is valued by the recipients (for example, Sherry, 1983; Robben, 1984). The theoretical analysis of Belk (1979) suggests that gifts from opposite-sex donors are more personal than gifts from same-sex donors, especially at one's birthday. Burgoyne and Routh's (1989) research suggests that the unacceptability of money as a gift is moderated by the status difference between donor and recipient. Specifically, it is more acceptable for the high status person in the relationship to give money to the low status person than the other way around. Furthermore, age differences are an important source of status differences. Accordingly, it was hypothesized that it is less unacceptable for older people to present younger ones with money as a gift, than vice versa. Research investigating the three factors jointly is absent. The effects of the amount of behavioural costs invested, the sex and age of the recipient, and the interactions of these effects, on the evaluation of a gift received on one's birthday were investigated.

Type of gift, degree of intimacy, and occasion

As several studies have shown, money tends to be less acceptable as a gift than a 'real' gift (for example, Hussein, 1985). Research suggests that the degree of intimacy between donor and recipient influences the evaluation of money as a gift (for example, Webley and Wilson, 1989). The more intimate the relationship, the less acceptable money seems to be as a gift. Although the analysis of Belk (1979) suggests that the type of gift occasion also influences the evaluation of money as a gift, hardly any research on this issue has been performed. The available studies have focused on gifts at either Christmas or Mother's day. Here, the difference between a personal life-cycle occasion (one's birthday) and an achievement occasion (passing an exam) are compared. It can be expected that on achievement occasions, money is more acceptable as a gift (that is, a 'reward') than on personal life-cycle occasions. The effects of the three factors and their interactions are explored.

Finally, the conditions that may make money an acceptable or even a preferable gift to recipients are explored.

METHOD

Subjects

A total of 103 students in Marketing and Consumer Behaviour at Erasmus University participated in one of two studies as a course requirement. The mean age of the students was 22 years. There were 40 women and 63 men. The subjects were randomly assigned to either study 1 (final N = 55) or study 2 (final N = 48).

Procedure

Both studies were designed as a gift evaluation task. The subjects received a ten-page booklet containing an explanatory page, a score form, descriptions of eight gift situations, questions concerning gift evaluation, several background questions, and some open-ended questions on the acceptability of money as a gift. Subjects were asked:

> Please read each description of a situation carefully. Try to imagine how you would feel and how you would react in that situation. Next, complete the questions below each description.

The situations in study 1 read:

> Imagine that you receive a present in this situation. Read the description carefully. From a 'X' person of 'Y' you receive a birthday present. You have the impression that the donor has invested 'Z' to choose a nice present.

In the original descriptions, the letters between quotes were replaced by:
X = 'younger' versus 'older' (AGE)
Y = 'the same sex' versus 'the opposite sex' (SEX)
Z = 'much effort' versus 'not much effort' (EFFORT)
The situations in study 2 read:

Imagine that you receive a present in this situation. Read the description carefully. For 'X' you receive a present from 'Y'. For this occasion you receive 'Z'.

In the original descriptions, the letters between quotes were replaced by:

X = 'your birthday' versus 'passing an examination' (OCCASION)

Y = 'a room-mate' versus 'your partner' (RELATIONSHIP)

Z = 'a nicely wrapped present' versus 'an envelope with money' (PRESENT)

The order of the eight situations was randomized, both in study 1 and study 2.

Questionnaire

Each description of a situation was followed by questions concerning the evaluation of the gift, the donor, the relationship, and the self (= personal reactions of recipient), and concerning the expectation to reciprocate. The questions were mainly based on Belk's model of gift-giving (Belk, 1979). The wording of the questions, together with the relevant labels, are presented below. Both in study 1 and in study 2, the subjects indicated on 7-point semantic differential scales whether they 'would find the gift in this situation' 'very good – very bad' (= Gift evaluation 1), and 'very suitable – very unsuitable' (=Gift evaluation 2), whether in this situation they would be 'very happy – very unhappy' (=Self evaluation 1), 'very satisfied – very unsatisfied' (=Self evaluation – 2), whether in this situation they would find the donor 'very kind – very unkind' (=Donor evaluation). Also, in both studies, the subjects indicated on a 4-point scale whether they would expect to reciprocate (return a gift) 'very much – not at all' (=Expect reciprocate). In study 1, the subjects indicated for each situation whether they felt their own status was 'higher', 'the same', or 'lower' than that of the donor (=Own relative status), and they indicated on a 4-point scale whether according to them the donor had put 'a lot of effort – no effort at all' in choosing the gift (=Donor effort). In study 2, subjects indicated on 5-point scales how close they would call the relationship with the donor in each particular situation: 'very close – very superficial' (=Relationship evaluation), and how personal they would find the gift: 'very personal – very unpersonal' (=Gift evaluation 3). Finally, the subjects in study 2 indicated on a 4-point scale how much they felt the gift was due to one's own effort: 'very much – not at all' (=Own effort). After evaluating each of the situations separately, subjects ordered the situations, from most to least liked/preferred. Finally, subjects were asked how suitable they felt money generally is as a gift, how they would define a gift in their own words, what the subjective meaning of a gift is, and what kind of gift they would prefer most.

EFFORT, SEX AND AGE OF THE DONOR

Two main analyses were carried out. Firstly, univariate analyses of variance with repeated measures (3 factors, 2 levels) were carried out to test the hypotheses. The summary results of the univariate analyses of variance with repeated measures are presented in Table 8.1. Since eight dependent variables were analysed, the appropriate Bonferroni correction was carried out to adjust the critical p-levels of the test statistics (adjusted p-level = critical p-level divided by 8). Secondly, preference scaling was carried out on the rank orders of the eight gift situations.

Table 8.1 Summary results of analyses of variance with repeated measures: Study 1

Criterion	Age	Sex	Factors Effort	Age x Sex	Age x Effort	Sex x Effort	Age x Sex x Effort
Gift evaluation (1)	.2	.2	252.9***	1.9	.9	.6	.9
Gift evaluation (2)	3.9	.5	102.9***	.2	.1	3.6	.7
Self evaluation (1)	.4	.3	198.5***	.7	.3	.3	.4
Self evaluation (2)	.1	1.1	180.9***	.2	.0	1.4	.0
Donor evaluation	.1	9.7*	243.1***	6.8	.1	1.0	.2
Donor effort	3.6	2.2	352.4***	.4	.2	.3	.2
Own relative status	20.6***	.2	1.3	.1	.3	.0	.3
Expect reciprocate	.5	.4	87.0***	.0	.0	3.9	.1

Notes: Numbers denote F-values. Asterisks denote Bonferroni p-levels:
*p less than .05; **p less than .01; ***p less than .005.
Degrees of freedom = 1/54.

The results of the analyses of variance are simple to interpret. Presents in which the donor has invested a great deal of effort are evaluated most positively. The gift is 'better', more 'suitable', the recipient is happier, more satisfied, the donor is rated as nicer. The donor is judged to have invested a great deal of effort (the manipulation check). As hypothesized, the relative status of the recipient is higher when the donor is younger, and the relative status of the recipient is lower when the donor is older. Finally, not unexpectedly, opposite-sex donors are always liked more than same-sex donors, irrespective of their age and their gift (effect of 'sex' on 'donor evaluation'). Subjects were also asked to rank order the eight gift situations on the basis of preference. The mean rank of the four 'high effort' gift situations was 6.4 (maximum = 8, minimum = 1), compared to a mean rank of 2.6 of the four 'low effort' gift situations. The highest mean rank was attained by the two gift situations describing a high-effort present from an opposite-sex donor (6.9). The rank orders of the individual preferences for the eight gift situations were subjected to a multidimensional analysis of preference data, MDPREF, (Green, Carmone and Smith, 1989). MDPREF is a metric model based on a principal components analysis. The analysis tries to plot both the subjects and the stimuli in a n-dimensional space. Specification of the number of dimensions to retain mirrors the process in ordinary principal components analysis. As expected, the first dimension in the solution was EFFORT. Gifts in which much effort was invested were evaluated most positively. The first dimension dominated the solution completely, accounting for 75 per cent of the variance (the second and third dimension accounted for respectively 8 and 5 per cent of the variance). To save space, the corresponding MDPREF solution will not be presented. To analyse potential sex differences in evaluating gifts, independent t-tests were carried out. Since 56 t-tests (8 situations x 7 variables) were carried out, the p-levels were adjusted accordingly (adjusted p-level = critical p-level divided by 56). Only four tests produced a significant result at the 5 per cent level or better. Interestingly, three of the four tests referred to the ascribed status of the donor. Women felt that their own status was similar to the status of a same-sex donor. Men felt that their own status was higher than the status of same-sex donors (irrespective of age and kind of gift). Other reliable sex differences were absent.

DEGREE OF INTIMACY, GIFT OCCASION, AND TYPE OF GIFT

Similar analyses as in study 1 were carried out. Since nine dependent variables were analysed in study 2, the p-levels of the test statistics were adjusted accordingly (adjusted p-level = critical p-level divided by 9). A summary of the Anovas is presented in Table 8.2.

Several results attract attention. First, as expected a real present is always evaluated more positively than money (factor: PRE). A real present is better, more suitable and more 'personal'. The recipient feels happier and more satisfied with a real present. Donors are perceived to be nicer when they give a real present. The relationship is closer with a real present. Interestingly, a real present is perceived to be more the result of one's own effort than money, and one expects more to reciprocate in the case of receiving a real gift. Second, a clear interaction between the relationship and the type of gift (RELxPRE) can be observed. A real present from one's partner is best, most personal, and most suitable. The least suitable and worst gift is money given by one's partner. This effect was amplified for 'Gift evaluation 1' when the gift occasion is taken into account (OCCxRELxPRE). On a 7-point scale from 'very bad' (1) to 'very good' (7), with the mid-point 'neither good nor bad' (4), the highest score was attained by the 'real gift' from the partner given on the occasion of one's birthday (mean score 4.1), while the lowest score was attained by money from the partner on one's birthday (mean score 1.6). Subjects expected more that they would reciprocate when they received a gift on the occasion of their birthday than for passing an exam. Expected reciprocation was also higher when the donor was one's partner than when the donor was a roommate, and when the gift was a real present than when the gift was money. Subjects were also asked to rank order the eight gift situations on the basis of preference. The highest mean ranks were attained by the two situations in which a nicely wrapped 'real' present was received from one's partner (6.9).

Table 8.2 Summary results of the analyses of variance with repeated measures: Study 2

Criterion	Occ	Rel	Factors Pre	Occ x Rel	Occ x Pre	Rel x Pre	Occ x Rel x Pre
Gift evaluation (1)	1.1	1.0	88.8***	2.1	9.3*	12.8**	9.3*
Gift evaluation (2)	18.0***	2.4	93.5***	13.9**	3.4	20.4***	3.4
Gift evaluation (3)	.2	9.5*	162.0***	2.4	.0	21.3***	.0
Self evaluation (1)	3.0	.5	52.6***	1.8	4.0	13.1**	4.0
Self evaluation (2)	.6	3.0	54.5***	6.2	8.0*	7.4	8.0*
Donor evaluation	3.3	4.3	42.8***	3.7	4.7	21.4***	4.7
Relation evaluation	1.0	128.1***	23.7***	6.0	.3	5.3	.3
Own effort	12.0**	28.2***	9.5**	5.9	.0	3.4	.2
Expect Reciprocate	34.6***	17.3***	38.9***	7.1	1.0	1.9	1.0

Notes: Occ=Occasion; Rel=Relationship; Pre=Present.
Numbers denote F-values.
Asterisks denote Bonferroni p-levels: *=p less than .05;
**=p less than .01; ***=p less than .005.
Degrees of freedom = 1/48.

The lowest mean ranks were attained by four situations in which money was received. Multidimensional preference scaling was carried out on the rank orders of the overall preference for the eight gift situations. The first four dimensions in the solution accounted for respectively 59, 18, 10, and 5 per cent of the variance. Accordingly, the three-dimensional solution, in which the first dimension dominates, was chosen. Since the location of the subject vectors did not reveal separate clusters, only the plots of the gift situations in the three-dimensional space are presented in Figure 8.1. To help in interpreting the solution, hierarchical cluster analyses (single linkage) were carried out. The analyses were carried out on the mean scores on the nine evaluations of each of the eight gift situations. As expected, the first dimension distinguishes between real gifts and money as a gift: The situations 1 to 4 are on the left in the plot, the situations 5 to 8 are on the right. The second dimension expresses the gift occasion, while the third dimension expresses the relationship between donor and recipient. These results confirm the results of the analyses of variance. Together, the two types of analyses strongly suggest the dominance of the type of gift in evaluating gifts. The analyses of variance reveal the interaction between the type of gift and the degree of intimacy in the relationship when evaluating gifts.

MONEY AS A GIFT

After completing the questions for the specific situations, subjects in both studies were asked to indicate whether money was acceptable to them as a gift, what kind of present they would prefer most, how they defined 'a gift', and what their subjective meaning of a gift was. The replies to these questions will be discussed for the two studies jointly (total $N = 111$). When asked: 'Do you think money is acceptable as a gift?', 10 per cent indicated that money was 'very acceptable'. For 33 per cent it was 'reasonably acceptable', for 16 per cent it was 'as good as a "normal" present', for 38 per cent it was 'not very acceptable' and for 4 per cent it was 'totally unacceptable'. Next, the subjects were asked 'Which gift would you like to receive most?'. A total of 85 per cent of the subjects indicated 'a normal gift'. A record token, a book token and a gift token were preferred by respectively 2, 2 and 6 per cent of the subjects. Money was preferred by 5 per cent of the subjects. Not unexpectedly, the (un)acceptability of money as a gift is associated with the preference for either money and tokens or a 'real' gift (chi-square $= 11.4$, df $= 4$, p $= .02$). Acceptability can be conceived as a 'lower bound' in evaluating gifts. Money may be quite acceptable, but this doesn't mean that it is also preferred as a gift. Preference can be conceived as an 'upper bound'. Clearly, a 'real' gift is preferred most. Content analyses on the open-ended questions support these notions. Our subjects indicated their answers to three open-ended questions:

1. 'Please indicate why you think money is acceptable or unacceptable as a gift'
2. 'When do you think money is equally suited as a real gift' and
3. 'When do you think it certainly is not'.

First, a subset of all protocols (n = 111) was used to arrive at a system to classify the free responses. Only in very few cases did the classification system have to be expanded with an extra category. Next, the responses to all three questions were jointly considered to obtain scores on the following categories:

(a) Is money an acceptable gift
(b) reasons for acceptability of money as a gift, and
(c) reasons for the unacceptability of money as a gift.

Dimension 1 by dimension 2   Dimension 1 by dimension 3

Figure 8.1 Preference scaling for Study 2:   Gift situations on dimension 1 by 2, and dimension 1 by 3.

Notes:
1 = birthday, roommate, money   5 = birthday, roommate, gift
2 = exam, roommate, money   6 = exam, roommate, gift
3 = birthday, partner, money   7 = birthday, partner, gift
4 = exam, partner, money   8 = exam, partner, gift

Category (a) contained two classes, acceptable and unacceptable. Category (b) consisted of 15 classes, 11 of which held nine responses or less. Finally, category (c) included seven classes. On the first question, a majority of the subjects indicated that according to them money was an acceptable gift (59 per cent). Sometimes participants mentioned specific conditions which are to be fulfilled before money was deemed allowable. For the present analyses, these subjects' responses were categorized as 'money is acceptable'. A little less than half of the participants thought money unacceptable (41 per cent). When is a money gift as appropriate as a real present? This second open-ended question elicited a total of 163 categorized responses. Some subjects' answers were so elaborate and rich that several classes within a category were necessary to accommodate the reasons presented. It appeared that three classes of the 15 contained 62 per cent of the responses. The most important reason for accepting money as a gift is when the recipient is in financial trouble, has specifically asked for it, or both (42 of 163 responses, 26 per cent). Next, a number of reasons were provided that pertain to the alleged inability of the donor to buy an appropriate present, because of old age, bad taste, or unfamiliarity with the recipient (34 of 163, 21 per cent). Finally, a group of reasons indicate that money is acceptable as a gift when the recipient is saving it up for a large purchase, or wants to do something special with the money (26 of 163, or 16 per cent). When should a donor definitely not consider giving money as a gift? Subjects generated 135 responses to this question. It appeared that financial gifts are seen as inappropriate when donor and recipient are involved in a close relationship with each other. Close relationship was the most salient group of reasons for not giving money as a gift (43 of 135 responses, or 32 per cent). A second reason for avoiding monetary gifts is that they convey a message of laziness, and an unwillingness to expend effort to shop for an appropriate present (36 of 135, 27 per cent). Finally, money gifts are not welcome because they are impersonal (26 of 135, 19 per cent).

CONCLUSION AND DISCUSSION

The results of the three analyses confirm and extend the results of prior research. The more effort is invested in the gift by the donor, the more it is valued by the recipient, as has been found in previous research (Robben, 1984). This behavioural cost effect dominates the evaluation. The sex and age of the donor had effects on the recipient's evaluation of the donor. Yet, these differences did not affect the evaluation of the gift. This may have been caused by the strong influence of the behavioural costs variable. The evaluation of money as a gift is influenced by the degree of intimacy of the relationship between donor and recipient. The more intimate the relationship, the less appropriate money is as a gift. Money is generally not strongly preferred as a gift by the recipients. Yet, an important result of the present study is that money is *not* unacceptable as a gift. Usually, it is not preferred, but it is welcomed just the same when received. Moreover, the content analysis of the free responses of our subjects reveal that in certain situations money is not only very acceptable, but even preferred. If one is in desperate need of money – as most students are most of the time – then obviously money is preferred. If one is saving for a large purchase, a considerable number of our students preferred money over a gift. Also, when a person is a notorious donor of inappropriate 'real' presents, one would rather have money from this donor than another 'garden-gnome'. These results confirm Burgoyne and Routh's (1989) finding that it is more acceptable to receive money as a gift than to give it. The expected reciprocation was stronger when one received a gift for one's birthday, than when one received a gift for passing an exam (study 2). In the latter case, the gift would have the meaning of a reward with the message 'you did a good job'. Usually, there is no need to reciprocate this, except when one wants to reward someone for his or her rewarding behaviour (in order to have future rewards). There is a strong norm to give gifts at birthdays. Yet, one does not give gifts at birthdays to reward a person, but to communicate friendship, thoughtfulness, dedication, love. The gift contains information about the meaning that the relationship (and the recipient) has for the donor. Money does not contain the right information, exactly because it is the universal medium of exchange. Receiving money as a gift from a person who we thought was close to us, tells us that we are universal to the donor, while our hope was that we were something special. As a final suggestion when donors want to give money as a gift, they should wrap it up, use ribbons, or fill a bottle with a large number of small coins. One of the authors once carefully glued several banknotes on a cheap poster and gave this as a present to someone at his birthday. This went down well. The donor should do things that will change the meaning of money from 'universal and low effort' to 'special and high effort'.

REFERENCES

Banks, S. K. (1979).   Gift-giving: A review and an interactive paradigm. *Advances in Consumer Behavior*, **6**, 319-324.

Belk, R. W. (1979).   Gift-giving behavior.   In J. N. Sheth (ed.), *Research in Marketing 2*. Greenwich, CT: JAI.

Belk, R.W. (1982).   Effects of gift-giving involvement on gift selection strategies. *Advances in Consumer Research*, **9**, 408-412.

Belshaw, C. S. (1965).   *Traditional exchange in modern markets*.   Englewood Cliffs, NJ: Prentice-Hall.

Burgoyne, C., & Routh, D. A. (1989).   Looking a gift horse in the mouth?   When and why money is unacceptable as a gift.   In T. Tyszka & P. Gasparski (eds.), *Homo Oeconomicus: Presumptions and Facts*.   pp.456-470.   Warzawa: Polish Academy of Science.

Clarke, K., & Belk, R. W. (1979).   The effects of product involvement and task definition on anticipated consumer effort. *Advances in Consumer Research*, **6**, 313-318.

DeVere, S. P., Scott, C. D., & Shulby, W. L. (1983).   Consumer perceptions of gift-giving occasions: Attribute saliency and structure. *Advances in Consumer Research*, **10**, 313-318.

Green, P. E., Carmone, F. J. Jr., & Smith, S. M. (1989). *Multidimensional scaling: Concepts and applications*.   Boston: Allyn and Bacon.

Grønhaug, K. (1972).   Buying situation and buyer's information behavior. *European Marketing Research Review*, **7**, 33-48.

Hussein, G. (1985).   Is money an unacceptable gift in Cyprus? *Perceptual and Motor Skills*, **61**, 1074.

Petty, R. E. & Cacioppo, J. T. (1986). *Communication and persuasion: Central and peripheral routes to attitude change*.   New York: Springer Verlag.

Robben, H. S. J. (1984).   Gift evaluation and behavioral costs.   Unpublished Master's thesis, Tilburg University.

Ryans, A. B. (1977).   Consumer gift buying behavior: An explanatory analysis.   In D. Bellinger & B. Greenberg (eds.), *Contemporary marketing thought*. Chicago: American Marketing Association.

Scammon, D. L., Shaw, R. T., & Bamossy, G. (1982).   Is a gift always a gift?   An investigation of flower purchasing behavior across situations. *Advances in Consumer Research*, **9**, 531-536.

Shapiro, B. P. (1970).   The effect of price on purchasing behavior.   In D.L. Sparks (ed.), *Broadening the concept of marketing*.   Chicago: American Marketing Association.

Sherry, J. F. (1983).   Gift-giving in anthropological perspective. *Journal of Consumer Research*, **10**, 157-168.

Tesser, A., Gatewood, R., & Driver, M. (1968).   Some determinants of gratitude. *Journal of Personality and Social Psychology*, **9**, 233-236.

Vincent, M. & Zikmund, W. G. (1976).   An experimental investigation of situational effects on risk perception. *Advances in Consumer Behavior*, **3**, 125-129.

Webley, P., Lea, S. E. G., & Portalska, R. (1983).   The unacceptability of money as a gift. *Journal of Economic Psychology*, **4**, 223-238.

Webley, P. & Wilson, R. (1989).   Social relationships and the unacceptability of money as a gift. *Journal of Social Psychology*, **129**, 85-91.

9. When is a cobweb model stable?

Alastair Fischer
University of Adelaide

INTRODUCTION

For many commodities, particularly in agriculture, supply must be determined some months in advance. The amount supplied depends on expectations of the future price, which in turn is influenced by past prices. One approach to these markets with a supply-response lag is the well-known cobweb model, but surprisingly few experiments have been carried out to test its predictions. Three main questions arise from experiments with such markets for a single commodity. How stable is the market? Is an equilibrium other than the theoretical competitive one approached, and if so, how quickly? What light does the model throw on the formation of expectations in general?

The first such experiments were set up by Carlson (1967) and, as far as the author knows, his lead has been followed only by Kreps and Scheinkman (1983), Holt and Villamil (1986) and Burns, Fischer and Meyler (1989). Carlson's experiments used linear supply and demand curves. He carried out two replicates with a steep demand curve and two with a shallow demand curve, and found that equilibrium was approached quickly in all four cases. Contrary to his expectations, the approach to equilibrium was if anything faster in the two replicates using the steep demand curve.

More recently, Burns *et al.* (1989) have run experiments using three commodities, which share some key common inputs, and where there is a supply response lag for each commodity. These markets turn out to be less stable than the markets for a single commodity. Their set of 22 replicates used the same basic design which was adapted to suit markets of between 5 and 12 participants. The participants could each produce in aggregate six units of output in each period, divided in any way (but using integers only) between three commodities (A, B and C). So the six units could be six of A and none of B and C; or five of A, one of B and none of C, etc. Participants made production decisions independently in advance, and the prices of the three commodities were then determined and announced by the experimenter, who added up the production of each commodity and read off the appropriate price from the demand curve for that commodity. The demand curves for the three commodities were linear and different. For simplicity costs were assumed to be zero.

In the experiments by Burns *et al.*, prices and quantities were much less likely to approach equilibrium than in Carlson's experiments. For the first five periods, participants were told only the price in each period, but in each of periods 6 to 10 they were told both the prices and aggregate quantities produced and in each of periods 11 to 15 (or 16) they were told price, aggregate quantities and the three demand curves being used. Prices fluctuated almost as much at the end of the experiment as at the beginning.

Such a result requires an explanation, as it contradicts the Carlson result for a single commodity. Burns *et al.* (1989) believed that the reason for the results lay in the difference between the explicit supply curve of Carlson's single commodity experiment and the supply curves (all zero price but stopping at a quantity between 0 and 6) of the three-commodity experiment.

This chapter reports on several different experiments which have been performed in order to try and shed further light on these and related matters. At this stage the work has looked mainly at the stability of equilibrium, and has not focused on expectation formation. The work of Holt and Villamil (1986) on a single person cobweb and of Kreps and Scheinkman (1983) on a two-stage production process are only peripherally related to the present work.

THE EXPERIMENTS

Six experiments were performed in the five months from December 1989. Ten students participated in each experiment. They were paid in proportion to their earnings in the experiment an average of A$25 (about £10) for a two hour period. Five of the six sets of participants were undergraduate students in Economics/Commerce and the sixth set consisted of Honours undergraduate students in Applied Mathematics, all at the University of Adelaide.

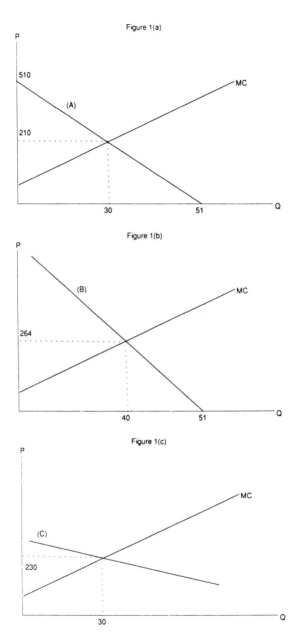

Figure 9.1 Supply and demand conditions for markets A, B, and C (experiments 1, 2, 3, and 4)

Experiments 1 and 2

In the first two experiments the market consisted of a single commodity, and took place in three parts. In all three parts and within each part, all participants had the same cost schedule. In the first part, the demand curve used (A) was of medium slope, in the second part (B), of steep slope and in the third part (C), of shallow slope. The cost curve for each participant was given in tabular form, the underlying equation being $TC = 75q + 25q^2$ for integer units from $q = 0$ to $q = 5$. The three demand curves were:

(A) $p = 510 - 10Q$
(B) $p = 1224 - 24Q$
(C) $p = 290 - 2Q$

for integer $Q > 0$ and $p > 0$, where $Q = \Sigma q$

The equilibrium in these markets was respectively:

(A) $p = 210$, $Q = 30$ (3 per participant)
(B) $p = 264$, $Q = 40$ (4 per participant)
(C) $p = 230$, $Q = 30$ (3 per participant)

Figures 9.1(a), 9.1(b) and 9.1(c) show these markets in continuous form, though in reality they are step-functions. In all cases the equilibria were attainable since q ranged up to 5 units per participant, or 50 overall. In experiment 1, the demand curve A was used first and the experiment ran for 36 periods, followed by curve B for 20 periods. In experiment 2, curve B was used first for 20 periods, followed by curve A for 34 periods (the competitive equilibrium having been attained for the last five periods) and curve C for 12 periods (equilibrium attained for the last three periods).

Results

In both experiments, equilibrium was approached quickly for each type of demand curve, but deviations were somewhat greater the steeper the curve (see Figure 9.2). The average amount produced over all periods was below the competitive equilibrium for each part of the experiment except for curve C in experiment 2, and the deviation was greater the steeper the demand curve. In all experiments, there was a relatively large initial variability for about the first four periods. Therefore, greater reliance is placed on the average quantity and its standard deviation, omitting the first four periods, as reported in Table 9.1.

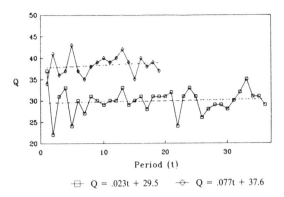

(a) Experiment 1, Demand curves A and B

$\boxdot$ Q = .023t + 29.5 $\diamond$ Q = .077t + 37.6

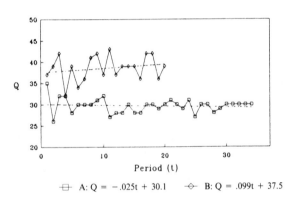

(b) Experiment 2, Demand curves A and B

$\boxdot$ A: Q = −.025t + 30.1 $\diamond$ B: Q = .099t + 37.5

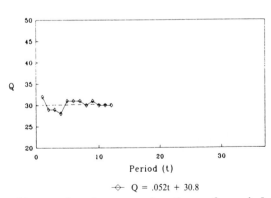

(c) Experiment 2, Demand curve C

$\diamond$ Q = .052t + 30.8

Figure 9.2 Quantity produced as a function of period (experiments 1 and 2)

Table 9.1 Summary of quantities produced for experiments 1 and 2

Demand curve	N of periods	Eqm Q	Ave Q	Ave Q#	SD	SD#
Experiment 1						
(1) A	36	30	29.9	29.8	2.9	2.3
(2) B	20	40	38.45	38.8	2.3	2.1
Experiment 2						
(1) B	20	40	38.55	38.8	2.9	2.6
(2) A	34	30	29.7	29.5	1.7	1.2
(3) C	12	30	30.4	30.5	0.8	0.5

Notes: 'Ave Q#' omits 4 periods
          'SD' is standard deviation
          'SD#' is standard deviation omitting
          4 periods

Experiments 3 and 4

As a result of experiments 1 and 2, it was decided that in the next experiments participants should make production decisions for the markets for the medium demand curve (curve *A*) and the steep demand curve (curve *B*) simultaneously. So that the learning task was not unduly complicated, participants started with a few rounds of the single market, market *C*.

Since the supply and demand conditions for each market were essentially unchanged, the equilibrium quantity for *A* was still 30 units (3 units each for 10 participants) and for *B* was 40 units (4 by 10). Each participant was able to produce up to ten units in total, (the cost curve for each market separately was $TC = 75q + 25q^2$, for $q = 0$ to $q = 10$) so the two equilibria were attainable, as the aggregate of *A* and *B* in equilibrium was seven units per participant.

In the last part of experiments 3 and 4, each participant was constrained to an aggregate production of six units, so that the two equilibria could not both be attained simultaneously. The constrained optimum quantities of *A* and *B* are 2.33 and 3.67 per participant respectively, as shown in Fischer (1990).

Results

Equilibrium was approached quickly in market *C* with the shallow demand curve, and on average, slight overproduction occurred in both experiments (see Table 9.2). Equilibrium was also approached quickly in markets *A* and *B* when the constraint on total production was not binding (see Figure 9.3). For market *A* (middling slope), there was slight underproduction on average in one and slight overproduction in the other experiment. Again in market *B* there was slight underproduction on average in both experiments.

Table 9.2 Summary of quantities produced for experiments 3 and 4

Demand curve	N of	Eqm periods	Ave Q Q	Ave Q#	SD	SD#
Experiment 3						
(1) C	28	30	*	30.4	*	1.6
(2) A	20	30	29.5	29.4	2.7	1.0
B	20	40	38.8	38.8	3.1	2.8
(3) A	12	23.3	23.3	23.4	2.6	2.9
B	12	36.7	35.6	36.1	3.0	2.8
Experiment 4						
(1) C	10	30	30.9	30.8	1.4	1.1
(2) A	19	30	30.2	30.8	4.2	3.5
B	19	40	39.9	39.5	5.3	3.9
(3) A	14	23.3	23.5	22.3	5.2	5.5
B	14	36.7	33.4	35.4	5.9	5.9

Notes: 'Ave Q#' omits four periods
'SD' is standard deviation
'SD#' is standard deviation omitting four periods
* denotes that a student made an error due to misunderstanding
instructions in the early periods, therefore making the overall average
and standard deviation meaningless.
In (2) participants made decisions for A and B simultaneously and in (3)
participants made decisions for A and B simultaneously and were
constrained to an aggregate production of six units per period.

In experiment 4, one participant tried to destabilize the market for profit in the middle of the second part, but on failing to achieve this, he then played essentially randomly out of boredom, spite or devilment in the second and third parts of the experiment. As a result, this market was relatively less stable than that of the first three

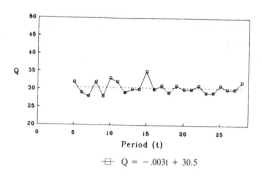

(a) Experiment 3, Demand curve C
student error corrected

⊟ Q = − .003t + 30.5

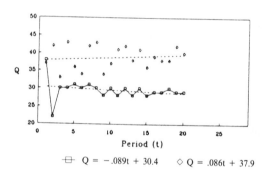

(b) Experiment 3, Demand curves A & B
no Q constraint

⊟ Q = − .089t + 30.4   ◇ Q = .086t + 37.9

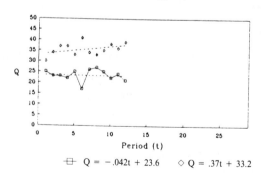

(c) Experiment 3, Demand curves A & B
constrained (Q<61)

⊟ Q = − .042t + 23.6   ◇ Q = .37t + 33.2

**Figure 9.3   Quantity   produced   as   a   function   of   period
(experiments 3 and 4)**

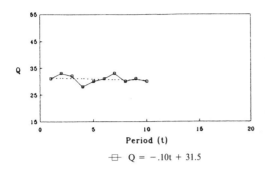

(d) Experiment 4, Demand curve C
student error corrected

$\boxplus$ $Q = -.10t + 31.5$

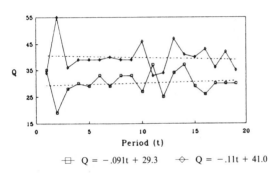

(e) Experiment 4, Demand curves A & B
unconstrained

$\boxplus$ $Q = -.091t + 29.3$ $\diamond$ $Q = -.11t + 41.0$

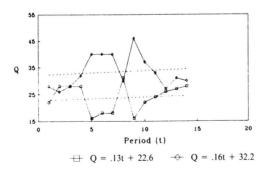

(e) Experiment 4, Demand curves A & B
constrained (Q<61)

$\boxplus$ $Q = .13t + 22.6$ $\diamond$ $Q = .16t + 32.2$

Figure 9.3 (concluded)

experiments, but in other respects the results were similar to those of experiment 3.

In part (3) of experiments 3 and 4, where total production was constrained to 60 units, the market was less stable than in part (2), where total production was not constrained. This is shown by the higher standard deviations of quantities over time in part (3). This ties in with the work done by Burns *et al.* (1989) on three commodities.

Experiments 5 and 6

Experiments 5 and 6 were constructed to overcome a design problem of experiments 3 and 4, to make the scale of the experiments closer to those of Carlson, and to investigate whether the same results for a single commodity market were observed for the elastic part of a steep demand curve as compared with the inelastic part of the same demand curve.

The design problem was that in experiments 1 and 2, participants could produce only up to five units of *A* and up to five units of *B*, whereas in experiments 3 and 4, they could produce up to ten units of *A* and *B* in aggregate. However, this meant that in experiments 3 and 4 they could produce more than five units of one of *A* or *B*, which occasionally someone did, thus resulting in experiments 1 and 2 not being equivalent to experiments 3 and 4. In experiments 5 and 6, participants were told that there was no limit to the amount of either *A* or *B* which could be produced.

To match Carlson's original experiments, the scale of production in the first four experiments was multiplied by five (so that for example equilibrium was at 20 units for each participant rather than at four units each for market *B*). This was done for two reasons. First, it was thought that a 0 to 5 range of production was a rather lumpy one, and that a 0 to 25 range allowed rather finer distinctions to be made between units. Second, there might be a 'scale effect' whereby people act differently with numbers such as 5, 10, 15, 20 compared with 1, 2, 3, 4.

Because the scale of the experimental numbers changed by a factor of five, but in other respects the experiments were unaltered, the demand curve formerly called *B* was now called *B2* in the new scale.

Finally, it was hypothesized that the average production was lower than the theoretical equilibrium for the steep demand curve due to the fact that the equilibrium occurred in the inelastic range of the demand curve in question, an increase in aggregate production leading to a decrease in aggregate revenue. According to the simplest of the theories regarding the cobweb model, the determinants of stability of the model are the slopes of the supply and demand curves. So by altering the position of the marginal cost curve parallel to itself, the slopes of supply and demand would be unaltered, but the equilibrium position could be put into the elastic part of the demand curve, where an increase in aggregate production (to above the equilibrium level) would lead to an increase in aggregate revenue. This was done in experiment 6 only. In experiment 5, a second marginal cost curve was introduced but with equilibrium remaining in the inelastic part of the demand curve, as it was thought that a change in stability could be caused by learning effects alone.

Experiments 5 and 6 consisted of two parts. In part (1), the individual cost equation was $TC = 55q + 5q^2$ (called $MC1$) and market demand equation (called $B2$, steeply-sloped) was $p = 1204.4 - 4.8Q$ (p expressed to nearest integer). In part (2) for experiment 5, the cost equation was replaced by $TC = 205q + 5q^2$ (called $MC2$) and in experiment 6, the cost equation was replaced by $TC = 905q + 5q^2$ (called $MC3$). The same demand curve was used as in part (1). (The equation for demand curve $B2$ is similar to that of B in experiments 1 to 4 but with $Q/5$ replacing Q, and having the same value of p at $Q=1$. The intersection of supply and demand is at $q = 198$ and $p = 254$ for part (1); at $q = 173$ and $p = 374$ for part (2) in experiment 5, and at $q = 50$, $p = 964$ for part (2) in experiment 6.

Results

Equilibrium was approached quickly in experiment 5 and very quickly in experiment 6 for cost curve $MC3$ (see Figure 9.4). There was no tendency in either the first part or the second part of either experiment 5 or 6 for underproduction. The increased range of production (relative to the equilibrium value) gave some increased instability for the first few periods of these two experiments. Even after the first four periods, and on dividing by five for comparability with demand curve B of experiments 1 to 4, the standard deviation of quantities for part (1) was higher than the equivalent standard deviation for experiments 1 to 4 (see Table 9.3). In the second part of the experiments, for experiment 5 a similar result pertained as in the first part, not surprisingly since the production remained in the inelastic part of the demand curve. In the second part of experiment 6 when the demand curve was elastic, the standard deviation was much lower. However this might have been because the equilibrium quantity was much lower, as the S.D. relative to equilibrium q did not change so much.

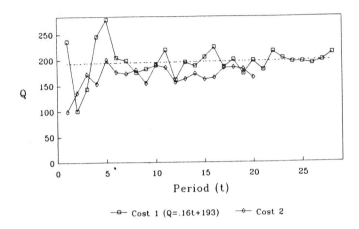

(a) Experiment 5, Demand B2
two cost curves

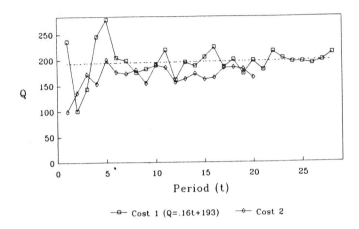

(b) Experiment 6, Demand B2
two cost curves

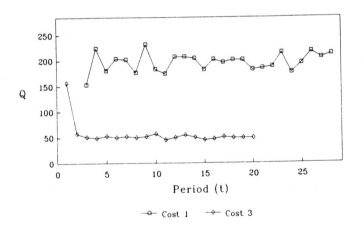

Figure 9.4 Quantity produced as a function of period (experiments 5 and 6)

**Table 9.3 Summary of quantities produced for
experiments 5 and 6**

Demand curve	N of periods	Eqm Q	Ave Q	Ave Q#	SD	SD#
Experiment 5						
(1) B2 & MC1	28	198	195.6	198	31.4	21.7
Q divided by 5	28	39.6	39.1	39.6	6.3	4.3
(2) B2 & MC2	20	173	166.9	173.8	21.3	12.9
Q divided by 5	20	34.6	33.4	34.8	4.3	2.6
Experiment 6						
(1) B2 & MC1	28	198	205.3	196.9	38.8	15.3
Q divided by 5	28	39.6	41.1	39.4	7.8	3.1
(2) B2 & MC3	20	50	55.6	49.8	23.5	3.0
Q divided by 5	20	10	11.1	10	4.7	0.6

Notes: 'Ave Q#' omits four periods
'SD' is standard deviation
'SD#' is standard deviation omitting four periods

GENERAL DISCUSSION

It is evident that all the markets investigated approached equilibrium moderately quickly when there were no binding constraints preventing equilibria from being attained and, judging by the standard deviation of quantities produced over time, the steeper the demand curve, the greater the fluctuations about the average production over time (see Table 9.4). There may be a tendency for average production to be slightly below the theoretical competitive equilibrium when the demand curve is very steep and inelastic. However, this does not appear to be a very large effect, if it exists at all. For this type of experiment, therefore, ten participants may proxy for the infinite number of perfectly competitive theory. There is virtually no support for a Cournot-type restriction of quantity. For example, in experiments 5(1) and 6(1) the Cournot equilibrium is 183, the competitive equilibrium is 198, and the experimental results were 198 and 197 respectively. For calculation of the Cournot Solution, see Varian (1987).

The results available in Table 9.4 give an indication that when the theoretical competitive equilibria cannot both be attained in the two markets taken together because total production is constrained, there is less stability in the markets. This was what was happening in the three-commodity market (Burns *et al.*, 1989), which had zero cost curves for the commodities for simplicity. Without a constraint on total production, the equilibria would have been reached at $p = 0$ (or slightly above 0 to avoid zero production). In Burns's case, therefore, the constraint on production was a binding one which did not allow the perfectly competitive equilibria to be reached.

Table 9.4 Standard deviations of production after period four

Shallow demand curve (C)

Expt No.	S.D.	Part of experiment (constrained)	S.D.
2	0.5	Third	
3	1.0	First	
4	1.1	First	
Average 0.9			

Middling demand curve (A)

1	2.3	First	
2	1.2	Second	
3	1.0	Second (together)	2.9
4	3.5*	Second (together)	5.5*
Average 1.5 (first 3)			

Steep demand curve (B)

1			
2	2.6	First	
3	2.8	Second (together)	2.8
4	3.9*	Second (together)	5.9*
5	4.3**	First	
6	3.1**	First	
Average 2.5 (first 3)			

Notes: *Student destabilized experiment
      ** S.D. for Demand curve B2 divided by 5.

This would appear to have some practical importance. For example, suppose that farmers have a choice of growing either crop *A*, crop *B* or a combination of both, and that in aggregate, both prices and quantities of production are relatively stable over time. Now suppose that there is a surge in the demand for *A*, and its price rises. Farmers will tend to begin producing more of *A* and less of *B* if the amount planted to *A* and *B* in aggregate remains unchanged. In time, it could be expected that there will be new entry – that is, increased total production of *A* and *B* taken together – until equilibrium in both markets is again approached. However, if entry is a relatively slow process, the experiments suggest that the markets will be less stable.

There is some evidence to suggest that the stability of the experimental market depends on the lumpiness of the commodity, as is shown at the end of Table 9.5 for commodity *B2* rather than *B*. Paradoxically, greater lumpiness appears to be associated with greater stability.

These experiments are continuing. Further replications are needed to firm up some of the results tentatively obtained so far, particularly those where the production constraint does not allow the competitive equilibria to be attained. More specifically, such experiments need to be carried out over more than 12 or 14 periods, to see whether there is greater convergence over a longer time period, and to measure all standard deviations using the same number of time periods. The present study does not do this, which weakens its validity somewhat. An obvious extension is to put a stochastic element into the supply and/or demand curves to see whether stability is maintained in these circumstances. More work also needs to be carried out to analyse the way in which expectations are formed by participants.

REFERENCES

Burns, J. P. A., Fischer, A. J., & Meyler, M. J. (1989). We could not get our cobweb to stop cycling: An experiment with increasing information. Paper presented to the Annual Conference of Economists, 10-13 July, Adelaide, South Australia.

Carlson, J. A. (1967). The stability of an experimental market with a supply-response lag. *Southern Economic Journal*, **23**, 308-321.

Fischer, A. (1990). When is a cobweb model stable? Some experimental results. In S. E. G. Lea, P. Webley, and B. M. Young (1990). *Applied Economic Psychology in the 1990s*. pp. 94-112. Exeter: Washington Singer Press.

Holt, C. A., & Villamil, A. (1986). A laboratory experiment with a single person cobweb. *Atlantic Economic Journal*, **14**, 51-54.

Kreps, D., & Scheinkman, J. (1983). Quantity precommitment and Bertrand competition yield Cournot outcomes. *Bell Journal of Economics*, **14**, 326-337.

Varian, H. R. (1987). *Intermediate microeconomics: A modern approach.* New York and London: Norton.

10. Distributive justice versus bargaining power

Werner Güth, Peter Ockenfels, and Reinhard Tietz
Johann Wolfgang Goethe-Universität

INTRODUCTION

We first review experimental results ranging from purely non-strategic allocation problems to simple bargaining situations. All situations have in common that the definition of fair division takes the simple form of a fifty-fifty solution and that exploitation of strategic power implies an extreme payoff result. In our new experiment this is only true, in general, if payoffs are restricted to monetary rewards which the players themselves can influence.

In the second section we describe three cake-dividing paradigms, namely dictatorship, reward allocation, and ultimatum bargaining, for which we briefly review the main experimental results in the third section. In the fourth section we introduce a new ultimatum bargaining experiment. The only difference to previous experiments is that player 2 receives a transfer payment t which does not depend at all on how the game is played. If this transfer payment t is equal to the size of the cake, the normative solution – which gives all the cake to player 1 – implies equal monetary payoffs that is, a fair allocation of rewards. We use a two-factorial experimental design with three different cake sizes c and $t = 0$, as in previous experiments, as well as $t = c$ in order to test some hypotheses, mainly concerning the influence of the parameters c and t.

The fifth section describes the experimental procedure. The experimental results are analysed in the sixth and seventh sections. We first use the bids – the player positions have been auctioned – and the actual bargaining decisions to test our basic hypotheses. In the seventh section psychological factors are also used to explain the observed decision behaviour. These factors have been calibrated from the answers to a rather detailed psychological personality questionnaire which is completely unrelated to the experimental situation. Güth, Ockenfels and Tietz (1990) analyse the psychological data with the help of factor analysis and try to explain bidding and bargaining decisions by these factors. The paper concludes with some final remarks.

The experimental results reveal that many subjects were frightened by the considerable monetary rewards. A major result is that, as compared to $t = 0$, transfer payments $t = c$ do not support strongly the game theoretic solution although it implies equal monetary payoffs. Here one should, of course, keep in mind that we have auctioned player positions. If player positions are assigned arbitrarily to subjects, the predictive power of the game theoretic solution might increase. The psychological factors affect the decision behaviour significantly but different decisions are always influenced by different psychological factors.

THREE CAKE DIVIDING PARADIGMS

In the following we want to consider the most simple kind of allocation conflicts with just two interacting individuals, called player 1 and player 2, who have to divide a positive amount c of a given divisible resource. We will refer to c as the cake which has to be allocated. It is assumed that both players prefer more to less of the cake and that this fact is common knowledge as it is nearly always common knowledge that most economic agents prefer a higher income to a smaller one. We will describe three types of cake-dividing paradigms which all yield the same extreme allocation of the cake c, if players are assumed to be completely selfish.

Dictatorship games

Here, player 1 is free to allocate the cake c in any way he wants, in other words, in this game player 1 can choose any amount d_1 with

(1) $0 \leq d_1 \leq c$

which implies the payoff vector $(d_1, c\text{-}d_1)$ where d_1 is player 1's payoff, and $c\text{-}d_1$ the payoff of player 2. Obviously, selfish behaviour by player 1 is determined by

(2) $d_1^* = c$ and the outcome $(c,0)$

according to which all the cake is consumed by player 1.

Reward allocation games

Here, both players are required first of all to perform a certain task for which they both together receive the reward c (>0). Usually the task is such that one can measure how much both players have individually contributed. In such a case, s with

(3) $0 \leq s \leq 1$

is player 1's share in the efforts to earn c. Player 2's contribution is the residual share $1 - s$.

Knowing that the task has been fulfilled and the share s is the amount that he has contributed, player 1 can allocate the cake as he wants to. Thus, given that the task has been completed, the reward allocation game has the same rules as the dictatorship games, that is, (2) describes also the outcome in reward allocation games if player 1 is completely selfish.

Ultimatum bargaining games

An ultimatum bargaining game is the most simple sequential bargaining procedure with two subsequent decision stages. First player 1 determines his demand d_1 satisfying (1), then knowing player 1's demand d_1 player 2 can decide whether he accepts it or not. In the case of acceptance the payoff result is $(d_1, c-d_1)$, that is, player 1 receives what he demanded and player 2 receives the residual amount. If player 2 does not accept, conflict results with 0 - payoffs for both players, that is, the cake has been lost.

If player 2 cares only for his share of the cake, then he will obviously accept any demand d_1 with $d_1 < c$. In the extreme case $d_1 = c$ he would be indifferent between accepting and the choice of conflict. Thus player 1 will choose the highest demand $d_1 < c$ which means that he obtains nearly all the cake if the smallest unit of measurement is sufficiently small as compared to c. Thus purely selfish behaviour on the part of both players implies an outcome which is very close to the one described by (2). It seems justified to say that, in case of selfish behaviour, all three cake-dividing paradigms imply the same extreme result, namely that all the cake is consumed by player 1 and that player 2 gets nothing.

EXPERIMENTAL RESULTS FOR THE DIFFERENT CAKE DIVIDING PARADIGMS

In the following we want to report briefly the main experimental results of previous studies with the three cake-dividing paradigms described in the second section, and compare them (for details of the experimental procedures see the original studies). We do not claim to include all previous experimental studies in our comparison since we may not be aware of some experimental studies of reward allocation which have been carried out by psychologists.

Dictatorship experiments

Experiments with dictatorship games have been performed by Forsythe, Horowitz, Savin, and Sefton (1988) with a constant pie of $5. We will concentrate on the experiments where the money was really paid to subjects and only briefly mention the results of the No Pay experiments (in the No Pay experiments no monetary rewards were given to subjects). In a total of 45 games only two players 1 asked for more than half of the cake, namely $d_1 = 3$, and only eight subjects proposed the equal distribution, in other words, 35 out of 45 subjects asked as player 1 for less than half of the cake.

The dominant behaviour is thus characterized by an impressive generosity of dictators which resembles the politeness ritual observed by Mikula (1972) in reward allocation experiments. According to the politeness ritual a superior player likes to display generosity, that is, to propose favourable results for the inferior player for which the inferior player would never ask. This is supported by the fact that in the No Pay experiments only 23 out of 46 subjects have asked for less than $c/2$. In the No Pay experiment it does not cost anything to be generous which might have prevented some subjects from displaying such a cheap kind of generosity.

Although the experimental situation is not quite a dictatorship game where a constant cake has to be allocated, the experimental results of Hoffman and Spitzer (1982, 1985) are worth mentioning. In this experiment, player 1 could unilaterally choose one of several payoff vectors, for example, the payoff vector ($12, 0) with $12 for himself and nothing for player 2 or more favourable payoff vectors for player 2 whose components could sum up to $14. The players were free to communicate and sign a mutually binding agreement specifying the payoff vector, which player 1 must choose, as well as possible side payments, for example, to compensate player 1 for giving up his most preferred payoff vector.

The main purpose of the first experiment (Hoffman & Spitzer, 1982) was to test the efficiency hypothesis, namely that both players will strive for the payoff vector with the highest sum of components. A somewhat surprising result was that all pairs of subjects did not only strive for the biggest pie of $14 but also shared it equally although player 1 could guarantee himself $12 by choosing the payoff vector ($12, 0). Thus players 1 invariably agreed to give up $5 in order to let player 2 enjoy $7 instead of nothing. Given that $5 is a considerable amount for a student subject, the politeness ritual requires quite a sacrifice from the superior player. The Hoffman and Spitzer results therefore provide strong evidence that in face-to-face experiments with asymmetric strategic power, superior players feel strongly pressed to induce more equal payoffs.

In their second study Hoffman and Spitzer (1985) did not assign the roles of player 1 and player 2 simply by an unbiased chance move as before, but gave the dictator position to the one of the two subjects who has won a purely strategic (hash mark) game which both subjects have played beforehand. The hash mark game starts with 17 hash marks of which player 1 and 2 can alternately cross out 1 to 4. The player who crosses out the last hash mark has lost the game. The main purpose was to test the hypothesis that dictators will be more willing to exploit their strategic power if they consider their more powerful position to be morally justified. Players 1, who have earned their position by winning the hash mark game, asked for higher payoffs for themselves than dictators due to chance moves: subjects appeared to treat their entitlements as rights to unequal payoff divisions when the experimental institutions led them to believe that they had "earned" those entitlements.

A similar observation has been made by Güth and Tietz (1985, 1986) who auctioned the positions of ultimatum bargainers before letting the auction winners play the ultimatum bargaining game. Since the price for the position of player 1 will usually be much higher (on average it was twice as high as the price for the position of player 2), players 1 will think that they deserve their more powerful position and will feel more justified to exploit it. As a matter of fact, Güth and Tietz (1986, Table 2) observed almost no equal payoff distributions whereas equal divisions of the cake c are quite frequent without auctioning the player positions (see Table 1 in the survey paper of Güth and Tietz, 1990).

In our view, auctioning the player positions is a more appropriate way to induce justified entitlements for more powerful strategic positions. Each player has earned his position in a strictly competitive situation and has to pay a competitive price for it, whereas the hash mark game is completely unrelated to the distribution problem. Furthermore, the bids in the auction as well as the auction prices can be used as additional data indicating aspiration levels etc. (see also Güth & Schwarze, 1983).

Reward allocation experiments

The typical way of performing a reward allocation experiment is as follows: two subjects work simultaneously but usually without seeing each other on the same task, for example, proof reading, writing addresses on envelopes. It is essential that the burden of the task is serious enough so that the difference of a superior individual contribution (for example, 60 per cent) to an inferior individual contribution (for example, 40 per cent) reflects a substantial difference in individual efforts. The allocator is informed about his share s and the residual share $1-s$ of his partner in fulfilling the task and has then to decide how to allocate the reward (almost always a positive amount of money). A similar situation with predetermined rewards where the allocator, who has to allocate the amount of work, has a comparative cost advantage in accomplishing the task, has been investigated by Güth (1984).

Here we do not try to review all experimental studies of reward allocation but restrict ourselves to mentioning some typical results. Even more than in dictatorship games one would not expect to observe selfish behaviour frequently. In the study of Güth (1984), for instance, only five of 62 subjects were completely selfish. The main purpose of reward allocation experiments is to explore which norms of social justice are actually used and whether one norm is substituted by another when certain environmental aspects change.

Shapiro (1975) distinguished allocators who anticipated further future interaction with their partner and allocators with no such perspective. With no further future interaction most allocators, whether superior ones with shares $s > 1/2$ or inferior ones with shares $s < 1/2$, predominantly used the contribution standard, according to which rewards have to be proportional to individual work amounts or contributions. The contribution standard is a very convincing theory of distributive justice with strong empirical support; it is known as equity theory among psychologists and as the behavioural theory of distributive justice among economists (see Homans, 1961; Walster, Berscheid, & Walster, 1973; Walster & Walster, 1975; Mikula & Schwinger, 1977/8). Güth (1988) has generalized this concept for situations with competing standards in measuring rewards and/or contributions.

But if allocators anticipated further interaction with their partner, the results were different for superior and inferior allocators (Shapiro, 1975; for similar observations see also Mikula & Schwinger, 1973). Whereas superior allocators tended to assign equal rewards as predicted by the politeness ritual, inferior allocators relied mainly on the contribution standard. According to Mikula and Schwinger (1973) as well as Mikula (1974) equal rewards were more often used by allocators who liked their partner than by allocators with disliked partners.

Overall, we can conclude that inferior allocators are morally strongly obliged to use the contribution standard, whereas superior allocators can use a wider range of allocation rules. They tend to choose equal rewards and this tendency is strengthened if they expect future interaction with their partner and if they personally like their partner.

It should be mentioned that the work in most reward allocation experiments was not very burdensome and it may even have been fun to perform the task. Furthermore, the total reward was usually not very high. Thus a superior allocator was never asked to make a substantial sacrifice if he chose equal rewards instead of allocating rewards proportionally to contributions. As far as we know, all sacrifices of superior allocators were considerably smaller than the $5-sacrifice by players 1 in the Hoffman and Spitzer experiment.

Ultimatum bargaining experiments

Again we will restrict ourselves to mentioning the general tendencies of the observed behaviour. We will ignore all results concerning bargaining with alternating offers (here only the last round is an ultimatum game in the narrow sense as defined in Ultimatum Bargaining games, above). More general surveys are Thaler (1988) and Güth and Tietz (1990). Furthermore, some of the recent studies survey most previous studies, for example, Kravitz and Gunto (1988) and Ochs and Roth (1989).

In spite of the apparent popularity of ultimatum bargaining few experiments have tried to explore the behaviour in the basic game situation described above in Ultimatum Bargaining games. To our knowledge this has been done only by Güth, Schmittberger and Schwarze (1982), Güth and Tietz (1985, 1986), Kravitz and Gunto (1988) and Prasnikar and Roth (1989). In all other studies the ultimatum bargaining decisions were either embedded in a larger game context (Binmore, Shaked & Sutton, 1984; Güth & Tietz, 1988; Neelin, Sonnenschein & Spiegel, 1988; Ochs & Roth, 1989; Weg, Rapoporto & Felsenthal, 1988) or subjects assumed the positions of both players in two different games (Güth *et al.*, 1982; Kahneman, Knetch & Thaler, 1986a and b; Bolle, 1988).

In game theory terminology the selfish behaviour, which we have derived for ultimatum bargaining games, is the only perfect equilibrium point of these games (Selten, 1975). It says that player 2 should accept any proposal d_1 with $d_1 < c$ and that player 1 can therefore ask for the highest amount $d_1 < c$ (due to limited divisibility such an amount always exists). Knowing the results for dictatorship and reward allocation experiments it will be no surprise that the selfish behaviour has only been rarely observed. Güth *et al.* (1982) observed several equal splits, that is, $d_1 = c/2$. Nearly always players 1 left a considerable share of c for player 2. Furthermore, many demands $d_1 > c/2$ were rejected. With more experience players 1 became more ambitious but earned less.

Güth and Tietz (1985, 1986) auctioned the positions of ultimatum bargainers before letting the auction winners play the ultimatum bargaining game. Furthermore, they used much bigger pies (a subject only earns the difference between what he wins in the ultimatum bargaining game and the price for his position). Since on average players 1 had to pay twice as much as players 2 for their position and since such an essential price difference had been expected, players 1 felt more justified in exploiting their more powerful position. This is revealed by the fact that contrary to Güth *et al.* (1982) an equal split of c was never observed (see Güth & Tietz, 1988, Table 1). Nevertheless, the overwhelming tendency was still to leave a substantial share of c for player 2 in order to make the choice of conflict too costly for player 2.

In the experiment of Kravitz and Gunto (1988) subjects did not play the ultimatum bargaining game properly but were confronted with (by the experimenters) predetermined demands. The main purpose of the experiment was to assess how the acceptance behaviour of player 2 is influenced by a comment attached to the proposal where the authors distinguished a power comment (a rather nasty hint to player 1 that he is strategically more powerful) and a need comment (which tries to justify a high demand by an urgent need for the money).

If a subject plays the ultimatum bargaining game twice, once as player 1 and once, with a different partner, as player 2, one usually observes more equal splits than in normal ultimatum bargaining experiments (see Güth *et al.*, 1982, and Kahneman *et al.*, 1986a and b, as well as Table 3 of Güth & Tietz, 1990, for a comparison of these results). Unfortunately, the amounts have been rather low and positions were not auctioned beforehand.

Overall, it seems fair to say that the game theory solution (selfish behaviour) is almost never observed and that players 1 try to leave enough for player 2 to prevent him from choosing conflict. For small cakes one usually observes many equal splits, especially when subjects assume the positions of both players. This tendency to share the cake equally becomes nearly extinct if the cake size increases and if positions of ultimatum bargainers have been auctioned.

ULTIMATUM BARGAINING WHEN SELFISH BEHAVIOUR IS FAIR

When positions of ultimatum bargainers are auctioned, an accepted demand $d_1 > c/2$ does not necessarily imply a higher net payment to the player 1 subject, than to the player 2 subject. If the prices of both positions were known before playing the ultimatum bargaining game, one might expect that subjects will try to induce equal net payments (payoff in ultimatum bargaining minus the price for the position of player 1 or 2, respectively). Güth and Tietz (1985, 1986) have informed each player only privately about his own price. Thus the prerequisites of equating net payments were not granted due to their experimental procedure (see Güth (1988) who discusses the prerequisites of certain justice norms more thoroughly).

In the following we want to describe an ultimatum bargaining experiment which does not only cover the previously analysed situations but also situations where selfish behaviour in the sense of perfect equilibrium behaviour (Selten, 1975) implies equal rewards for both players. The main idea is to introduce a transfer payment t which is given to player 2 irrespective of how the ultimatum bargaining game is played. In Table 10.1 we have described the two-factorial design of the new experiment.

If player 1's demand is accepted by player 2 the resulting payoff vector is $(d_1, t+c-d_1)$, that is, player 2 receives the residual amount $c - d_1$ in addition to his transfer payment t. If player 2 chooses conflict, this results in the payoff vector $(0,t)$. Obviously, these rules coincide with those described in Ultimatum Bargaining games above, only in case of $t = 0$. For $t = c$ player 2 is sure to win at least c.

The cake parameter c is varied in order to explore whether and how the allocation behaviour changes with the size of the cake. In case of $t = 0$ we have the usual conditions of previous ultimatum bargaining experiments. But for $t = c$ we have the special result that the game theory solution implies equal payoffs for both players since both players essentially receive c. Player 1 receives c since this is implied by the game theory solution of an ultimatum bargaining game with cake size c; player 2 obtains c in form of his transfer payment $t = c$. Thus in the $t = c$ games, the selfish demand $d_1^* = c$ of player 1 does not contradict the equal reward principle but is suggested by this principle. The $t = c$ ultimatum bargaining games provide probably the most favourable conditions for observing experimentally the game theory solution in ultimatum bargaining games. Obvious hypotheses to be tested are therefore:

Table 10.1 The two-factorial design of the new experiment (c is the cake size, t the transfer payment to player 2)

Transfer t Cake c	t = 0	t = c
c = DM 18		
c = DM 32		
c = DM 54		

Hypothesis A: For all cake sizes c the demanded share d_1/c by player 1 will be higher for $t = c$ than for $t = 0$.

Believing in our previous results of ultimatum bargaining experiments makes us, of course, suspicious whether player 1 will really dare to demand all of c in case of $t = c$. After all, unlike dictatorship games or reward allocation experiments, player 1 still needs player 2's agreement. This leads us to postulate:

Hypothesis B: For all cake sizes c the demanded share d_1/c by player 1 will be less than .85, that is, considerably smaller than the game theory prediction.

Since player 2's critical payoff level for choosing conflict (in the sense that 2 chooses conflict if his payoff falls below this level) will be mainly determined by the time invested, one might also conjecture that d_1/c increases with c:

Hypothesis C: The demanded share d_1/c by player 1 will increase with c.

Here we will not be able to test all these hypotheses in a statistically appropriate way but will confine ourselves to some crude empirical statements. Our experiments yielded some rather unexpected results. Apparently many of our subjects have been frightened by the relatively high amounts which induced them to avoid – partly – non-existent risks. Part of our empirical analysis will concentrate on these unexpected findings.

EXPERIMENTAL PROCEDURE

We have carried out three experimental sessions, session 1 with 30 subjects, session 2 with 62 subjects, and session 3 with 57 subjects. In all sessions subjects were students of economics or business administration attending the same course for introductory microeconomics. Before the experimental session no game theory concepts were mentioned. Since all subjects answered the rather detailed personality questionnaire 16-PA based on the well-known 16 PF (Brandstätter, 1988), more detailed information about the subjects is available.

Subjects were placed at maximum distance from each other in a large lecture room to avoid communication among subjects. Each subject received a code number to identify all his decision data over the experiment and was asked to answer fully the personality questionnaire 16-PA which has no special relation to the experiment at hand. After this subjects were informed about the rules and the optimal bidding behaviour in second highest bid-price auctions (Vickrey, 1961; Güth, 1986). By a simple graphical proof it was shown to them that bidding truthfully is never worse but sometimes better than any other bidding strategy. We especially indicated to the subjects that they can never lose in such an auction if they do not overbid, but that overbidding their true value might result in a loss. After this all subjects participated in an auction with not more than four bidders and with predetermined monetary true values. We refer to these auctions as the pretest since their main purpose is to control whether and to what degree the instructions about the optimal bidding behaviour have been accepted. The proportion of essentially truthful bidders (deviating at most 5 per cent from the value) was 73 per cent (in the previous experiments of Güth & Schwarze 1983, and Güth & Tietz, 1985, 1986, this share was about 83 per cent).

Only after the pre-test were subjects informed about the rules of c,t ultimatum bargaining games with cake size c and transfer payment t to player 2. The rules were, furthermore, exemplified by numerical examples with values of c and t other than the ones used in the experiment. Knowing the rules of c,t ultimatum bargaining games, subjects were told that they were now going to bid for the positions of ultimatum bargainers. For each of the six games in Table 10.2, that is, for 12 player positions, an independent auction took place. Again subjects were told that they would lose money if their position price exceeded what they won in ultimatum bargaining but that they could avoid any risk of losing money if subjects, bidding for position 1, bid only 0 and if subjects, bidding for the position of player 2, did not bid more than t.

On his bidding form each subject was informed about the parameters c and t of the game and whether he was selected to bid for the position of player 1 or player 2 in this game. In other words: the set of subjects had been partitioned by chance into 12 subsets with all subjects in the same subset bidding for the same player position. In addition to their bid, subjects were asked what they would have bid for the other player position in their c,t game (potential bid) and which prices they expect for both positions.

After collecting all bidding forms we quickly determined the 12 auction winners who were only privately informed about their position price (the second highest bid for this position). Knowing his own position price but not the one of his anonymous opponent, player 1 has to determine his demand d_1. Player 2, after learning about his own position price and player 1's previous demand d_1, could then choose between accepting player 1's proposal or not. The experiment concluded by paying privately the net win (the difference between the payoff in ultimatum bargaining and the position price) to all auction winners. The auction winners of the pre-test were paid at the end of the experiment to save time. Since the net win can be negative, especially in the case of conflict in ultimatum bargaining, quite often we had to collect money rather than to pay money to the subjects.

Unfortunately, we were not able to repeat the experiment with the same subjects. But note that, since subjects had already bid for ultimatum bargaining positions, their ultimatum bargaining behaviour should not have been completely naive (however, Güth & Tietz, 1985, 1986, who also auctioned ultimatum bargaining positions, did not observe clear effects of experience). Subjects were not debriefed after the experiment.

EXPERIMENTAL RESULTS

In this section we restrict ourselves to analysing the bidding behaviour for ultimatum bargaining positions as well as the plays of c,t ultimatum bargaining games. Table 10.2 describes the mean bid $\bar{b}_1$ for position 1 and the mean net bid $\bar{b}_2\text{-}t$ for position 2 for the six c,t ultimatum bargaining games and about the numbers n_1 and n_2 of bids underlying these averages where the results of all three experimental sessions are aggregated.

Table 10.2 Mean bids $\bar{b}_i$ for player positions i and numbers of observations n_i (i = 1, 2)

$\bar{b}_1$ $\bar{b}_2$-t n_1 n_2	t = 0		t = c		both t	
c = DM 18	7.84 12	5.02 12	8.27 12	3.18 12	8.05 24	4.10 24
c = DM 32	12.37 12	9.52 11	15.62 14	-1.15 13	14.37 26	3.74 24
c = DM 54	28.23 -14	10.70 13	14.66 12	-6.67 12	21.97 26	3.00 25
all c	16.78 38	8.45 36	13.00 38	-1.54 37	14.89 76	3.60 73

According to Hypothesis A we should have:

(4) $\bar{b}_1(t{=}0) < \bar{b}_1(t{=}c)$ and $\bar{b}_2(t{=}0) > \bar{b}_2(t{=}c) - t$.

Unfortunately, the prediction (4) is not true for player 1 under the condition c = DM 54. In this case we have $\bar{b}_1(t{=}0) > \bar{b}_1(t{=}c)$. Thus the bidding behaviour does not always conform to Hypothesis A.

Since the second highest bid-price auctions it pays to bid truthfully the bids b_1 can be interpreted as what player 1 thinks he can earn in the position of player 1. As a crude test of Hypothesis B we therefore can examine whether:

(5) $\bar{b}_1/c < .85$

for all c as well as for t = 0 and t = c. It can be seen from Table 10.2 that condition (5) is always satisfied. This also holds for the individual decisions in eight of 76 cases. Unfortunately, this does not really confirm our hypothesis that players 1 want to leave a considerable share for player 2 to prevent him from choosing conflict. If conflict has to be feared only in case of demands $d_1 > c/2$ then what one really should expect instead of (5) is:

(5) $.5 \leq \bar{b}_1/c < .85$

Only for c = DM 54 and $t = 0$ is this more refined hypothesis satisfied. Many subjects must have doubted that demands $d_1 = c/2$ will certainly be accepted.

Even more striking is that several subjects, bidding for the position of player 2 in a $t = c$ ultimatum bargaining game, have chosen bids $b_2 < t$ although they can be sure to receive at least $t = c$ as player 2. In Table 10.2 the mean net bid $\bar{b}_2 - c$ is positive only for c = DM 18. Table 10.3 gives the number m_1 of bids $b_1 < c/2$ and the total number n_1 of bids b_1 as well as the number m_2 of bids $b_2 < t$ and the total number n_2 of bids b_2.

At least subjects with $b_2 < t = c$ tried to avoid a non-existent risk. But, as can be seen from Table 1 of Güth and Tietz (1990), demands $d_1 \leq c/2$ also do not face an essential risk of conflict. In our view the m_i subjects listed in Table 10.3 have been frightened by the high monetary amounts (for students) and not by actual risks.

In view of these results it is interesting to compare the bidding quota:

(6) $\dfrac{\bar{b}_1 + \bar{b}_2 - t}{c}$

for the various c, t games and this is given in Table 10.4.

For c = DM 32 and c = DM 54 and $t = c$ the bidding quota is extremely low. Normatively this quota should be 1. But since one cannot exclude the possibility of conflict, it is quite natural to expect a bidding quota smaller than 1 as it is true for all c, t games in Table 10.4. If, however, this quota is smaller than 1/2, this hardly can be explained by the naturally existing risk of conflict. After all the subjects themselves are mainly responsible for whether conflict will result or not. In particular the subjects in the position of player 1 can nearly always avoid conflict by choosing a moderate demand.

In our view, the very low bidding quota for c = DM 32 and DM 54 and $t = c$ reveals that subjects were frightened by the rather high monetary amounts involved. Since such fears should vary from one individual to another, it is interesting to compare the standard deviation σ for the various c, t games. In Table 10.5 one can find all standard deviations σ_i of bids b_i ($i=1,2$) as well as the number of observations n_i for all c, t games. Except for player 1 with c = DM 18 the standard deviation for $t = c$ is larger than the one for $t = 0$. Furthermore, the standard deviation increases with c. Since the change from $t = 0$ to $t = c$ also implies a larger total monetary reward, the variance of bids is strongly (positively) related to the total monetary reward.

Table 10.3 Numbers m_i of subjects with bids $b_1 < c/2$ and $b_2 < t$, respectively, and total numbers n_i of bids

	$t = 0$				$t = c$			
	m_1	n_1	m_2	n_2	m_1	n_1	m_2	n_2
$c = $ DM 18	6	12	0	12	7	12	2	12
$c = $ DM 32	7	12	0	11	4	14	3	13
$c = $ DM 54	6	14	0	13	9	12	5	12

Table 10.4 The bidding quota $(\bar{b}_1+\bar{b}_2-t)/c$ and the total number of bids $n = n_1 + n_2$

$(\bar{b}_1+\bar{b}_2-t)/c$ $n=n_1+n_2$	$t = 0$	$t = c$
$c = $ DM 18	.71 24	.64 24
$c = $ DM 32	.68 23	.45 27
$c = $ DM 54	.72 27	.15 24

For Hypothesis C with the help of bid data, we list the mean intended demanded shares $\bar{b}_1/c$ of players 1 in Table 10.6. Hypothesis C is not validated. For $t = 0$ the demanded share b_1/c first decreases and then increases when c becomes larger, whereas for $t = c$ the contrary is true. Subjects must have seen the $t = 0$ situations as quite different from the $t = c$ situations. A possible interpretation is that subjects were very puzzled by the $t = c$ transfer payment to player 2 and therefore became very careful, especially when large amounts were involved. After all player 1 could argue: "Well, player 2 will receive $t = c$ in any case. So he is sure to make quite a lot of money. Probably that will make him even more greedy since his $t = c$ payment does not depend at all on his behaviour and since he wants to prove that he is a clever bargainer". A more psychologically oriented experiment where subjects would think aloud, indicate their reasoning procedure by written statements, or are debriefed after the experiment, might have found out whether this was the typical argument.

Table 10.5 Standard deviations σ_i and number n_i of bids b_i for player positions i = 1,2

σ_1 σ_1 n_1 n_2	$t = 0$		$t = c$	
c = DM 18	5.66 12	2.76 12	5.34 12	5.98 12
c = DM 32	7.42 12	9.69 11	8.50 14	13.16 13
c = DM 54	13.89 14	11.11 13	16.27 12	21.22 12

Table 10.6 The mean intended demanded shares $\bar{b}_1/c$ with bids b_1 being interpreted as intended demands d_1

$\bar{b}_1/c$	$t = 0$	$t = c$	both t
c = DM 18	.43	.45	.44
c = DM 32	.38	.48	.44
c = DM 54	.52	.27	.41

The actual plays of ultimatum bargaining as well as all previous decision variables of auction winners are listed in Table 10.7.

If we neglect minor deviations with $|\alpha-\beta| <$ DM .10 from the true value, seven of the 34 subjects did not accept in the pre-test that bidding truthfully is optimal.

The auction winners bid higher amounts for the more powerful position (position 1 for $t = 0$ and position 2 for $t = c$).

(7) $b_1 > b_2$ for $t = 0$ and $b_1 < b_2$ for $t = c$

Table 10.7 The decision data and plays of ultimatum bargainers

| Game | | Player 1 | | | | Player 2 | | | | Decision | |
c	t	α	β	b_1	P_1	α	β	b_2	P_2	d_1	δ_2
18	0	5.43	5.43	18.00	10.50	8.18	5.00	8.20	7.50	11.00	0
		*	*	9.02	5.00	4.82	4.82	9.01	8.00	14.00	1
		9.82	9.00	15.00	12.01	5.27	3.43	5.00	4.50	13.00	1
18	18	2.57	2.50	17.00	11.00	7.88	7.88	32.00	23.00	18.00	1
		6.25	6.25	8.00	5.00	5.03	5.03	27.14	22.00	13.00	0
		9.46	3.00	20.50	10.00	8.94	8.94	27.00	18.00	10.00	1
32	0	6.18	6.18	17.00	11.00	4.80	4.75	3.75	1.00	16.00	1
		4.44	5.50	25.00	20.00	*	*	16.00	16.00	20.00	1
		3.63	3.63	18.00	12.00	5.36	5.30	32.00	15.00	16.00	1
32	32	2.02	2.02	18.00	17.00	6.46	6.46	48.00	32.00	22.00	1
		6.59	6.58	16.00	16.00	8.15	8.15	49.00	36.00	24.00	1
		7.21	7.21	32.00	29.01	9.29	9.29	39.00	35.00	32.00	0
54	0	5.79	6.09	50.00	40.50	8.62	8.62	22.00	15.00	20.00	1
		8.99	10.50	54.00	35.00	8.24	8.24	27.00	27.00	47.00	0
		9.89	9.90	35.00	26.00	7.14	7.20	25.00	10.00	40.00	1
54	54	9.37	9.37	53.00	16.00	9.65	10.50	68.00	34.00	50.00	1
		8.89	8.89	27.00	10.00	5.19	5.19	74.00	60.00	27.00	1
		8.35	6.89	30.00	23.95	6.18	3.00	70.00	54.00	30.00	1

Notes: c,t are the parameters of the ultimatum bargaining game
  $\alpha(\beta)$ is the true value (bid) in the pre-test
  b_1 and p_1 (b_2 and p_2) is the bid, respectively, the price for the position of player 1(2)
  d_1 is the demand of player 1 and δ_2 player 2's acceptance decision, $\delta_2 = 1$ means acceptance, $\delta = 0$ conflict
  in the case of "*" the pre-test's results are not available

Equation 7 is significant in the means by the Mann-Whitney U test in five of the six *c,t* parameter constellation at a level of .05. The same is true for the prices p_i in four of the six cases. For the actual demands d_1, Hypothesis A is not significant at a .1 level by this test, but holds in the average ($d_1/c = .636$ ($t = 0$) $< d_1/c = .744$ ($t = c$)).

Hypothesis B is fulfilled in 14 of the 18 observations. A minority of subjects seemed to apply game theory reasoning (see also Table 1 of Güth & Tietz, 1990, which contains most previous experimental

results). Two of these four demands d_1 with $d_1/c > .85$ have been
rejected. The fact that the demand $d_1 = $ DM 47 in the game with $c = $
54 and $t = 0$ has been rejected whereas a higher demand for $t = c$ has
been accepted conforms to the basic argument underlying Hypothesis
A.

The conflict ratio (five of 36 plays ended in conflict) is not
unusual. All rejected demands d_1 were demands for more than half of
the cake. The minimum quota d_1/c of the rejected demands is 0.61.
Only four of 36 players 1 did not ask for more than $c/2$. Thus most
players 1 tried to exploit their bargaining power. But doing so seems
to be quite a gamble since in two of the five cases of conflict a higher
demand for the same c,t constellation was accepted.

The average demanded quota $\bar{d}_1/c$ does not conform to Hypothesis
C as Table 10.8 illustrates. Although the ordering of the values in
Table 10.8 is similar to one in Table 10.6, the demanded quotas are
considerably higher than the bid quotas $\bar{b}_1/c$. Thus the bid quota
predicts well the sign of the influence of the parameters c and t on
demand decisions but it underestimates the size of demands. This
underestimation is quite natural since the auction winners evaluate the
position as more profitable than their competing bidders. Only six of
the 18 auction winners have chosen a demand d_1 exceeding their own
bid b_1; for nine the demand was smaller than b_1, and for three players
1 bid and demand were equal. Some of the differences $b_1 - d_1$ are
quite considerable. Demands d_1 with $b_1 > d_1$ clearly reveal that these
auction winners have revised their aspirations.

Table 10.8 The average demanded quota for all plays

$\bar{d}_1/c$	$t = 0$	$t = c$
$c = $ DM 18	.70	.76
$c = $ DM 32	.54	.81
$c = $ DM 54	.60	.66

THE INFLUENCE OF PSYCHOLOGICAL FACTORS

In the following we want to report on the purely exploratory attempt
to explain ultimatum bargaining behaviour by psychological factors.

Beside the sociological items (age, sex, and education) subjects had to rank themselves according to 33 discrete bipolar scales, where the last item is not a psychological one since it only asks how one can trust the answers of the previous items. Our approach relies on combining two opposing items into one aspect as suggested by Brandstätter (1988). Instead of psychological factors (see Güth, Ockenfels & Tietz, 1990) we use the 16 psychological aspects as explanatory variables in our regression analysis. The two questions underlying one aspect have the two related psychological characteristics on opposite sides. By coding in an increasing order once from left to right and once from right to left and taking the mean of both codes one makes sure that extreme values can only be observed if both questions are answered in a consistent way (see Brandstätter, 1988).

Regressions with psychological aspects a_i as regressors yield:

(8) $b_1 = 5.12 + .44c - .14t - 1.38a_8 - 1.21a_{16} - .99a_{15} + .87a_{11}$
     (1.7) (5.5) (-2.33) (-4.06) (-3.18)   (-2.52)   (2.35)

$r^2 = .48$ $N = 72$

Except for the constant term all regression coefficients are significant ($\alpha < .05$). Aspect a_4 is related to sensitivity, a_{11} to the way of approaching others, a_{15} to self control and a_{16} to emotional stability. For the demands by players 1 a different psychological aspect becomes relevant:

(9) $d_1 = -3.48 + .67c + 1.25a_4$
      (-.79) (5.92) (2.45)

$r^2 = .73$ $N = 17$

The new aspect a_4 appearing in (9) refers to the feeling of dominance in social interaction. Although (9) does not include t as an exploratory variable, the coefficient of determination is with $r^2 = .73$ much larger than in (8). Also here all regression coefficients, except for the constant term, are significant.

For the bids b_2 for the position of player 2 we obtain:

(10) $b_2 = 10.89 + .75t - 1.10a_6$
       (5.13) (10.99) (-2.69)

$r^2 = .65$ $N = 70$

and for the acceptance decisions δ_2 by players 2

(11) $\delta_2 = .40 + .11a_{13}$
        (2.81) (3.24)

$r^2 = .41 \quad N = 17$

Whereas a_6 is related to feeling easy or not, the aspect a_{13} in (11) refers to curiosity versus conservatism. Thus psychological variables are shown to be important but either due to differences in the groups of subjects who decide about b_1, d_1, b_2, or δ_2 or due to the perceived difference in the problem to decide about b_1, d_1, b_2, or δ_2 different psychological variables seem to matter for different decision variables.

A rather speculative interpretation of our results could be that different decision problems call on different psychological aspects and that one can define bargaining cleverness by combining all the psychological aspects which improve the decisions and its payoff implications in the various decision problems. In the case of δ_2 one could, for instance, argue that it does not pay to reject a demand still leaving something for player 2. Psychological aspects favouring such a behaviour therefore indicate bargaining cleverness.

FINAL REMARKS

Dictatorship and reward allocation experiments show that considerations of distributive justice can be very powerful even when bargaining power is given to one party only. One might object that the monetary motivation in these experiments was rather low and that the politeness ritual will rarely be observed for very high monetary rewards. For ultimatum bargaining at least, relatively high payments have also been used. Although equal splits are rarely observed for high monetary payments, ultimatum bargaining behaviour is still characterized by the conflict between complying with norms of distributive justice and exploiting bargaining power, since most demands ask for more than half of the cake but leave a considerable part also for player 2.

The main innovation of the new experiment is that the game theory solution with its extreme payoff implication is supported by the fairness principle of equal monetary rewards. But as our results show this does not suffice to make the game theory solution a good prediction. Unfortunately, many experimentally observed decisions do not satisfy the most basic requirements for reasonable decision behaviour. This might be due to the fact that we did not provide opportunities for learning how to play such games.

Another innovative aspect of our work is the exploratory use of personality questionnaire. Although psychological factors significantly influence the observed decision behaviour, it is surprising that different decisions are affected by different factors. In our view, it would be premature at this stage to judge whether it is good or bad to control for individual psychological differences by using the personality questionnaire 16 PA. We plan to use the personality questionnaire in future experiments in order to see whether the psychological factors remain constant from experiment to experiment or whether the relevance of factors depends on the experimental situation. At least in our study the psychological factors have been fairly stable since almost the same factors result if one of the three experimental sessions is excluded.

REFERENCES

Binmore, K. G., Shaked, A. & Sutton, J. (1984). Fairness of gamesmanship in bargaining?: An experimental study. Unpublished Working Paper. London: The London School of Economics and Political Science.

Binmore, K. G., Shaked, A. & Sutton, J. (1985). Testing noncooperative bargaining theory: A preliminary study. *American Economic Review*, **75**, 1178-1180.

Binmore, K. G., Shaked, A. & Sutton, J. (1988). A further test of noncooperative bargaining theory: Reply. *American Economic Review*, **78**, 837-839.

Bolle, F. (1988). Are there high reward experiments without high expenditure for the experimenter? *Journal of Economic Psychology*, **11**, 157-168.

Brandstätter, H. (1988). Sechzehn persönlichkeits-adjekivskalen (16PA) als forschungsinstrument anstelle des 16 PF. *Zeitschrift für experimentelle und angewandte Psychologie*, **35**, 370-391.

Forsythe, R., Horowitz, J.L., Savin, N.E. & Sefton, M. (1988). Replicability, fairness and pay in experiments with simple bargaining games. University of Iowa, Working Paper 88-30.

Güth, W. (1984). Egoismus und altuismus: Eine speiltheoretische und experimentelle analyse. In H. Todt (ed.), *Normengeleitetes verhalten in den sozialwissenschaften*. Schriften des Vereins für Socialpolitik, N.F. Bd. 141, 35-58.

Güth, W. (1986). Auctions, public tenders and fair division games – an axiomatic approach. *Mathematical Social Sciences*, **11**, 283-294.

Güth, W. (1988). On the behavioral approach to distributive justice: A theoretical and experimental investigation. In S. Maital (ed.), *Applied behavioral economics, Vol. II*. Brighton, Sussex (1988), 703-717.

Güth, W., Ockenfels, P. & Tietz, R. (1990). Distributive justice versus bargaining power: Some experimental results. In S. E. G. Lea, P. Webley & B. M. Young (eds), *Applied economic psychology in the 1990s, Vol. 2*. Exeter: Washington Singer Press, 840-860.

Güth, W., Schmittberger, R. & Schwarze, B. (1982). An experimental study of ultimatum bargaining. *Journal of Economic Behavior and Organizations*, **3**, 367-388.

Güth, W. & Schwarze, B. (1983). Auctioning strategic roles to observed aspiration levels for conflict situations. In R. Tietz (ed.) *Aspiration levels in bargaining and economic decision. Lecture notes in economics and mathematical systems.* Berlin. 217-230.

Güth, W. & Tietz, R. (1985). Strategic power versus distributive justice: An experimental analysis of ultimatum bargaining. In H. Brandstätter & E. Kirchler (eds), *Economic psychology.* Linz. 129-137.

Güth, W. & Tietz, R. (1986). Auctioning ultimatum bargaining positions: How to decide if rational decisions are unacceptable? In R. W. Scholz (ed.), *Current issues in West German decision research.* Frankfurt, Bern, New York. 173-185.

Güth, W. & Tietz, R. (1988). Ultimatum bargaining for a shrinking cake: An experimental analysis. In R. Tietz, W. Albers, and R. Selten (eds), *Bounded rational behavior in experimental games and markets. Lecture notes in economics and mathematical systems, Vol. 314.* Berlin, Heidelberg, New York, Tokyo. 111-128.

Güth, W. & Tietz, R. (1990). Ultimatum bargaining behavior: A survey. *Journal of Economic Psychology.*

Hoffman, E. & Spitzer, M. L. (1982). The coase theorem: Some experimental tests. *Journal of Law and Economics*, **25**, 73-98.

Hoffman, E. & Spitzer, M. L. (1985). Entitlements, rights and fairness: An experimental examination of subjects concepts of distributive justice. *Journal of Legal Studies*, **14**, 259-297.

Homans, G. C. (1961). *Social behavior: Its elementary forms.* London: Harcourt Brace.

Kahneman, D., Knetsch, J. L. & Thaler, R. H. (1986a). Fairness as a constraint on profit-seeking: Entitlements in the market. *American Economic Review*, **76**, 728-741.

Kahneman, D., Knetsch, J. L. & Thaler, R. H. (1986b). Fairness and the assumptions of economics. *Journal of Business*, **59**, 285-300.

Kravitz, D. A. & Gunto, S. (1988). Decisions and perceptions of recipients in ultimatum bargaining games. Manuscript, Department of Psychology, Bowling Green State University, Bowling Green, OH. 43403-0228.

Mikula, G. (1972). Gewinnaufteilungsverhalten in dyaden bei variiertem leistungsverhältnis. *Zeitschrift für Sozialpsychologie*, **3**, 126-133.

Mikula, G. (1974). Gewinnhöhe, gewinnerwartung und die aufteilung gemeinsam erzielter gewinne. Berichte aus dem Institut für Psychologie der Universität Graz.

Mikula, G. & Schwinger, T. (1973). Sympathie zum partner and bedürfnis nach sozialer anerkennung als determinaten der aufteilung gemeinsam erzielter gewinne. *Psychologische Beiträge*, 136-144.

Mikula, G. & Schwinger, T. (1977/8). Affective inter-member relations and the reward allocation in groups: Some theoretical considerations. In H. Brandstätter (ed.) *Social decision process.* Beverly Hills CA: Sage.

Neelin, J., Sonnenschein, H. & Spiegel, M. (1988). A further test of noncooperative bargaining theory: Comment. *American Economic Review*, **78**, 824-836.

Ochs, J. & Roth, A. E. (1989). An experimental study of sequential bargaining. *American Economic Review,* **79,** 355-384.

Prasnikar, V. & Roth, A. E. (1989). Fairness and considerations of strategy in bargaining: Some experimental data. University of Pittsburgh.

Selten, R. (1975). Reexamination of the perfectness concept for equilibrium points in extensive games. *International Journal of Game Theory,* **4,** 25-55.

Shapiro, E. G. (1975). Effects of future interaction on reward allocation in dyads: Equity or equality. *Journal of Personality and Social Psychology,* **31,** 873-880.

Thaler, R.H. (1988). Anomalies: The ultimatum games. *Journal of Economic Perspectives,* **2(4),** 195-206.

Vickrey, W. (1961). Counterspeculation, auctions and competitive sealed tenders. *Journal of Finance,* **16,** 8-37.

Walster, E., Berscheid, E. & Walster, G. W. (1973). New directions in equity research. *Journal of Personality and Social Psychology,* 151-176.

Walster, E. & Walster, G. W. (1975). Equity and social justice. *Journal of Social Issues,* 21-43.

Weg, E., Rapoporto, A. & Felsenthal, D. S. (1988). Two-person bargaining behavior in fixed discounting factors games with infinite horizon. Department of Psychology, University of North Carolina.

11. Customer reactions to automated teller machines (ATMs): A field study in a UK building society

Carole B. Burgoyne, A. Lewis and D. A. Routh
The University of Bath

P. Webley
The University of Exeter

INTRODUCTION

In recent years several Western countries have witnessed a very rapid growth in the installation of automated teller machines (ATMs), not only in banks and building societies, but also in settings such as airports, supermarkets and shopping centres. The current generation of ATMs is able to handle deposits and withdrawals, orders for cheque-books and statements, as well as direct debits and standing orders, and these facilities are being offered by both the banks and the building societies. For the banking institutions the rapid development of automated services is an economically sound policy, since a combination of falling machine costs and rising labour costs has meant that transactions by machine have become relatively cheaper. Thus, a competitive edge can be retained, both by cutting costs, and by matching the range of services available elsewhere.

However, as Cockcroft (1984) points out, there is a danger that the rapid proliferation of new technology may not be geared to the genuine needs of the consumer. An indication that this might be so is provided by evidence of resistance to the new technology by a significant proportion of customers. For example, Scobie and O'Donnell (1989) cite a report in the ABA Banking Journal which refers to a '33% wall' of ATM usage, which implies that use of the new technology is restricted to a minority of the banks' customer base. In the UK, a 1985 survey suggested that only 40 per cent of customers were using an ATM to withdraw cash (Hartley, Metcalfe, Evans, Simnett, Georghiou and Gibbons 1985). According to a MORI poll (1985) users of ATMs appear to be drawn predominantly from people in the younger age groups with a higher socio-economic status. Thus, whilst there is some demographic information available concerning non-use of automated services, it does not appear to be allied with any adequate understanding of the underlying reasons for non-use.

The development of such understanding is of considerable interest to economic psychology, for, as the present case study illustrates, consumer resistance and consumer attitudes can have wide-ranging economic implications. As Smyth and Reynolds (1987) have pointed out, the use of technology is double-edged, and whilst Government deregulation and technology push the UK financial institutions in one direction, 'the widening power of the customer – pulls in another' (p. 22). Thus, although it is in the interests of the financial institutions to maximize efficiency by promoting the use of automated services, the importance of consumer choice means that such economic and technological change cannot be imposed upon an unwilling clientele.

The increasing competition between UK banks and building societies means that they are now operating in a buyer's market, and are having to reconsider the image that they present to the public. Banks have traditionally been places of 'aura and grandeur' (Gorvin, 1987) and have sometimes been accused of being somewhat indifferent to the needs of their clients, with inconvenient opening hours and locations. They are now attempting to give banking a 'human face' with 'open plan' decor and a more welcoming atmosphere. By contrast, building societies have always been viewed as more friendly and approachable, which may make them a more attractive option to the less financially sophisticated customer (NCC, 1983). This presents the building societies with a dilemma: they may have more to lose than the banks by pressing ahead with further automation, yet they must exploit advances in technology in order to remain competitive. Thus, the purpose of the present study was to explore the impact of some of the new technology upon customers of a leading UK building society (which provided partial funding). The study was considered to be timely in the light of forthcoming innovations, such as the installation of fully automated branches.

More specifically, we aimed to gain some insight into customers' perceptions and attitudes concerning the automated services. It was hoped to elucidate a range of psychological and pragmatic issues, but especially those with a potential bearing upon non-use of ATMs. These included the following: the general types of problems encountered by users; the bases of people's mistrust of 'machines' and computer technology; and the more specific ergonomic problems associated with features of the human-machine interface. To this end, a qualitative methodology was adopted, employing semi-structured interviews in four different settings. The purpose of this strategy was to maximize our coverage of the range of views available from both users and non-users of ATMs, together with their supporting reasons, rather than to compare the locations themselves.

METHOD

Locations
In order to meet the foregoing aims of our qualitative methodology, four contrasting locations were selected in Bristol and Oxford. These comprised two smart, city centre branches, a well-established branch in a community shopping area, and a small out-of-town branch attached to a relatively new superstore complex. Both the city centre branches had at least one ATM; an external one in Oxford, and both an external and an internal one in Bristol. The community shopping area branch was in the process of installing its first (external) ATM and the out-of-town branch had no immediate plans for installation since it was likely to be a target for vandalism at night. By interviewing in these diverse locations, opinions were solicited from a range of clients including those with access to both personal and automated services and those with immediate access solely to personal services.

Semi-structured interviews
A pilot study was carried out in order to ascertain customers' willingness to talk about their financial affairs, and to discover which aspects appeared to be most important to them. The interviewer introduced herself as a researcher interested in customer's perceptions of banking services and asked a structured set of questions about services, experiences with ATMs, satisfaction with the building society and so on. It became clear during this initial study that many people held quite strong opinions about two particular topics embedded in the questions. These topics were attitudes to automated services and views about banks *vis-á-vis* building societies.

Therefore, the final form of the interview consisted of more open-ended questions, concerning automation in banking services and similarities and differences between banks and building societies. These questions included the following: 'You may have noticed that some services are now available through automation, such as the cash machines. Do you have any feelings about this?' and 'How similar do you feel that banks and building societies have become?' Depending upon the respondent's initial answers, further questions were posed in order to explore the reasons for the views expressed. At the end of the interview respondents were asked the following question: 'Who would you consult (if anyone) if you needed to make an important financial decision, such as depositing or investing a large sum of money?'

Interviews were carried out indoors at each of the four branches during the normal opening hours (9.00 a.m. to 5.00 p.m). In the case of branches with an external ATM, some interviews also took place outside in the street. As well as recording respondents' views about the above topics, details of age, occupation and possession and use of ATM cards were obtained.

In order to maintain eye-contact and encourage disclosure, respondents' comments were not written down during the interview but immediately afterwards. The use of a tape-recorder had been ruled out as being too intrusive and impractical in a noisy public setting. Although many people were in a hurry, and not willing to spare much more than a few minutes, most of those interviewed were surprisingly open and willing to express their views, sometimes in strong terms. Some clients who could not spare the time for an interview were willing to take questionnaires which could be completed at home and returned by post. In so far as possible, the questionnaire was carefully designed to cover the same ground as the semi-structured interview.

Respondents

135 respondents participated in the study, 120 by means of an interview, and 15 via a questionnaire. The sample comprised 73 women, 61 men, and one questionnaire respondent who omitted to specify sex. Further details of age, sex, and occupation are given in Table 11.1.

RESULTS AND DISCUSSION

For the purposes of analysis it was decided to aggregate the data from the interviews and questionnaires. Inspection of the questionnaire responses suggested that these data were broadly comparable to the interviews, though lacking in the qualitative richness of most of the latter. A content analysis was used to identify the major themes and issues that respondents raised concerning the automated services and perceptions of banks and building societies. These are considered in turn in the next two sections, each of which begins with a presentation of our major qualitative findings supplemented by a number of relevant findings obtained by means of correspondence analysis (CA), now increasingly used in marketing and consumer research (Hoffman and Franke, 1986). The purpose of the latter exploratory data analyses was to uncover potentially interesting and important associations between the qualitative categories and various demographic and behavioural characteristics.

Table 11.1 Age, sex and occupation of respondents

Age group	16-29		30-49		50-75			
Sex	F	M	F	M	F	M	Mi	Σ
Occupation								
Not employed	4	2	6	1	6	3	0	22
Employed	4	9	9	7	4	3	0	36
Professional/skilled	17	16	13	9	9	9	1	74
Missing	1	0	0	1	0	0	1	3
Totals	26	27	28	18	19	15	2	135

Note: 'Mi' is 'Missing'

Attitudes towards automated services
Qualitative findings

Just over 55.5 per cent of the respondents were in favour of automated services, 32 per cent were against, and 12.5 per cent either had no strong views or regarded ATMs as irrelevant. Amongst the latter were some pensioners who had very little cash to invest and did not need access to instant cash and balance statements. Around 56 per cent of respondents were ATM users (possessing bank and/or building society ATM cards), about 15 per cent possessed ATM cards but never used them, and about 29 per cent did not possess any ATM cards. In general, respondents' attitudes were reflected in their use of the automated services. Table 11.2 provides the details. The main advantages and disadvantages of ATMs, according to our respondents, are summarized in Table 11.3.

Many respondents, both users and non-users of ATMs, could see advantages and disadvantages associated with the automated services, although the perceived disadvantages differed for the two groups. Those in favour of automation, and especially those who were users of ATMs, were more likely to see 'convenience' as the major advantage and 'inconvenience' as the major disadvantage. Users of ATMs appreciated having access to their accounts at any hour of the day and night, and felt that machine transactions were speedier and involved less queuing than traditional, over-the-counter transactions. For these respondents, the major drawback was the inconvenience experienced when the machine failed to deliver the service, as a result of breaking down or running out of cash. Other sources of inconvenience included the length of time taken to clear automated deposits of cheques and cash, and their location out-of-doors during inclement weather. This supports the finding of Stanley and Moschis (1983) that potential ATM users are more 'time-sensitive'. Very few ergonomic problems were mentioned, though a few respondents had experienced 'card-swallowing' and incorrect amounts of cash had occasionally been delivered by the machine. Generally speaking, users were well satisfied with the automated service.

Those against automation conceded that ATMs provided a convenient service for those who wished to use it, but some felt no need of out-of-hours service. Others had building society accounts mainly with the intention of saving, and for these respondents, the facility of withdrawing cash was almost too convenient, and likely to lead to potential loss of financial control, such as overspending. One woman aged 42, and working as a kitchen assistant, claimed that she was a determined saver, and the temptation to draw out money when 'in town' would be just too great. She had also had experience of relatives getting into debt using cash cards. Some equated ATM cards with 'plastic' money, or credit 'debts' and were against these on principle.

Since non-users had not been attracted by the acknowledged convenience of ATMs, they were unaffected by factors which caused inconvenience to users. However, they were concerned about several risks associated with using a machine. These included lack of control in the event of machine malfunction and perceived lack of redress should the machine fail to deliver the correct sum of money. There were also fears about security, such as fraud, theft of the card, and the potential risk of robbery when drawing cash in the street, especially at night. Such anxieties are not groundless, as shown by Scobie and O'Donnell (1989). In their study, 4 per cent of respondents had found errors in their accounts, and 7 per cent had experienced theft of their cards. Some of our respondents expressed reservations about the fact that deposits made via an ATM are not verified at the time, whilst others were against automation in general because they felt that the spread of technology represented a threat to the quality of life. Some were suspicious of the institutions' motives for increasing automation of banking services. For example, one man said:

> I don't believe in cards because they make spending too easy – which after all is the ultimate aim of banks and building societies – to get people to take out overdrafts in order to charge them interest.

Other views expressed by users were:

> If we deal only with machines we shall lose out on personal contact, and although I don't have sleepless nights about it – it is important. (Male probation officer, aged 55).

Table 11.2 Attitudes towards automation

Possession of B.Soc. ATM card	NO (but use bank ATM)	NO (not used)	YES (used)	YES	Σ
Attitude					
For	1	14	6	54	75
Neutral	10	2	5	0	17
Against	28	5	9	1	43
Totals	39	21	20	55	135

Note: *two missing values

> There is a good deal of suspicion about machines but they make mistakes far less than humans. (Male town planner, aged 30).

> I believe other people can use the card as well – people can see you put your number in if you're tiny. (Woman shelf filler, aged 45)

> I only use it if I'm absolutely desperate because I've come across so many people having problems. One bloke put in his card and requested £20, and the machine gave him a receipt but no money. He said 'I'd like to see what happens when you try', but I said 'Not likely!' (Man aged 29)

Other views expressed by non-users included:

> Building societies are getting as bad as the banks now with all this technology – you don't feel welcome any more. (Unemployed woman)

Table 11.3 Advantages and disadvantages of ATMs

Advantages

Convenience:	Quicker; less queueing; out-of hours service.
Security:	More reliable; less error; no need to carry cash.
System:	More competition between institutions; no need to deal with people

Disadvantages

Inconvenience:	Inflexible; too long to clear cheques; machine breakdown; out of money; longer to solve problems; minimum payout; wet weather; forget PIN
Insecurity:	Theft of card; fraud; mugging; unauthorized access to personal information.
Quality of life:	Impersonal; leads to unemployment; anti-machine feelings.
Loss of Control:	No verification of deposits; overspending; card 'gobbling'; system errors.

. . . only thing is, downtown – if you get clobbered on the head and get robbed – that's happened to a couple of my mates downtown. (Male student, aged 17)

Personally, I don't like machines. I think we are moving towards a society where nobody ever talks to each other any more. (Male sales representative, aged 53)

It puts people out of work – good for the businesses, but bad for people. (Retired man, aged 73)

I don't like computers, I know how to use them, but they go wrong. And there's never anyone around when they do go wrong. (Housewife, aged 43)

I wouldn't be happy about putting money in the machine . . . I like to see it put on the book. (Retired woman, aged 66)

Technology is fine for some, but I prefer eyeball to eyeball contact when performing my transactions. (Male clerk, aged 36)

It seems then, that anticipation of ergonomic problems was not an especially important factor in deterring people from using ATMs. The major deterrents were both pragmatic and psychological: not enough financial activity or need for out-of-hours service to justify the perceived risks associated with using the machine; justifiable fears about robbery – especially salient to older customers and women; a desire to control both spending and the process of making transactions; and a preference for personal service as a value in its own right. Scobie and O'Donnell (1989) found that a range of perceived problems diminished with increasing card use. It seems likely that non-users may develop an availability bias (Kahneman, Slovic and Tversky, 1982) based upon frequency, recency, and so on, of reports of problems and errors in the mass media. Scobie and O'Donnell's finding implies that actual card use may be a necessary requirement for overcoming this bias. However, if people neither want nor need access to instant cash or information, then it is difficult to see how this may be achieved.

Quantitative findings
The foregoing quotations capture the flavour of our respondents' views about automation. However, it is also important to explore the extent to which these may be associated with various demographic and behavioural characteristics. Thus, as described below, the data were coded categorically so as to create several contingency tables suitable for exploration by means of correspondence analysis (CA).

In order to carry out these analyses we made use of the particular version of CA proposed by Carroll, Green and Schaffer (1986). According to their treatment, CA is a form of metric multidimensional internal unfolding for categorical data. In its two-way form, it uses separate sets of points to represent the row and column profiles in the same space based upon a chi-square metric. However, unlike followers of the 'French school' of data analysis (Greenacre, 1984; Lebart, Morineau and Warwick, 1984), Carroll *et al.* scale the axes of their CA plots in such a way that both the within- and between-set (squared) distances are comparable. Also orthogonal rotation of the axes and translation of the coordinate system are permissible. In passing, it should be noted that the differing scaling conventions available in CA have been a source of some confusion (Carroll, Green and Schaffer, 1987).

ATM card use in relation to age, sex and occupation
As is well-known to users of CA, the presence of a 'sparse' row or column profile in the data tends to generate an outlier in the solution, which possesses too much influence in determining its dimensions. In order to avoid this problem in our analyses, it was necessary to aggregate our data over at least one of the three variables available for defining row profiles, viz., age-group (younger, 16–29 years; middle,

30–49 years; older, 50–75 years); sex; and occupational group (not employed, unskilled, skilled/professional).

For the first CA, the row profiles were obtained by crossing age-group and sex, whilst pooling over occupational groups, and the column profiles comprised the four categories of ATM card-use (no card; card not used; bank card used; building society card used). Figure 11.1 depicts the two-dimensional CA solution obtained, which accounted for 98 per cent of the variance. The horizontal axis contrasts users and non-users of building society ATMs, and shows that users tended to be the younger males and females. Users of bank ATMs were males in the middle age-group, whilst older males and females were respectively associated with non-use and non-possession of an ATM card. But females in the middle age-group were associated fairly equally with both use and non-use of ATMs.

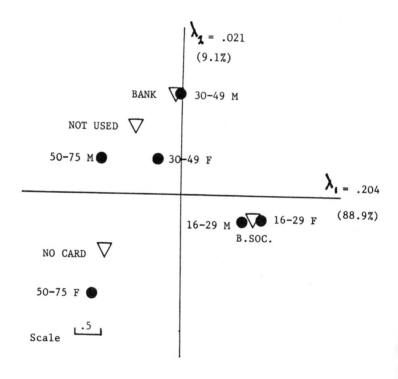

Figure 11.1 Card use in relation to age and sex

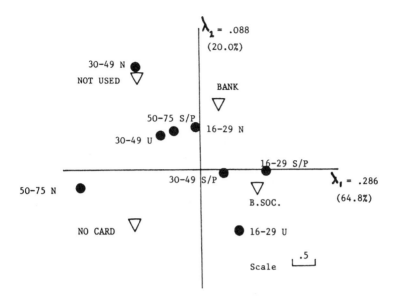

Figure 11.2 Card use in relation to age and occupation
Notes: N = not employed
U = unskilled employment
S/P = skilled/professional employment

In the second CA, the row profiles were obtained by crossing age and occupational group, whilst pooling over sex, and the column profiles again comprised the types of card-use. A two-dimensional solution accounted for almost 85 per cent of the variance, and is depicted in Figure 11.2. The horizontal axis shows a clear contrast between users and non-users of ATMs. It also reveals that all the younger-age groups as well as those in skilled and professional occupations in the middle age-group were associated with some form of card use. However, non-employment in the middle age-range was associated with possessing but not using a building society card, whilst non-employment and unskilled employment in the older age-group tended to be associated with non-possession of an ATM card of either type. To summarize, then, the evidence presented in Figures 11.1 and 11.2 suggests that our ATM users were most likely to be found amongst the men and women who were under 30 years, irrespective of their employment status, or in the 30–49 age group with skilled or professional occupations, especially if male. In contrast, non-users were more likely to be female, over 30, and either non-employed or in an unskilled occupation.

Card use in relation to advantages and disadvantages of ATMs
For the next correspondence analysis, the four categories of card use provided the row profiles, whilst six categories of positive and negative statements about automated services (shown in Table 11.3) were used to create the column profiles. Owing to the problem of sparsity mentioned earlier, it was necessary to aggregate two of the advantage categories, namely security and system. Here, a one-dimensional solution accounted for nearly 95 per cent of the variance, and it is depicted in Figure 11.3.

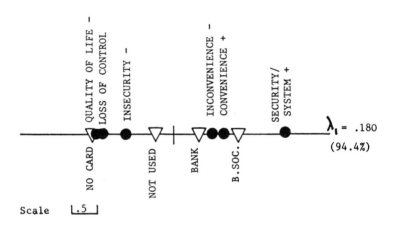

Figure 11.3 Card use in relation to advantages and disadvantages of ATMs

From left to right, Figure 11.3 shows an ordering for card use ranging from non-possession of an ATM card through to use of a building society ATM card. It also shows that the advantages of ATMs tended to be mentioned by ATM users, whereas, with the exception of inconvenience, most of the disadvantages (negative views concerning security, quality of life and control) were emphasized by non-users of ATMs, but especially by non cardholders.

Attitudes in relation to age and occupation.
In this case, we pooled over sex and crossed age and occupational groups to form the row profiles, whilst the positive and negative statements were again used to create the column profiles. In this instance, however, even aggregation over the security and system advantages did not overcome the problems associated with sparsity. Therefore, we report a CA solution which was obtained after eliminating these two advantages. The outcome was a good two-dimensional solution, depicted in Figure 11.4 and accounting for 85 per cent of the variance.

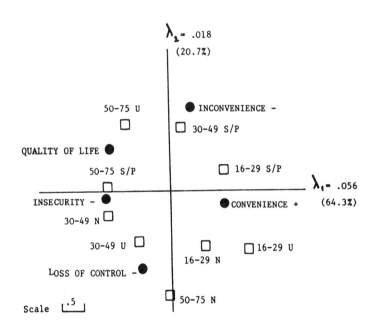

Figure 11.4 Attitudes in relation to age and occupation

Notes: N = Not employed
          U = Unskilled employment
          S/P = Skilled/professional employment

Figure 11.4 shows that convenience tended to be emphasized by the younger groups, whereas inconvenience was associated with skilled and professional people in the middle age-group. Other disadvantages were stressed by the remaining middle and older age-groups, but without there being any clear pattern in terms of occupational group.

Perceptions of banks *vis-à-vis* building societies

Qualitative findings

Nearly all respondents preferred building societies to banks, although this may reflect, in part, the choice of setting. Many respondents perceived little difference between the financial institutions, but their main reason for keeping a building society account was the higher rate of interest offered. Others perceived important differences in favour of building societies, which they felt were less formal, more helpful and friendly, and more accessible. These respondents were more comfortable in dealing with the building society, and felt that it was more responsive to the needs of the individual investor, whereas banks were perceived as favouring the more profitable business accounts.

> The building society staff are more polite and helpful. Banks are rude to their customers.

> I prefer the building society. It's more approachable, less hassle.

> I suspect the banks are not really interested in us – the small customer.

A few respondents expressed a marked antipathy towards banks, which were seen as making an unacceptably high level of profits, 'They're really raking it in', and many resented paying bank charges for the 'privilege' of allowing the banks to use their money. The majority of those in favour of automation saw very little difference between the two financial institutions, and most of these said that they would also be willing to trust a financial expert when making a major financial decision. Half of those not willing to trust an expert preferred using a building society rather than a bank. Some of the most negative statements came from those opposed to automation, and these attitudes were also associated with a mistrust of experts:

> Banks, all built on slavery, ruining people's lives, making money by treading on people . . . and supporting oppressive regimes.

No, I wouldn't trust a financial expert, I've seen too many fiddles at X [name of a leading bank].

. . . these people don't live in the real world . . . they all come out of the same mould.

Basically, I hate banks – they are just a load of crooks in pin-stripes.

The most extreme views about banks were, however, expressed by only a minority of respondents, and more than half the sample felt that any difference between the two institutions were small. None the less, one important distinction was made by a large proportion of respondents, both young and old, and this concerned the building societies' 'guardianship' of their clients' money. Not only was the building society seen as a safe custodian, but also as socially more responsible, safe-guarding clients against overspending, and not allowing them to get into debt. For example:

Banks don't help people to be responsible for their money. They allow people, e.g. students, to run up huge debts, and this is not in the clients' interest.

The building societies are changing for the better and represent a better deal for the working classes . . . more friendly, helpful, look after their clients' interests and help them to keep their money, whereas banks encourage overspending.

It is better to invest in other people's houses than in the commercial sphere.

Up to a point, these findings are consistent with those reported by the NCC in 1983. At that time a building society was seen primarily as a place to deposit savings, especially by those aged 40 and over. This was still largely the view of older customers in the present study, but not of younger customers, who made little distinction between the institutions. The 1983 survey found that consumers were concerned about opening hours and speed of transactions, but few mentioned these in the present study, perhaps because the provision of ATMs has reduced the differences between banks and building societies in these respects. Consumers in 1983 had wanted to see a number of improvements: better access to funds, clearer statements, sufficient information, standing orders and cash dispensers. Respondents in the present study felt that some of these improvements had been made by building societies, and that they were only awaiting the provision of a cheque account before moving all their funds to the building society. At the time of writing this facility has now been made available by the building society which was involved in funding the research.

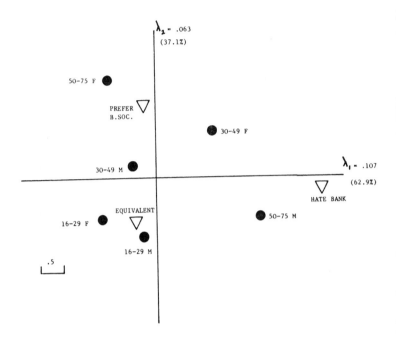

**Figure 11.5 Perceptions of banks and building societies in relation
to age and sex**

Quantitative Findings

On the issue of respondents' perceptions of banks *vis-à-vis* building
societies, there appeared to be three primary attitudes. Some viewed
the two institutions as being equivalent, but some much preferred
building societies, whereas the remainder were antipathetic towards
banks. For our final CA, we pooled over occupational group and
crossed sex and age group to create the row profiles, whilst the
column profiles represented the above three attitudes. A two-
dimensional solution necessarily accounted for all of the variance, and
is exhibited in Figure 11.5. This reveals that the modal response for
the younger groups was to view banks and building societies as being
equivalent. Males in the middle age range were intermediate between
seeing the institutions as being equivalent and preferring building
societies, whilst older males were associated with a strong antipathy

for banks. But for women over 30 the modal response tended to be a preference for building societies.

Implications
In principle, it is clear that banks and building societies should be able to reduce the costs of many of their transactions by installing ATMs. This forms part of a general trend towards an increasing use of technology in banking and a reduction in the use of cash, for example, by means of EFTPOS (Electronic Funds Transfer at Point of Sale), and Home Banking. However, whilst the technology is available for further innovations, these 'advances' are curtailed to some extent by the interests of consumers, interests which the 'suppliers' cannot ignore. As the present case study shows, these changes are not primarily consumer-led: it is not simply a question of satisfying customer wants, but, in part, an exercise in moulding and changing them.

According to Stanley and Moschis (1983) the resistance to new technology is more common among older customers, those in non-professional occupations, and with fewer years of formal education. This is further exemplified by the present findings. However, it is not only demographic characteristics which determine this resistance but also customers' perceptions and attitudes: non-users are particularly concerned about machine malfunction, lack of redress, insecurity, and 'lack of control' (c.f. Scobie and O'Donnell, 1989). Our results suggest that customers who dislike ATMs are less trusting of experts and more antipathetic towards banks. Whilst younger people are more in favour of new technology and see fewer differences between banks and building societies, the changing role of building societies is likely to upset those customers most loyal to the traditional, 'friendly' values of the building societies.

Marketing strategies stressing convenience and ease of access are unlikely to be successful as these are attributes already associated with the requirements of existing users. As Stanley and Moschis (1983) put it, existing users are more 'price' and 'time' sensitive. Marketing directed at traditional building society customers should be aimed instead at reducing anxiety, for example, by producing ATMs which verify deposits at the time deposits are made. They also need to find ways of countering the 'availability bias' (Kahneman, Slovic and Tversky; 1982) of customers whose perceptions are coloured by the few errors that occur in ATM transactions as compared with the millions of successful ones. Alternatively, the marketing strategy for banks might be to win over disaffected building society customers by reducing their forbidding image and appearing to be more socially responsible.

194   *Carole B. Burgoyne, A. Lewis, D. A. Routh and P. Webley*

Thus, whilst all financial institutions need to aim for increases in efficiency, any such moves will have to be traded off against the possibility of losing customers. In a competing market it is interesting to speculate whether technological change can simply be imposed, or whether a market will develop (as has happened in the case of the UK Post Office) in which 'old-fashioned' values will prevail.

ACKNOWLEDGEMENTS

We are grateful to the ESRC and a leading UK building society for their financial support.

REFERENCES

Carroll, J. D., Green, P. E. & Schaffer, C. M. (1986). Interpoint distance comparisons in correspondence analysis. *Journal of Marketing Research*, **23**, 271-80.

Carroll, J. D., Green, P. E. & Schaffer, C. M. (1987). Comparing interpoint distances in correspondence analysis: A clarification. *Journal of Marketing Research*, **24**, 445-450.

Cockcroft, J. (1984). Microtechnology in banking. London: Economist Intelligence Unit, Special Report No. 169.

Gorvin, R. (1987). The Co-operative bank. *Banking World*, December, 31.

Greenacre, M. J. (1984). *Theory and applications of correspondence analysis.* London: Academic Press.

Hartley, J., Metcalfe, J. S., Evans, J., Simnett, J., Georghiou, J. & Gibbons, M. (1985). *Public acceptance of new technologies: New communications technology and the consumer.* PREST, University of Manchester.

Hoffman, D. L. & Franke, G. R. (1986). Correspondence analysis: Graphical representation of categorical data in marketing research. *Journal of Marketing Research*, **23**, 213-227.

Kahneman, D., Slovic, P. & Tversky, A. (1982). *Judgement under uncertainty: Heuristics and biases.* Cambridge: Cambridge University Press.

Lebart, L., Morineau, A. & Warwick, K. M. (1984). *Multivariate descriptive statistical analysis.* Chichester: John Wiley and Sons.

MORI (1985). ATM opinion poll.

National Consumer Council (1983). *Banking services and the consumer.* London: Methuen.

Scobie, G. E. W. & O'Donnell, P. (1989). Electronic cash dispensers versus bank cashiers. Paper presented to British Psychology Society Annual Conference, St. Andrews, Scotland.

Smyth, A. & Reynolds, M. (1987). Banking – A way to the future. *Banking World*, December, 22-23.

Stanley, T. J. & Moschis, G. P. (1983). The ATM-prone consumer: A profile and implications. *Journal of Retail Banking*, **5**(1), 45-51.

12. The fax machine: A revolution in communication?

Karl-Erik Wärneryd and P. G. Holmlöv
The Stockholm School of Economics

INFORMATION SOCIETY AND THE DIFFUSION OF THE FAX

Is there an information revolution?

It is often asserted there is a revolution in information due to the introduction and adoption of new information technology. The word revolution instils a feeling of sudden changes that are met with heavy resistance from some of the concerned parties, that people protest against what they hold to be further dehumanization and alienation. The rapid adoption of the telefacsimile which, with hindsight, may be interpreted at some time in the future as a major revolution is hardly debated at all.

There has been an explosion in the use of the fax during the last three or four years but no exact statistical data are available. Japan has the largest number of fax machines per 1000 inhabitants, followed by the US, and probably Sweden. The major increase began in 1984–85. In Sweden in 1978, there were about 500–600 fax machines. In 1990, the number is estimated to be over 130 000 and is increasing rapidly. While the early fax machines were slow, clumsy, noisy, and spread a foul smell of burning paper, the third and fourth generations now in use are handy, noiseless, have no specific odour, and work fast.

Everyday observation leads to the notion that the use of the fax is not seen as a revolution, but rather as a peaceful change towards better efficiency and capacity for dealing with urgent messages. The fax is presumably adopted as a replacement for something that can be done in other ways. The really novel uses appear gradually and at a later stage. With hindsight, they may seem like a revolution.

The purpose of this chapter is to elucidate the adoption and use of the fax machine in Sweden. First, a theoretical background is given which leads to some assumptions about factors that possibly influence the acceptance of the innovation. Second, a survey carried out among fax users that attempts to assess the importance of these factors is reported. The results are discussed with a view towards how much (or little) of a communication revolution the fax means.

THEORETICAL BACKGROUND

Types of adoption patterns
In principle, three types of adoption patterns for innovation in information technology can be distinguished:

1. The adoption of a single unit. Purchasing a PC for use by a single person or a small group of people may not change much within the administrative structure of a business firm or a government agency.
2. Introducing a set of information innovations that must be accompanied by far-reaching work routine and perhaps also staff changes. Computerization of departments and whole companies is a case in point.
3. A change in information carriers makes it possible and even mandatory to change the use of information media. The increasing availability of ISDN is an example. The digital networks provide new broadband services with extremely rapid transfer that was previously very expensive or impossible. This involves modernization that may occur piecemeal or in a more global fashion.

The telefacsimile mainly belongs in the first group. A single unit can be purchased, it is easily installed, and no dramatic changes in work routines are necessary. In some cases, though, the fax is adopted as part of a more comprehensive introduction of information technology in attempts to make most information handling electronic.

Adoption as a function of the number of adopters
Some of the fax machines available in 1978 were rarely used according to a study made at the Stockholm School of Economics (Jundin & Lindqvist, 1978). The 1978 study indicated that there were essentially two types of purchase motives. The majority had bought the fax for a very specific purpose and they communicated almost

exclusively with one single partner with a high frequency. They were very satisfied with the innovation which, for example, replaced a messenger between a hospital and a testing laboratory or between an advertising agency and a publisher. The second group bought the fax for general communication purposes, to communicate with other holders of fax machines. Since those were few and, despite a directory published by the leading marketer of fax machines, largely unknown to one another, the purchase was not considered to be a success.

The study clearly indicated that a minimum critical mass of holders was necessary for the fax to become a general means of communication. Introduction curves are often described as S-shaped. The assumption is that the number of new adopters during a certain period is a function of how many have already adopted the innovation because of a demonstration effect. In the case of the fax there is at a later stage the additional effect of getting more and more potential communicants. Around 1985 the fax may have reached a critical mass of adopters after having been hampered earlier by a deficiency of fax holders to communicate with.

The interplay between external and internal factors: Adopter categories

Buying the first fax machine is, for a company or organization, a function of two sets of factors. There are external factors such as the properties of the fax, the paradigm set by other communicators, and the availability of information. There are internal factors like the need for certain communication services, the nature of the internal and external communication networks, and the structure of the organization. The internal and the external factors can combine in many more or less subtle ways (Meyer & Goes, 1988). The purchase of the second and later faxes is likely to be more dependent on internal factors than purchasing the first one.

If there is a communication flow between the company and one or a few fixed receivers and this flow transfers pictorial material or data where accuracy and fast transfer are essential, there is a high probability for early adoption of the fax. The alternatives are usually not wholly satisfactory. For short distances, messengers can be used at the risk of incurring high expenses. The mail service is relatively slow, even with fast parcel service.

When there is no such fixed communication flow to a partner, the usefulness of a fax depends on whether enough target receivers can be reached via the fax. Critical mass is specific to each firm or other organization. Some firms will reach critical mass much earlier than others because a sufficiently large number of their contacts are early adopters either for specific purposes or out of general innovativeness.

On the basis of these considerations, which are largely supported by earlier research, it is here postulated that there exist four groups of adopters, listed in order of fax acquisition:

1. Firms and organizations with fixed communication flows to a partner and a time constraint for the transfer of messages. They are characterized by a need factor which they share with one or a few other communicants.
2. Firms and organizations that are eager to adopt technological innovations at an early stage. They are characterized by innovativeness. (See Meyer & Goes, 1988)
3. Firms and organizations having networks in which there has been widespread adoption of the fax attaining a 'critical mass' at an early stage in the introduction process and who have some time or pictorial constraints for the transfer of messages.
4. Firms and organizations which have external communications with a wide variety of other firms and organizations. They will hesitate until the use of the fax is already quite widespread. This means that there must be a general critical mass of adopters before this group adopts. Ultimately, they will face external pressure to adopt.

While on average the groups may show this order of adoption, organizational factors will decide how early or late the individual adoption will be. In the literature on adoption of innovation, there is some theory about relevant organizational factors (for example, Zaltman and Wallendorf, 1983; Meyer and Goes, 1988; von Hippel, 1988).

Four important organizational factors are often mentioned. These are; innovativeness, degree of decentralization of the organization, degree of formalization of the organization, and the complexity of the organization. Complexity essentially involves how many kinds of experts there are in the organization. While decentralization and complexity encourage adoption and formalization works against innovation, the effects with respect to implementation are reversed. An innovation is more easily implemented in a more formalized organization. These findings of earlier research may also be expected to hold true for the adoption of the fax.

METHOD

The fax survey

Several informal interviews with people who were knowledgeable about the fax were conducted first. A mail questionnaire was then developed, using a number of questions borrowed from a 1978 study (Jundin & Lindqvist, 1978). After a pre-test, the questionnaire was sent via fax to a sample of fax telephone numbers systematically sampled from the Swedish fax directory (published by Swedish Telecommunications). The directory lists most of the fax telephone numbers in Sweden. The probability of being selected was proportional to the number of fax telephone numbers listed for an organization. For the analyses that will be reported here this bias has little importance.

Before the questionnaires were faxed to the sample members, the fax holder was telephoned and asked the name of the appropriate person in the organization to receive the questionnaire.

The response rate was high and 76 per cent of the fax holders approached sent in completed questionnaires, in practically all cases via fax. In all, 283 usable questionnaires were returned. A report on major aspects of the survey is available in Swedish (Lindberg, Holmlöv & Wärneryd, 1989).

Four groups of respondents were distinguished: executives (26.5 per cent), middle management (18.4 per cent), secretaries and switchboard operators (38.9 per cent), and firm owners and miscellaneous specialists (15.5 per cent). In the analyses reported below no significant differences were found between the groups.

Hypotheses

Based on the discussion above, the following questions are directed to the data:

1. What are the characteristics of the adoption process with respect to the initiation stage and the time when the adoption is made? The theoretical background suggests that firms and organizations with specific communication purposes, with frequent messages under time pressure, and with a predominance for pictorial and complex messages would be first to initiate adoption.
2. Are there differences between adopters who differ in terms of the degree of innovativeness, decentralization, and complexity? The more innovative, decentralized, and complex the firm the earlier the adoption should be.

3.   What are the attitudes towards the fax?   Fax use for more
      specific purposes should foster more positive attitudes.   What
      are the attitudes towards advertising via the fax?   Those who use
      the fax for specific purposes or are heavy users are expected to
      be more negative towards advertising received via the fax,
      whereas those who use the fax as part of an open communication
      network would tend to be more acquiescent.
4.   Is the fax only a better way of solving certain message transfer
      problems or does it mean something radically new?   The
      expectation is that the fax is adopted because of its relative
      advantage (Rogers, 1983) and that new uses are a secondary
      idea.

RESULTS

The purchase motive

Differences in the time when the fax was adopted will here be related
to differences in needs.   The idea of the importance of a minimum
size critical mass for the expansion of the telefacsimile cannot be
strictly tested on the type of cross-sectional data presented here.   The
idea indicates that there should be a development from purchases for
specific purposes, with one or a few partners, to purchases for general
communication purposes.   Table 12.1 reports the answers given to the
question about purchase objectives, cross-tabulated with how many
years the work unit had had a fax.   While an inspection of the Table
reveals that there is some tendency in the expected direction, a chi-
square test is far from significant.   In comparison with the 1978 study
(Jundin & Lindqvist, 1978) there is a marked change.   In 1978, 68 per
cent of the respondents stated that the fax machine had been bought
for a specific purpose; an additional ten per cent stated that the
purchase had been made for mixed purposes, including a specific use.
The category 'external pressure' was not at all applicable in 1978.   It
is interesting to note that counter to expectation there is little
difference between early and later adopters in the use of this category
in Table 12.1.

   A comparison between the stated purpose for the acquisition of the
fax machine and the present network is shown in Table 12.2.   Routine
use here refers to the use of the fax for fixed and regular contacts with
one or only a few receivers.   The category 'General contacts' means
that the fax is employed for contacts with many receivers in an open
network.   The data bear out the expectation that when the fax is
bought for a specific purpose, it involves a communication link with a

Table 12.1 Adoption time and the purchase motive

	Specific purposes		General purposes		External pressure		Total	
	N	%	N	%	N	%	N	%
< 3 years ago	50	39.4	53	41.7	24	18.9	127	100
3 to 4 years ago	27	43.6	27	43.6	8	12.9	62	100
> 4 years ago	23	52.3	14	31.8	7	15.9	44	100
Total	100	42.9	94	40.3	39	16.7	233	100

few receivers. When the purchase means giving in to an external pressure, the fax provides a communication link to an open network. A chi-square test shows that there is a significant relationship (chi-square = 15.24, df = 2, $p < 0.001$). When the advantages of the fax are discussed, its speed is often mentioned first. The higher the need for conveying urgent messages, the earlier the adoption of the fax should be. About half of the sample reported that they used the fax primarily for urgent messages. There is an insignificant tendency for those who have mostly urgent messages to report earlier adoption. With respect to the type of documents mostly transmitted via fax there is a tendency, but no significant difference, in adoption date between those who send more pictures, drawings and so on, and those who send little.

In sum, the differences between those who purchased the fax more than four years ago and those who bought more recently are on the whole quite small, although pointing in the expected direction, for the variables related to need: need for a fixed communication link to another party or a few specific receivers, the frequency of urgent messages, need for sending and receiving complex messages (pictures, drawings and so on).

Organizational factors

The adoption time is expected to show some correlation with organizational factors. Three types of indicators will be used: The degree of innovativeness, the degree of decentralization, and the complexity of the organization.

Table 12.2 The purchase purpose and present use

	Present Use					
Reason for purchase	Mostly Routine		General Contacts		Total Contacts	
	N	%	N	%	N	%
Specific purpose	60	54.6	50	45.4	110	100
General purposes	31	32.3	65	67.7	96	100
External pressure	11	26.2	31	73.8	42	100
Total	102	41.1	146	58.9	248	100

The degree of innovativeness is assessed in two ways. The questionnaire had an attitude statement relating to the organization's willingness to try technical innovations. The answers were given on a four-point Likert-type scale. In another question the respondents were asked about the work unit's access to a number of technological devices like answering machines, PCs, mobile telephone, electronic mail, and videotex. An index was computed on the basis of the number of devices (excluding the fax machine) that were reported as being available. All of the innovations belonged within the area of communication technology. Meyer and Goes' (1988) objection against general innovativeness indices thus does not apply.

While Table 12.3 shows no difference in organizational attitude towards technological innovations related to the time of acquisition, Table 12.4 which reports on the adoption of communication technology indicates a clear difference (chi-square = 14.76, df = 4, p = 0.005). The early adopters have shown more innovativeness in the sense that they have acquired other technological facilities to a larger extent than the later adopters. To some extent this is a function of the size of the organizations.

On average the larger firms have been earlier adopters and they also tend to have the largest number of technological innovations. When the respondents are grouped into four size groups the same pattern is visible in each group. In the group with between 50 and 499 employees the relationship between adoption time and innovativeness is significant. In the largest size group (more than

Table 12.3 Innovativeness as measured through the statement 'In this firm we are eager to try technological innovations'

Purchase	Wholly true		On the whole true		Partially true		Not at all true		Total	
	N	%	N	%	N	%	N	%	N	%
< 3 years ago	17	13.4	37	29.1	62	48.8	11	8.7	127	100
3 to 4 years ago	11	16.4	25	37.3	29	43.3	2	3.0	67	100
> 4 years ago	6	12.0	17	34.0	20	40.0	7	14.0	50	100
Total	34	13.9	79	32.4	111	45.5	20	8.2	244	100

500 employees), chi-square yields $p = 0.10$. In the other two groups the tendency is not significant.

Table 12.4 Innovativeness according to the Innovation Index, based on number of communication innovations available in the organization

Purchase	Less than 5		5 to 9		10 and More		Total	
	N	%	N	%	N	%	N	%
< 3 years ago	31	24.0	89	69.0	9	7.0	129	100
3 to 4 years ago	16	23.9	46	68.7	5	7.5	67	100
> 4 years ago	8	16.0	29	58.0	13	26.0	50	100
Total	55	22.4	164	66.7	27	11.0	246	100

The degree of decentralization is indicated by the answers to the question concerning where the decision to purchase was taken. If the decision was made in the work unit itself, this was taken as a sign of decentralization. All other answers were coded as indicating higher degree of centralization.

Table 12.5 Adoption time and the degree of decentralization in the organization

Purchase	More decentralized		More centralized		Total	
	N	%	N	%	N	%
< 3 years ago	38	29.5	91	70.5	129	100
3 to 4 years ago	23	35.9	41	64.1	64	100
> 4 years ago	19	38.0	31	62.0	50	100
Total	80	32.9	163	67.1	243	100

Table 12.5 shows the adoption times for decentralized and centralized organizations. There is a slight, not significant tendency in the expected direction. The tendency is somewhat stronger in the small firms and organizations, but is still insignificant. Small firms are almost by definition decentralized; the small firm may consist of one single work unit.

The complexity of an organization refers to the number of experts of various kinds. The more experts in different specialties, the better the scanning of the environment for innovations will be. An admittedly crude indicator is given by the answers to a question about who brought up the idea of acquiring the fax. If the idea was suggested by the prospective users or by the purchasing department, the organization is considered to be less complex. If the purchase was initiated by other hierarchical levels or experts or a number of sources, this is interpreted as an indication of a more complex organization. Table 12.6 shows the results. There is a slight tendency in the opposite direction to that expected. With the indicator used the more complex organizations did not adopt earlier. The indicator is certainly a very crude one and should in further studies be replaced with something more substantial.

In sum, among the three investigated organizational factors of innovativeness, degree of decentralization, and degree of complexity, only the first one turned out to be significant for the time of adoption.

Table 12.6 Adoption time and the complexity of the organization

	Less complex		More complex		Total	
Purchase	N	%	N	%	N	%
< 3 years ago	34	32.3	95	67.7	129	100
3 to 4 years ago	24	26.3	43	73.7	67	100
> 4 years ago	18	37.1	32	62.9	50	100
Total	76	30.9	170	69.1	246	100

Attitudes towards the fax

A number of questions were aimed at finding out the evaluation of the fax. Three indicators will be reported. One question concerned whether the working unit would be able to manage without the fax.

Answers were requested on a four-point scale running from 'yes, definitely' to 'no, definitely not'. The answers are cross-tabulated with adoption time in Table 12.7. There is a tendency that those who have had the fax the longest time find it more indispensable (chi-square = 12.19, df = 6, $p = 0.06$).

The second indicator is provided through the answer to a question about problems with the use of the fax. Table 12.8 reports the results. It appears that most respondents either do not perceive any problems or think that the problems are negligible. As to adoption time, no significant tendencies can be distinguished in this analysis.

Seven attitude statements regarding the fax were factor analysed and combined into an attitude index. The factor analysis gave two factors, together explaining 46 per cent of the variance. The first factor reflected attitude towards the fax as a means of communication. The second concerned attitude towards the increased use of technology. An index was based on the three items that had high loadings on the first factor. According to the index the attitudes towards the fax do not differ significantly among the adopter groups. They were all highly positive. The results are not shown here. Those respondents who recognized a personal use for the fax (20 per cent) were even more favourable than the others. It is interesting to note that people could sometimes be very favourable towards the fax but at the same time dislike the increased use of technology.

Table 12.7 Adoption time and answers to the question 'Would you in your working unit manage your work without the fax today?'

Purchase	Yes, definitely		With some problems		With great problems		No, definitely not		Total	
	N	%	N	%	N	%	N	%	N	%
< 3 years ago	15	12.0	64	51.2	39	31.2	7	5.6	125	100
3 to 4 years ago	5	7.5	32	47.8	25	37.3	5	7.5	67	100
> 4 years ago	2	4.0	24	48.0	14	28.0	10	20.0	50	100
Total	22	9.1	120	49.6	78	32.2	22	9.1	242	100

Table 12.8 Time of adoption and answers to the question 'How do you perceive the problems that the fax has meant?'

Purchase	Serious, frequent		Frequent, not serious		Serious, infrequent		Negligible, no problems		Total	
	N	%	N	%	N	%	N	%	N	%
< 3 years ago	2	1.6	21	16.3	9	7.0	97	75.2	129	100
3 to 4 years ago	3	4.5	14	20.9	7	10.4	43	64.2	67	100
> 4 years ago	1	2.0	12	24.0	4	28.0	33	66.0	50	100
Total	6	2.4	47	19.1	20	32.2	173	70.3	246	100

Attitudes towards advertising by fax

The fax produces two-way communication services. The outgoing services are controlled by the holder of the fax (in principle, although in practice there seems to be some private social communication according to anecdotal material). The incoming service is controlled by a sender who may send messages that are not welcomed by the receiver. There are complaints about 'junk' fax, that is, mail that is not wanted. Unsolicited advertising is the foremost example of such mail. In the US there is talk about legislation against unsolicited advertising by fax. The further adoption and use of the fax in an open communication network is by some experts seen as being jeopardized through injudicious use of advertising by fax.

The questionnaire comprised a few questions about the reception of advertising via fax, the respondent's attitude towards such advertising, and about his/her attitude towards using the fax for sending advertising.

Table 12.9 Reception of advertising via fax and attitudes towards such advertising

Reception of Advertising	Positive		Indifferent		Negative		Total	
	N	%	N	%	N	%	N	%
Yes, often	3	27.3	4	36.4	4	36.4	11	100
Yes, sometimes	26	17.9	83	57.2	36	24.8	145	100
Seldom	6	7.5	45	56.2	29	36.3	80	100
No, never	4	8.5	16	34.0	27	57.5	47	100
Total	39	13.8	148	52.3	96	33.9	283	100

Reception of advertising via fax was apparently not a very frequent phenomenon at the time of the interview (November, 1988). The most common answer is 'yes, sometimes' according to Table 12.9. A check against adoption time, number of pages sent per day, and type of respondent shows no relationship with the frequency of reception. As can be seen in the Table, there is a significant relationship between reception and attitude. Although on the whole the attitude towards advertising through the fax is rather cool, those who receive advertising more frequently tend to be more kindly disposed towards it (chi-square = 22.30, df = 6, p = 0.001). Cross-tabulations of attitude towards advertising and adoption time, purchase motive, number of pages sent daily, and respondent group indicated some tendencies in the expected direction, but none were strong enough to reach significance.

The answers to the question: 'Would you personally think of sending advertising by fax?' give another indication of some hesitation about advertising via fax. If the 'don't knows' are added to the 'no' answers, 75 per cent do not want to use the fax for sending advertising. There is a significant difference among the respondent groups. The group that represents the executives and the owner-dominated group are more willing to use the medium than routine personnel, but those who are positive are still few.

In sum, the attitudes towards advertising by fax were negative rather than positive. Interestingly, those who had more often received advertising by their fax were more favourable. This may have to do with the fact that the advertising so far received may have been of use, for example, representing interesting purchase opportunities. According to some reports, the first advertisements sent by fax concerned office equipment, computer accessories and paper. If the fax is more indiscriminately used for unsolicited advertising, the positive correlation between reception and attitude may change.

The fax as a replacement

A common assumption is that an innovation will be accepted more easily if it replaces in a better way something already existing. Obviously the fax can to a certain extent replace such means of communication as telephone, telex, messenger boys, and mail service. A pure replacement should not cause much resistance if it means an improvement and at the same time is easy to implement. If the innovation offers a totally new kind of service and replaces something in a rather unclear way, there will be more hesitation. If the innovation is introduced as part of a thorough revision of an administrative system, there will also be more concern and resistance.

The apparently easy acceptance of the fax and the explosion in its use over the last few years can be a consequence of the fact that the fax is a convenient replacement for other means of communication, especially for transferring urgent messages with a certain degree of complexity. In the second place, it offers possibilities for developing new services. There are inventories of fax uses that by now are impressively long.

The questionnaire comprised questions about the replacing function of the fax machine, changes in work routines, and about possible new uses. Table 12.10 reports the answers to the question as to what means of communication the fax had replaced. Five such means were listed in the questionnaire together with an open category. This question was followed by a question about the extent to which the fax had replaced the earlier media. According to the Table the early adopters tended more often to replace telex by fax. They also tend to use the fax to replace or supplement more means of communication than the later adopters. They, more often than later adopters, considered the fax to be a minor supplement rather than a major replacement. About one-third of the respondents reported changes in work routines, but none mentioned radical changes. Roughly half of the respondents reported an increasing number of uses for the fax.

Table 12.10 The fax as a replacement for earlier media: 'What did you use earlier to transfer the messages that are sent by fax today?'

	Telex N	Telex %	Mail N	Mail %	Messenger N	Messenger %	Courier N	Courier %	Telephone N	Telephone %	Other N	Other %
< 3 yrs ago	40	31.0	117	90.7	19	14.7	4	3.1	84	65.1	2	1.6
3 to 4 years ago	29	43.3	56	83.6	15	22.4	4	6.0	45	67.2	2	3.0
> 4 yrs ago	24	48.0	44	88.0	13	26.0	10	20.0	25	50.0	6	12.0
Total	93	37.8	217	88.2	47	19.1	18	7.3	154	62.6	10	4.1
Chi-sq. (df = 2)	5.60		2.15		3.60		15.42		4.34		10.36	
p	0.06		0.34		0.16		0.00		0.11		0.01	

Multivariate analysis of adoption time

In the preceding analyses some variables have shown correlation with the dependent variable of adoption time. It is desirable to see which variables contribute most to the variance in adoption time. In principle, such an analysis should be based on measures that were obtained before the adoption. In a retrospective interview it is evidently not possible to get reliable information on, for example, attitudes towards the fax and towards the purchase at the time of the acquisition. Some variables may not have changed in any significant way after the purchase whereas others have. This means that the variables used in the regression analysis which will be reported here are something of a mixture. The results are tentative and serve primarily to sort out variables for continued examination in other studies.

The multiple regression proceeded in two steps. In the first step the procedure yielded five variables that contributed to the variance of the dependent variable above a criterion value (0.15). In the second step the coefficients for these variables were determined. The five variables are: The number of pages sent per day, the percentage of external communication (to receivers outside the organization), the number of means of communication that were replaced at least partly through the fax, whether the contacts were primarily with one or a few receivers rather than in an open system, and the number of employees in the organization. The variables thrown out from the analysis were the index for attitude towards the fax, the index of innovativeness, and the frequency of contacts with foreign receivers. Table 12.11 shows the results of the regression analysis. The explanatory value of the five significant variables is not great, but there are some interesting indications. Early acquisition was more likely when there were specific needs for communicating with a certain party, when the organization was large, and when the degree of external communication was high. The number of pages sent per day may be an indication of need prior to the acquisition. It may be a result of increased use of the new fax machine after the acquisition, but this seems less likely.

Table 12.11. Regression analysis of adoption time (in years)

Variable	Stand.coeff.	T	P(two-tail)
Constant	0.000	1.954	0.05
Number of pages sent per day	0.252	3.863	0.00
Percentage external fax communication	0.136	2.026	0.04
Number of communication means replaced	0.170	2.709	0.01
Types of contacts (routine= 1; open network=0)	0.121	1.927	0.05
Size of organization	0.136	1.954	0.05

Notes: R-square= 0.196; Adjusted R-square= 0.177

DISCUSSION OF THE RESULTS

There were three key ideas behind the present study:

1. The more an innovation improves on earlier devices and better serves special needs, the earlier and the more easily will it be adopted in comparison with other innovations that have less relative advantage to the potential adopter.
2. The adoption over time and space of an innovation in communication depends on whether it is used for specific purposes with few parties involved or depends for its function on wide access.
3. In addition to need and product characteristics as indicated under 1 and 2, characteristics of the organization will play a role for the

adoption time. Here the dissemination of information is a factor to consider.

The slow beginning of fax adoption may have been a consequence of the characteristics of the first variants of the product. They had some definite disadvantages in that they were slow (one page required a transfer time of three minutes in 1978), noisy, foul-smelling, and rather expensive. With the third generation of fax machines most of these inconveniences were gone and the fax could replace in a superior way some other means of communication. At first the acquisitions were made primarily for specific connections and later when a critical mass of machines was reached, the development exploded.

One can speculate that when there were enough acquisitions for communicating with specific parties and specific purposes, enough fax machines were around suddenly so that a partial network function could be served. The attainment of a critical mass was probably expedited through pioneers who at an early stage expected a network function for the fax, but who had to wait longer than expected for enough of a network to materialize. Our 1978 study (Jundin & Lindqvist, 1978) gives some clues to the later development. It distinguished between two types of users. Those can be seen as 'lead users' (von Hippel, 1988), though with different needs. Early users with high needs for the product are according to von Hippel (1988) especially interesting to study perceptively. They signal future needs and uses and can thus give important clues to the development of demand for the product.

The results of the present study indicate that there is some foundation for these ideas. A comparison with the 1978 study shows that the reasons for acquiring a fax machine changed from a clear dominance of specific communication purposes to a much more mixed setup of purposes in 1988, with yielding to external pressure as a wholly new category of buying motive.

The analysis of adopter characteristics against adoption time on the whole confirmed expectations. There is a tendency that those who adopted earlier were more often characterized by a need to serve specific communication purposes. Those who had acquired earlier showed more innovativeness, as measured by an index of possession of communication technology. To some extent the differences are explained by differences in organization size, but the tendency remains within most size groups.

Typically no important changes in work routines were reported by the respondents. There was a slight tendency for those who reported such changes to be less satisfied with the fax. Within the limits of this study, it was not possible to ask any penetrating questions about organizational characteristics such as complexity and decentralization. The two crude indicators used, in the case of decentralization yielded a weak tendency in the expected direction, while in the other case complexity did not seem to have any influence. It may be that a simple innovation like the fax is quite independent of the complexity of the organization in the sense used here.

CONCLUSIONS

Judging from the informal interviews made before the survey and anecdotal evidence from many sources, there is a fascination with the fax among many users. Some of these users seem to entertain worries about the future information society and the consequences of increased use of information technology. The attitude statements that covered such aspects were sometimes endorsed by people who were quite enthusiastic about the properties of the fax.

Advertising by fax is a new use which is seen as a potential menace to further development in fax use unless there is some self-imposed restraint or judicial regulation. Many of the new uses seem to involve selling services and goods in ways that are considered favourably by the receivers as, for example, restaurants and retailers sending special offers or daily menus to office personnel in nearby offices. In the long run it will be interesting to see what proportion of the messages will be new, earlier unforeseen types of messages.

In the longer run, what is most interesting about the fax are the new, not foreseen uses. The study reported here has only to a very limited extent been able to deal with this aspect. The use of the fax for social communication which judging from everyday observation is rapidly increasing is for example not covered.

REFERENCES

von Hippel, E. (1988). Lead users: A source of novel product concepts. In, K. Grönhaug & G. Kaufmann (eds), *Innovation: A cross-disciplinary perspective*. Oslo: Norwegian University Press. Pp.387-406.

Jundin, S. & A. Lindqvist (1978). Telefonen som brevlåda (The telephone as a mail box). Stockholm: The Economic Research Institute, The Stockholm School of Economics.

Lindberg, C., Holmlöv, P. G. & Wärneryd, K-E (1989). Telefaxen och användarna (The fax and the users). Stockholm: The Economic Research Institute, The Stockholm School of Economics. Dupl. report.

Meyer, A. D. & Goes, J. B. (1988). Organizational assimilation of innovations: A multilevel contextual analysis. *Academy of Management Journal*, **31**, 897-923.

Rogers, E. M. (1983). *Diffusion of innovations. 3rd edition.* New York: Free Press.

Zaltman, G. & Wallendorf, W. (1983). *Consumer behavior.* New York: John Wiley.

13. Entrepreneurial motivation and the smaller business

Colin Gray
School of Management, Open University

INTRODUCTION

Large corporations have long recognized that motivation of both workforce and management is a key factor in corporate success. Attempting to apply these lessons from the private sector to the task of reversing Britain's long term economic decline, policy makers have spent much of the past decade pursuing the publicly declared aim of creating an 'enterprise culture'. Apart from a tendency to seek a 'market solution' to most social problems and a number of profound changes to industrial relations law, the main thrust of this policy has been the promotion of self-employment and new small businesses. Two of the implicit assumptions of this policy are that self-employed small business managers are entrepreneurs and that the absolute growth in number of these small firms will boost the national motivation to succeed. These form the backdrop to this paper but its main purpose is to examine them in terms of motivation in relation to the smaller business rather than assess the overall effectiveness of the 'enterprise culture' policy.

It is worth pointing out, however, that there are valid empirical reasons to be sceptical about the assumptions that starting a business or becoming self-employed is entrepreneurial in itself and that the growth of the self-employed sector as a whole will generate more positive attitudes towards enterprise and promote more widespread entrepreneurial activities. Despite a record growth in self-employment over the past ten years, Britain has actually under-performed compared with rival economies and there are strong suggestions that, as in the 1930s, the growth of self-employment reflects high unemployment rather than entrepreneurial growth (Binks and Jennings, 1986). There also appear to be strong reasons to doubt that personal business motivations can be manipulated collectively to serve the needs of targeted public policy. Indeed, although a number of economic development theories make a strong case for viewing the innovating entrepreneur as the motor of economic change, the implicit theory underlying the enterprise-creation policy – that anti-entrepreneurial attitudes have been allowed to dominate social consciousness leading to the 'demotivation' of otherwise potential entrepreneurs – finds little support in the treatment of motivation in economic or psychological theory and less in the actual behaviour of the self-employed or small business managers.

Before demonstrating this lack of theoretical and empirical support, it should be emphasized that a proper understanding of motivational issues in small business development is extremely important. In recent years, most other European governments have begun to seek ways of motivating their citizens to start their own businesses. With as many as one third of western Europe's 18 million or so firms likely to disappear in the approaching Single Market, governments have been increasingly keen to promote the growth of dynamic small firms to produce innovative products, create demand and avoid a return to mass unemployment. In eastern Europe, governments have also been looking to a more entrepreneurial spirit to take up the slack of the collapsed centrally planned economies by encouraging the formation of new small firms.

It is essential, however, not to reduce small business development policies merely to the promotion of more and better entrepreneurs. The term 'entrepreneurial' is often used rather loosely to describe all small businesses despite the fact that few small firms and even fewer self-employed are actually entrepreneurial in any economical or psychological sense of the term (Gray, 1989a). The current technical usage of the term applies to a person who is strongly motivated to initiate their own enterprise and manages to do so successfully. Although an enterprise need not be an independent business (instead, perhaps, a division of a large organization or an activity in the voluntary sector), the entrepreneur is increasingly taken to mean someone who has successfully started their own business.

For the purposes of this paper, therefore, the definition of the entrepreneur conforms to Schumpeter's (1934) entrepreneur as someone who actively seeks to gain an advantage over competitors by initiating changes (in processes, inputs, products, finances, organization, and so on) to their business. The key features of entrepreneurial behaviour are competition and innovation. By implication, entrepreneurs must also be decision-makers and it is important to keep in mind that businesses are social organizations.

One of the key skills of the entrepreneur is an ability to co-ordinate, or even manipulate, the activities of others. Therefore, entrepreneurs only begin to be distinguished from the mass of other small businesses when they have sufficient resources, both labour and capital, to compete and innovate effectively.

Apart from the few that develop their enterprises into more complex organizations (formal or otherwise), self-employed or very small firms employing one or two people are not likely to be entrepreneurial. In turn, this implies that many of the features of the self-employed will not be those of the entrepreneur. For instance, unless the entrepreneur also provides the capital, risk-taking is not a necessary feature (Schumpeter, 1934; Brockhaus, 1980; Chell, 1985). Also, energetic behaviour is not necessarily entrepreneurial, especially when it is non-focused and aimed more at survival than growth. Therefore, although the self-employed are legally responsible for their own business decisions and many are active, inventive and motivated, the lack of the potential or desire for growth remains as a blocking, non-entrepreneurial feature.

On these criteria, it is clear that, although most entrepreneurs are likely to be heading a small or medium-sized enterprise, only a tiny proportion of all smaller enterprises will be entrepreneurial. Indeed, small business failure rates are rather high and the business world is peppered with failed high-risk ventures and badly managed inventors. Most of the self-employed and many small firm owners either replicate other existing businesses or respond reactively to external demand and they seem decidedly non-entrepreneurial in their motivation. However, if most small business managers do not appear to be entrepreneurs, most managers in large organizations should also be excluded. Large organizations seem to depend more on administrative rather than entrepreneurial skills. Even the few exceptions are often organizationally constrained from fully exercising their entrepreneurial decision-making talents.

Business success in large corporations is more likely to rest on planning and strong organization, with individual skills only able to flourish in a team or group context. For this reason, smaller firms – where the decision-making and management style is more individual and personal – provide a 'cleaner' research environment to examine entrepreneurial behaviour and motivation. However, it is wise not to forget the fact that it is usually the frustrated corporate entrepreneurs who have the greatest business success when they decide to be truly entrepreneurial and leave the big organizations to start their own businesses.

BUSINESS MOTIVATION IN SMALL FIRMS

Psychological motivation

Early debates in psychology over whether motivation is caused by an internal driving force (drives or needs) or the conscious striving towards external goals have been replaced by a more dynamic synthesis which takes into account not only the importance of goals (valence) and the power of needs but also the degree of expectation (expectancy) that certain behaviours or outcomes will lead to an attainment of a goal and the satisfaction of a need (Vroom, 1964; Atkinson and Feather, 1966; Schein, 1981). This basic model of motivation also allows for goals having negative valence and the motivation relating not to need-satisfaction but to anxiety-reduction. Although there is plenty of debate in management literature over the links between motivation, satisfaction and performance, the focus of this paper is more on how these elements of the basic motivational model apply to the small business entrepreneur.

A further distinction is usually made between primary drives which are physiologically based and acquired needs learnt socially. As there has never been a serious suggestion that business or entrepreneurial success is due to an innate 'business drive', however, this chapter is more concerned with socially learned needs. However, socially learned needs may reflect inner, psychological desires such as status or social esteem (the satisfaction of which is said to be intrinsic) or may be attached to the attainment of external goals such as money (extrinsic satisfaction). Finally, in dealing with business motivation, it is important to make the distinction between personal motivation and the target objectives set for the business.

Of course, this distinction does not discount the possibility that entrepreneurs may treat their businesses instrumentally as the means to enable them to achieve non-business goals (such as status or life-style) but modern management experts are agreed in linking business success which is the ultimate goal of the entrepreneur, to the setting of clear, measurable and appropriate business objectives. Indeed, there is evidence to suggest that entrepreneurs actually enjoy business and that their firms are central to their lives (Timmons *et al.*, 1977; Stanworth and Curran, 1973; Brockhaus and Horwitz, 1986). It is also clear that many self-employed people and owners of smaller businesses, particularly those seeking to avoid unemployment or failure in larger organizations, do not view their business as central to their lives and their eventual lack of success may be due to this lack of focus. The present survey (see pp. 220–8), addresses the split between personal motives and business objectives and casts some further light upon the significance of intrinsic motivational factors (status, life-style, securing the future, and so on) compared with the most common extrinsic motivator, money.

In spite of the importance of setting appropriate goals for business success, it is the other side of the motivational equation, the side concerned with entrepreneurs' needs, that is of greater psychological interest. Although there is still plenty of scope for more focused psychological studies of the entrepreneur, there are a number of key elements in the entrepreneurial profile. These include internal locus of control, need for achievement, controlled risk-taking, setting attainable goals, money as measure of success, persistence, and keen problem solvers (Timmons *et al.*, 1977; Chell, 1985; Brockhaus and Horwitz, 1986; Gray, 1989b). At first sight, most of these features are more descriptive of attitudes and behaviour than of psychological needs but, especially in the context of work, psychological needs reflect a variety of situations.

A commonly used motivational model in management and business literature is Maslow's (1954) 'hierarchy of motives'. Essentially, Maslow describes a process whereby people move from needing to satisfy primary drives through increasingly more complex secondary needs until they reach a stage of needing to arrive at full self-awareness or self-actualization. Although there is little empirical evidence that people actually do pass sequentially from one level to another, the notion that there are different levels or broad types of motives and needs seems reasonable. For the purposes of this chapter, Maslow's original five stages of needs may be reduced to three broad types. These are: basic primary needs such as hunger, thirst, sex, safety, physical security, and shelter; social transactional needs such as love, affection, appreciation, company, esteem, respect, and power; and personal development needs (self-actualization, creativity, altruism and, possibly, need for achievement).

It is not too difficult to see how different career choices could result from having to satisfy these different types of needs. For instance, it is clear that a large proportion of the self-employed, pushed into self-employment by the fear of unemployment, are mainly satisfying their more basic, lower-level needs for psychological and material security. Their principal business objective is usually survival rather than growth (Gray, 1989a). Also, it seems reasonable to hypothesize that, having satisfied their basic and social transactional needs through a successful business career, erstwhile entrepreneurs could well be drawn to non-business pursuits as a means for satisfying their personal development in a manner reminiscent of many Victorian philanthropists.

Entrepreneurs do not seem to be motivated by basic needs and, to the extent that money is regarded as the means to material and psychological security rather than a measure of success, money as an extrinsic goal does not seem likely to lead to entrepreneurial behaviour. The need most commonly associated with successful businesses and entrepreneurs is McClelland's (1961) need for achievement or 'n-Ach'. This 'desire to do well for the sake of inner feeling of personal accomplishment' seems to be a personal development need but, to the extent that it may be connected with the need to earn the esteem of others such as parents or peer groups, it may also be a social-transactional type of need. N-Ach is one of three main so-called 'psychogenic' needs first identified by Murray (1938) and used later by McClelland and his colleagues to analyse economic, business, educational and other social behaviour. N-Ach appears to be mainly a personal development need while the need for social contact or affiliation (n-Aff) and the need for power (n-Pow) seem to be mainly second level social transactional needs.

Entrepreneurs and top managers are distinguished in both big and small firms by their strong n-Ach and comparatively higher n-Pow and lower n-Aff (Murray, 1938; Atkinson and Feather, 1966; McClelland, 1961; McClelland and Winter, 1971; Davidsson, 1989). N-Pow constructs predominate among both top and bottom level managers while N-Aff constructs characterize non-entrepreneurial mid-level managers (Stewart and Stewart, 1981). However, a number of studies have suggested that n-Ach is not one single need but is multi-dimensional with as many as seven different factors, clustered into social transactional factors (work ethic, pursuit of excellence and problem solving mastery) and personal development factors (status aspiration, dominance, competitiveness and acquisitiveness) (Cassidy and Lynn, 1989). There is little doubt that n-Ach is a fairly complex construct, likely to reflect different processes of development in different individuals.

Therefore, even though n-Ach is useful as a broad construct to examine entrepreneurial behaviour, its complexity poses some problems, such as completely separating the small business owner's extrinsic goals (business objectives) from the intrinsic goals, or of disentangling short term business achievements (social transactional) from the longer term satisfaction of developing a successful business venture (personal development). Furthermore, the identification of fear of failure as an opposite concept to n-Ach suggests that the other psychogenic needs may also be multi- or bi-dimensional with related counter-concepts that are also important in analysing small business behaviour. For instance, people with high n-Ach also have a low fear of failure and tend to take calculated rather than reckless risks.

People with high fear of failure set themselves tasks with unrealistic levels of aspiration set too high (reckless) or too low (risk-averse), contrasting strongly with successful entrepreneurs who tend to set themselves high but attainable goals (Atkinson, 1957; Brockhaus, 1980).

These findings conform with Schumpeter's view of the entrepreneur and fit current patterns of small business behaviour in Britain. With few exceptions, low levels of growth and high failure rates characterize Britain's small business sector (see pp. 217–8). Very few small business failures admit that they set their sights too high or too low and virtually none, apart from certain self-employed who had previously been unemployed, state that they are motivated by a fear of failure. However, analyses of small business failure point to unrealistic targets and a failure to match their finances to their expectations (London Business School, 1987). Indeed, even the well-known small business goal of independence (another apparently simple yet multi-dimensional construct) is likely to be an unreal aspiration in most cases, reflecting more a desire to be left alone than any real prospect of growth to a sufficient size where independent action is a genuine possibility (Bolton Report, 1971; Curran, 1987).

Certainly, the desire for independence which is linked to resentment at the power of larger organizations or at not attaining the expected status within larger organizations, has long been identified as an important factor in the career choice of many self-employed (Bolton, 1971; Stanworth and Curran, 1973; Gray, 1989a). In seeking to escape from these unequal power relations, the stated objective of independence is an assertion for control over one's own destiny and can be seen as an expression of n-Pow. By analogy with fear of failure it could be termed fear of dominance. However, the essentially anti-social or isolated nature of a great deal of self-employment has also been well-documented and expressions of desire for independence of this type can be seen as the opposite pole of an n-Aff dimension (Gray and Stanworth, 1986; Curran, 1987; Curran and Burrows, 1988).

Thus, self-employment may offer a career-choice of least resistance for many people. This may explain why so many non-entrepreneurial self-employed are reactive rather than pro-active (Osipow, 1983). On a more positive note, however, independence can also refer to an ultimate state of self-control and defeat of alienation which, as a personal development goal beyond business objectives, would be an appropriate target for someone with high n-Ach who had succeeded in satisfying basic and social transactional needs. Indeed, this may explain why many early entrepreneurial careers reach a plateau and, as Schumpeter observed, cease being entrepreneurial. As mentioned earlier, on achieving a certain level of wealth or security, this type of entrepreneur would seek new challenges of a non-business kind.

Therefore, there are at least three different types of independence as a motivational goal. Actual patterns of business behaviour suggest that the fear of dominance (n-Pow) and fear of social exposure (n-Aff) types of independence are dominant among the self-employed with fear of dominance and, to a lesser extent n-Ach, present among many small firm owners. This ambiguity over the psychological meaning of independence, when reported by the self-employed and the owners of smaller businesses as a motive for being in business on their own account, indicates that the psychodynamic development of entrepreneurs and other small business owners may hold the key to understanding entrepreneurial motivation.

The psychological development of the entrepreneur

Detailed analysis of the relevant family and local cultural dynamics is beyond the scope of this chapter but it is instructive to note that strong fear of failure is associated with lack of parental, particularly maternal, support and a critical, over-structured upbringing (Atkinson and Feather, 1966). This is the same background process described by Kets de Vries (1980) for his neurotic 'entrepreneurs' whom he dooms to ultimate self-created business failure (or, in other words, setting their levels of aspiration unrealistically high). The dimensions of acceptance/rejection and support/non-support that Kets de Vries uses to analyse the role of their families in the psychodynamic development of small business owners, together with the phenomenon he describes (inability to function in large organizations and setting unrealistic levels of aspiration) are very similar to those described by Atkinson and Feather (1966) in relation to the development of fear of failure (hence, by reverse extension, n-Ach). Also, the psychodynamic conditions for developing high n-Ach of supportive parents (especially the mother) such as use of praise for achievements rather than blame for failures, and acceptance and the encouragement of independence and self-reliance, are very similar to the processes that produce internal locus of control defined here as the key entrepreneurial belief in self-control over one's own behaviour and destiny (Atkinson and Feather, 1966; Rotter, 1966). This suggests that entrepreneurs differ from other small business owners not only in their business behaviour but also in their family backgrounds (see Table 13.1) and, probably, in their psychological maturity.

Therefore, the hypothesis that entrepreneurs may be seeking to satisfy higher personal development needs than other small business owners seems to have some support. Research into career development, especially into personality/job congruence, self concept, occupational concept, and job search, also highlights the importance of family and cultural background in developing exploratory behaviour, reality testing and an ability to deal with ambiguity, frustration, tension and unmet expectations (Super, 1980). Encouraging such self-reliance and exploratory behaviour in their children is characteristic of mothers who themselves have high n-Ach and is linked to educational levels, social class and parental (especially paternal) occupation (Atkinson and Feather, 1966; Curran and Burrows, 1988). Not surprisingly, given these links between education, family backgrounds and social class, n-Ach is a feature not only of the more bourgeois occupations of the professions, managers, and capitalists, but also of the upward socially mobile (Atkinson and Feather, 1966). Table 13.1 shows clear differences in family occupational backgrounds.

The fundamental difference between the self-employed and the small business owners is relative proportions of fathers from occupations that allow for some degree of independent decision-taking. More than half the self-employed fathers were in 'order-receiving' occupations. A significantly higher proportion of small business owners (and the female self-employed) come from families where the father held a managerial position or ran his own business. Also, a comparatively high proportion of male self-employed had fathers who were also self-employed. Family links have long been recognized as a factor in the choice of self-employment as a career (Bolton, 1971; Curran and Burrows, 1988; Hakim, 1988; Bannock and Stanworth, 1990). In fact, specific large national-sample studies into these inter-generational links suggest that the family background effects are even stronger. More than one third (36 per cent) of the self-employed and small business owners come from families with self-employed parents and these links appear to be stronger – more than 40 per cent – among the more dynamic 15–25 employee firms (Bannock and Stanworth, 1990). It seems clear, therefore, that there are several categories of self-employed and that self-employed careers may have different meanings for different socio-economic classes.

As well as family and cultural background, the criteria of success and achievement actually used by entrepreneurs themselves is another area that requires further research. In some cases, the performance standards are likely to be directly related to the business objectives and, provided the level of aspiration remains the same, the satisfaction – the feeling of achievement – will come with the attainment of those objectives. In other cases, the satisfaction derived from successfully creating the enterprise itself rather than the goods or services produced by the business could provide the spur. However, in

Table 13.1 Family backgrounds 1984: self-employed, small business owners and employees

Father's work	Self-emp. (no emp.)		Small bus. (1-25)		Employees	
	Male %	Fem %	Male %	Fem %	Male %	Fem %
Employer/manager	16	28	28	33	15	16
Professional	4	6	2	4	3	4
Self-employed	10	3	7	4	4	5
Clerical/supervisory	17	14	18	16	17	14
Skilled manual	24	22	19	22	30	31
Unskilled manual	18	14	9	8	20	21
Rural/military	11	13	17	14	10	11

Source: Curran and Burrows, 1988

many other cases (and these are arguably the more interesting cases) the entrepreneur's own goals may be even more intrinsic, even though business success will demand that the business objectives be personally valid.

It may be that entrepreneurs with family or cultural business backgrounds (see Table 13.1) find the business world a natural arena for their talents and see business objectives as wholly natural and satisfying personal targets. Other entrepreneurs, perhaps those with managerial or professional backgrounds, may feel that business offers them an opportunity to acquire sufficient wealth to afford an expected high standard of living. Furthermore they may recognize that this means only a profitable business will enable them to achieve their ultimate goal. For yet another type of entrepreneur, however, the choice of a business career might itself have been an expression of a deeper level motivation. Whatever their degree of intrinsic motivation, entrepreneurs will distinguish themselves from other small businesses by their strong motivation and clear goals.

Of course, high motivation on the part of business owners clearly is not a sufficient condition for business success. Actual ability and opportunities, as well as their perception of their own abilities and opportunities, are obviously also vital elements in the success of any small business (Carswell, 1987; Davidsson, 1989). It is also vital that they set themselves appropriate business goals and that they realize that the objectives they set are determined by external economic realities. Ultimately, and maybe this is where the true significance of the psychodynamic development of entrepreneur lies, entrepreneurs are distinguished from other imaginative and energetic small business owners by their ability to perceive and respond effectively to changing economic realities.

Economic motivation

Few economists have given much thought to individual motivation but have preferred to explain both macro- and micro-economic behaviour on the basis of general assumptions about economic behaviour. Even in micro-economics with its emphasis on the theory of the firm, analysis tends to be mathematical, relying on abstracted assumptions rather than real business behaviour. For instance, many economists tend to 'explain' small firm behaviour by reference to models of oligopoly competition (a few firms that know each other) rather than perfect competition (many firms unknown to each other) or monopoly competition (dominant supplier). While each of these models assumes economic rationality, oligopolistic firms are said to base their price and volume decisions on the behaviour of their rivals which would be impossible under perfect competition (too diffused) or monopoly competition (small firms are price takers).

Leaving aside the fact that there is little evidence that business managers' behaviour in general is economically rational (involving profit-maximizing behaviour, prices discounting market information, the ability to calculate current marginal break-even points), the reality of small business competition suggests a world far removed from these micro-economic models. Even the more sophisticated versions which take into account market constraints, informational imperfections and refer to bounded rationality remain at heart market-clearing models based on the assumption that firms follow profit-maximizing strategies (Curwen, 1976). Virtually all smaller businesses operate under conditions of severely limited information that is not merely 'imperfect'. The majority are price takers and many, especially the newer businesses and certain self-employed, eventually fail because they over-compete on prices.

In these terms, the entrepreneurial small businesses are those that would register atypical curves on any of these models because of their ability to gain informational or cost advantages over their rivals. Indeed, the fact that many small businesses do not appear to be economically rational does not mean that profit-maximization is irrelevant as a business motive. On the contrary, economists tend to use the profit-maximization model not as a representation of actual business decision-making but as a benchmark of economically rational business behaviour. Indeed, economic efficiency is synonymous with profit optimization and, if entrepreneurial owners of relatively new small businesses have continued to grow successfully (in turnover, profits, and/or employment), it is likely that they measure their success in terms of increased profits because they recognize that profits are the best measure of business efficiency. Accepting the significance of profits targets to small business success and the active use of profits as appropriate business performance measures can, therefore, be taken as evidence of entrepreneurial behaviour. This enables the concept of entrepreneurship to be operationalized without recourse to psychological states of mind, behavioural patterns or personality profiles, thus avoiding any circular arguments when discussing entrepreneurial motivation.

However, this does not imply that profits exclude all other motives in the lives of busy entrepreneurs. Modern theories of the firm recognize that firms behave in response to both internal goals and external market conditions. Agency and managerial theories point out that managers are agents of the owners and that managers often have different goals, such as status, power, independence, and market share, from profit-maximizing owners (Marris, 1964). Thus sales-maximization or growth in workforce or accumulation of capital assets may better describe the actual behaviour of firms and independence-maximization the behaviour of many managers. It is worth noting, however, that most of the classical political economists from Adam Smith to Karl Marx recognized the central importance of profits to business performance even when they differed over their interpretation of the fundamental driving forces or motivations in human affairs.

Empirically, numerous research studies have confirmed that small business owner-managers rate independence, autonomy, self-awareness, self-actualization and achievement far higher than financial reasons for starting their business (Bolton Report, 1971; Stanworth and Curran, 1973; Curran and Stanworth, 1981; Gray and Stanworth, 1986). However, more than half of new small businesses also fail within five years, mainly for financial reasons. In general, therefore, small business behaviour should not be regarded as particularly entrepreneurial. Instead, if business development is seen as a life-cycle of rapid growth followed by productive expansion, stability, then eventual decline, many non-entrepreneurial businesses may have been entrepreneurial during their formative stages and their periods of transition may provide useful information about entrepreneurship and business development. For instance, the business behaviour associated with some business motivations such as profit-maximization may be more likely to lead to success whereas other common business motivations such as turnover targets and break-even points may lead to stagnation if not outright failure. The key to isolating typical entrepreneurial motivation may lie in establishing how closely business success is linked to appropriate motivation.

THE SMALL BUSINESS ENTREPRENEUR

The socio-economic profile

A massive increase in self-employment and new businesses has been a feature of most industrialized economies for much of the past decade. Britain has seen the numbers of self-employed climb from 2 000 000 to over 3 000 000 since 1980 while the net increase of new businesses registered for VAT has risen steadily by an average annual rate of 22 per cent to around 1 700 000. In Italy and Germany the increases, especially for small businesses, have been even more pronounced. Demographic projections predict a continuation of this trend albeit at a decreasing rate. With the collapse of the centrally planned economies in eastern Europe, the scope for small business entrepreneurs is expected to increase even further.

However, analyses of VAT registrations show high volatility with 1.7 million new registrations and 1.4 de-registrations from 1980 to 1988. Since 1980, the number of services firms have increased by 47 per cent, financial services (including property and professional services) by 40 per cent, wholesalers by 23 per cent, construction by 13 per cent but manufacturing by only 10 per cent (just 2 per cent since 1983). Retailing has suffered a net decline (Business Monitor, 1989). Given the wide differences between industries in entrepreneurial opportunities (existence of niche markets, scope for selling a going concern at peak performance, mass markets, high margins, and so on), part of being entrepreneurial lies in picking the right line of business in which to operate and the right size of operation.

The aggregated figures hide many conflicting trends and obscure important differences between the self-employed, small business managers, and entrepreneurs. For instance, small businesses with one to two dozen employees are net job-creators but less than one third of Britain's self-employed provide jobs for other people and many of those jobs are part-time (Creigh *et al.*, 1986; Gray, 1989a). Indeed, only 2 per cent of Britain's self-employed have more than 25 employees and very few small businesses employing up to 20 people manage to expand into the 20 to 50 employee band (Creigh *et al.*, 1986; Doyle and Gallagher, 1986). A number of smaller-scale but more specific studies suggest that the 15 to 25 employee firms are the most dynamic (Curran, 1987; Gray and Bannock, 1988).

An entrepreneur, whether of product, process, organization or marketing, is always an innovator. Few small businesses, however, and even fewer self-employed can claim to be genuinely innovative (Keeble, 1987). Indeed, few small firms and even fewer self-employed seem seriously interested in growth. For most self-employed, the primary motive is to retain their autonomy and independence (Curran, 1987; Gray, 1988). Thus, although firms employing fewer than 20 people account for more than 95 per cent of all firms, they account for only one third of all employment and just one fifth of sales turnover.

Taking exporting as a proxy for reasonably entrepreneurial activity, only around 5 per cent of British firms (roughly 100 000) export, compared with around 30 per cent in Italy. Although most of these exporters are small businesses, they only represent a tiny proportion of firms with fewer than 25 employees. Furthermore, many of these (as many as 50 per cent) appear to be passive exporters responding to orders from overseas customers but not actively seeking to increase exports for their businesses. This suggests that only a few firms have any pretensions to entrepreneurial behaviour. Indeed, if the 2.5 per cent of active exporters are a reliable proxy, this means that little more than 60 000 of Britain's estimated 2.5 million independent firms are headed by entrepreneurs. With such low numbers, it is important to be able to identify not only these active firms, but also the potentially active firms and those that can offer useful support.

Small business typologies and the entrepreneur

The differences between the self-employed and small business owner-managers go beyond variations in workforce size. Some of the more interesting differences lie in social origins, age, gender, types of industry and qualifications. Sociological studies have identified certain entrepreneurs who lack formal qualifications yet have started their own businesses out of frustration at not achieving promotion or due status (Curran and Stanworth, 1981). There is also some support for the 'outsider' theory of entrepreneurial development, namely, that competent outsiders blocked from entering mainstream careers successfully create their own businesses. Another useful distinction is between those who are in business for active reasons – to grow, accumulate capital, attain an expected status as a measure of personal achievement, and so on – and those who are reactive in the face of such adversities as redundancy, economic survival, poor employment prospects and so on (Gray and Stanworth, 1986). Most self-employed operate reactive businesses in the secondary (non-advanced) sector of the labour market (Gray, 1989a) and many small business owners, even in more central sectors of the labour market, are also reactive because they have little desire for growth.

A widely used three-way classification divides the self-employed and small firm owners into artisans (technical skills), classic entrepreneurs (marketing skills) and managers (administrative skills) (Stanworth and Curran, 1973). This model was later extended to include what was termed 'defensive opportunists' but may be better termed survivors – people who have turned to working on their own account as a result of redundancy, career blockage or lack of alternative opportunities (Gray and Stanworth, 1986). The self-employed tend to be non-entrepreneurial artisans or survivors. Most entrepreneurs are small business owners but even those who begin as entrepreneurs through founding their own firm frequently lose their entrepreneurial qualities when they achieve relative stability (Schumpeter, 1934; Davidsson, 1989).

Indeed, many small business owners are only entrepreneurial during the initial startup phase of their enterprise, preferring to restrict further growth so as to preserve their autonomy. This suggests a life-stage model of small business development with different types of business clustering at the different stages. It is widely recognized that small firms which do manage to grow successfully pass through roughly five stages – startup (establishing or extending from self-employment), survival (personal control over the business and employees), take-off (more formalized control), consolidation of the expansion (formal structures) and, in the absence of new product development, decline.

Although only a minority of firms actually grow and actual growth curves are not likely to be so smooth, the life-stage model provides a useful description of the process of growth. It provides the first startup stage as a convenient home for the vast majority of the self-employed. It identifies where entrepreneurial firms fit on the curve, in relation to other businesses, and it clearly outlines the points at which more professional management structures need to be introduced as the business expands. Failure to introduce appropriate management systems is one major reason why expanding firms fail and fall off the curve.

Of more immediate interest, this life-stage model places the entrepreneur on the steeply rising curve just above the point of maximum vulnerability for most firms but, at the upper limit, below the point where internal delegation becomes a necessity. This provides a clue as to why so few firms pass beyond the 20 to 25 employee growth barrier. Under about five employees, management can remain fairly informal but from about five employees to around 20, there has to be a certain amount of sub-division of labour and the delegation of specific tasks to key employees or partners. Beyond this point it becomes organizationally and psychologically difficult to delegate without also delegating some authority to make independent decisions. Indeed, the co-ordination of all these employees may be one of the entrepreneur's main skills.

At this point, the entrepreneur is faced with the choice of growing and gradually losing direct power, or limiting growth and retaining total power. The majority lose much of their entrepreneurial *élan* at this point and opt for the rather non-entrepreneurial position of restraining growth but retaining full power. Those entrepreneurs who do decide to begin setting up more professional management structures and to go for growth soon find that delegation can actually enhance their resources and range of options, and present them with more interesting, novel challenges. The ultimate research objective, beyond the scope of this chapter, is to explore what impels all entrepreneurs to move up the growth curve without falling off and to identify the characteristics of those who pass through the growth barrier.

BUSINESS MOTIVATION SURVEY

Description

For the past six years, the Small Business Research Trust (SBRT) which is an independent educational and research charity, has been conducting regular quarterly surveys on small business performance and aspirations. Because of the heterogeneous nature of the small business sector and the well-documented difficulties in reaching the very smallest businesses, the SBRT makes no claim that the results of the surveys represent the views of 'typical' small business owners or the sector as a whole. Rather, the quarterly surveys monitor general trends in the performance and attitudes of the members of small business representative organizations and, from one quarter to another, address specific issues of interest to small business support organizations. The SBRT, through separate surveys conducted more randomly (via National Westminster Bank), has established that there are no statistically significant differences between the responses of those who belong to representative organizations (roughly 25 per cent of the total) and the non-joiners.

Although the smallest end of the small business sector is notoriously difficult to research, there are strong grounds for believing that the trends identified through the quarterly surveys do, in fact, represent actual shifts in opinion and performance taking place in

Britain's small business sector as a whole. For instance, respondents' expected sales turnover and employment levels correlate highly with subsequent levels of actual annual sales and employment performance which, in turn, have provided accurate predictions of subsequent official measures of industrial activity in the retail, manufacturing and construction industries. Analyses of specific issues such as the financial needs of small firms or the effects of skilled labour shortages, have been confirmed by subsequent national surveys conducted by bodies like the National Economic Development Office (1986), the Institute of Employment Research (1987), and the Department of Employment (1989).

For instance, a special question on the problem of finance and interest rates in the first issue of the 1987 SBRT survey revealed that, while this was the major problem for 21 per cent of the respondents, nearly half (48 per cent) admitted to having some problems over finance. The likelihood of experiencing this problem did not appear to be related to size of firm. However, the age of the firm did seem to be significant with 59 per cent of startups (less than 2 years old) and only 44 per cent of established firms (more than 5 years old) reporting problems with finance. Declining businesses also suffered fairly strongly from this problem. Although finance and interest rates also represent their most important problem, the second most important problem has been consistently lack of demand and low turnover and, as many of them are self-employed sole traders, they have remained relatively unaffected by shortages of skilled and trained employees.

The most important problem for growing businesses over this entire period has been finance and interest rates. This has been felt more strongly by the growers, with an average of 25 per cent of all mentions over the period compared with 20 per cent for non-growers. The second most serious problems for the growers has been the total tax burden. Here, there is an average 17 per cent of mentions compared with 16 per cent for non-growers. Shortages of skilled and trained employees follows with an average 13 per cent of mentions over the period. This was only the sixth most important problem for all the non-growers (7 per cent of mentions). Another fairly evident contrast between the growers and non-growers was that lack of business and low turnover did not feature as an important problem for growers (6 per cent of mentions) but was number two for non-growers (16 per cent).

The above average importance of finance and interest rates to growing firms and the lower importance of low turnover and lack of business may be signs of working capital bottlenecks as growth hits organizational constraints in the expanding firms. One third of the respondents affected by slow payments, according to the responses to the special question in the third quarter of 1987, were from expanding firms, in terms of both their sales and their workforce, lending support to the view that the problem of securing sufficient working capital seems to be partly a side effect of growth itself.

A special analysis in the last quarter of 1986 of expanding firms revealed that manufacturers, wholesalers, and transport firms were strongest growers while the national decline in retailing was reflected in the lowest proportion of growers among retailing respondents to the Quarterly Survey. A later analysis of job-generation in the second and third surveys of 1987 confirmed this pattern and added the modern sector of business and financial services to the list of growers. Thus, the third 1986 survey, which examined the problems of debt control and found that small manufacturers, wholesalers and construction firms had the worst problems with slow payers, provided some oblique evidence of the need to control the turmoil which often accompanies growth. Before moving on to discuss briefly the significance of these trends, it is worth noting that the growers tend to be the firms with 10 to 50 employees rather than the smaller firms.

Two specific questions relating to business motivation were inserted in the quarterly survey (Vol. 6; No. 2) conducted during the second quarter of 1990 (April, May, June). To facilitate coding and to encourage a high response rate, quarterly survey questionnaires are confined to one single sheet of A4 and the questions tend to take the format of a forced choice between listed alternative replies with a blank space for non-standard responses. The listed alternatives to both questions reflect the issues discussed in this paper. The first question asked respondents to state their main motivation for being in business and offered response categories of: no alternative; family tradition; independence; to create security; making money; other. The second question asked about the respondents' main business objectives and offered response categories of: growth in sales; growth in profit; growth in employment; achieve a certain standard of living; protect your future; build up asset for your children; life style; other.

The most frequently mentioned general business problems concerned finance. Interest rates rated 26 per cent of mentions, cashflow/bad debts got 12 per cent, access to finance received 4 per cent, followed by lack of business (14 per cent), government regulations (7 per cent), and lack of skilled labour (6 per cent). More than half (56 per cent) reported that their sales turnover during the past year had increased but only one quarter (25 per cent) reported that they had taken on more staff. Because of increased use of labour-saving technologies and the quicker reactions of entrepreneurs to the downturn in the economy over much of the past year, it may be that some of the more entrepreneurial respondents have been shedding staff or using existing staff more productively. Nevertheless, the 21 per cent of all respondents who reported that they had grown in both sales turnover and employment should be regarded as entrepreneurial given the present economic climate.

Results

Some 1,350 small business owners from all over Britain responded to the quarterly survey. More than two-thirds (68 per cent) had fewer than ten employees which, although below the national distribution of 90 per cent of all firms in this size-bracket, means this national survey is the biggest of its type conducted amongst Britain's smaller firms. Just over half the respondents had businesses in the manufacturing (22 per cent) or business services (29 per cent) industries which, because many active (entrepreneurial) businesses are in these industries, was welcome but it does mean that small retailers, haulage, and construction firms were under-represented.

A more complete analysis of these growing businesses has not yet been completed and the present results represent only the initial analysis of the survey. Still, as Table 13.2 shows, there are interesting differences in the personal motivations of small business owners from different industries. The most notable result is the strong importance of independence as a motive for being in business across all industries although there are clear differences between industries. The interdependent nature of the building trade, with a considerable amount of cross sub-contracting and many skilled workers only nominally self-employed (often working almost exclusively for former employers), shows in the relatively less importance attached to independence and comparative importance given to creating security for themselves. The high concern over their independence and lack of concern over making money of the small transport firms is also apparent and hints at a fairly non-entrepreneurial approach. Indeed, apart from logistics management and courier services (which, in any case, could be classified as business services), there have been few innovations in small local transport firms. By comparison, wholesaling, which places less emphasis on security and more on making money, is a sector that has seen considerable new technological innovation.

The more instrumental and less idealistic approach of the small manufacturers is clear from their slightly lower concern over maintaining their independence (though, at 48 per cent, this is clearly their dominant personal motivation) and their comparatively more frequently expressed desire to make money as a prime personal business motivation. This fits the picture of the more task-oriented manufacturer compared with the more traditionally minded small retailers or the probable 'lifestyle' independence of small restauranteurs (see Table 13.7). It is worth noting that restaurants and shops are popular for startup businesses (which can be entrepreneurial, especially if they discover new niches) but that for the most part these types of business, in replicating existing businesses tend not to be entrepreneurial. As Table 13.3 shows, in terms of profit-orientation, manufacturing and wholesaling stand out as the two most entrepreneurial industries.

Table 13.2 Main personal motivations of small firm owners
(row percentages)

Business sector	No choice	Family trad'n	Indep.	Create security	Make money	Total (100%)
Manufacture	5	7	48	8	25	289
Transport	10	3	62	10	7	29
Construction	1	8	45	22	19	78
Wholesale	10	7	50	6	21	112
Retail	9	13	48	8	16	228
Catering/Rest.	7	0	59	7	19	27
Business serv.	5	0	53	6	16	387
Other serv.	5	4	56	9	16	153
Total No	80	71	678	111	251	1349
%	6	5	50	8	19	100

As discussed already, the most fundamentally entrepreneurial approach for a small business is that of maximizing profits. The maximization of sales may lead to a bigger sized firm or to a bigger market share but it can also eventually lead to inefficient growth, overtrading and possible failure or takeover. In larger firms, this is a policy that some managers might prefer in opposition to the owners' preference for profits if they stand to gain certain collateral benefits. In small firms, however, a policy of sales-maximization without ensuring the profitability of sales is a recipe for disaster and, as such, decidely non-entrepreneurial. Similarly, concern over status and life-style may be valid overall life objectives but they imply that the firm is not the owner's primary interest and that it lacks a suitable business objective.

Only the manufacturers and wholesalers reported that profit-maximization was their main objective while respondents from the other industries were more inclined to view their businesses as vehicles to support a preferred life-style or to enhance their status.

Table 13.3 Main business objectives of small firm owners
(row percentages)

Business sector	Sales growth	Profit growth	Staff growth	Status	Protect assets	Future growth	Life-style	Total (100%)
Manufacture	10	34	1	9	11	6	22	289
Transport	7	14	0	24	14	3	31	29
Construction	10	22	1	14	19	1	31	78
Wholesale	5	32	0	15	13	6	23	112
Retail	6	22	0	19	14	5	29	228
Catering/rest.	4	15	0	19	22	4	33	27
Business serv.	6	15	5	17	11	2	33	387
Other serv.	2	11	3	18	10	1	48	153
TOTAL No:	88	289	30	209	164	50	409	1349
%	7	21	2	16	12	4	30	100

Small transport firms, with a high concern over status and low interest in profit growth, appear to be the least entrepreneurial industry though the removal of any status-conscious, high-margin, up-market restaurateurs and retailers is likely to expose the rest of these industries as rather non-entrepreneurial. Indeed, the relatively non-entrepreneurial nature of most very small firms employing fewer than five people is clearly demonstrated in Table 13.4. There is a marked positive relation between the profit motive and size and almost equally strong inverse relations between size and both life-style and status. The self-employed and mini-firms in the one to four employee band, where lifestyle (42 per cent) is the dominant business objective, are clearly less entrepreneurial than the more dynamic firms in the 15 to 49 employee band, where 37 per cent have growth in profits as their main business objective. Certainly, this view is further supported by the results in Table 13.5 which shows making money as a personal motive for being in business increasing with the size of firm coupled with an equally distinct decline in independence as a personal motive.

Obviously, making money as a personal motive is strongly linked to having increased profits as a business objective, but it is interesting to note that money is often seen as a badge of success by entrepreneurs (Timmons *et al.*, 1977). It is also important to note the increase with firm-size of family tradition as motive. It may be that these respondents represent a stable, non-entrepreneurial sub-group of the generally more active 15 to 25 employee businesses. On the other hand, active later generations can put an established business to new

Table 13.4 Business objectives by firm size
(row percentages)

Number of employees	Sales growth	Profit growth	Staff growth	Status	Protect assets	Future growth	Life-style	Total (100%)
1 – 4	7	12	1	18	11	3	42	595
5 – 9	7	21	4	16	14	5	24	324
10 – 14	4	27	1	15	19	3	23	124
15 – 49	8	37	3	11	11	4	19	233
50 – 99	8	54	0	8	6	4	16	50
100+	6	38	0	6	19	0	19	16
Total No:	88	289	30	209	164	50	409	1349
%	7	21	2	16	12	4	30	100

Table 13.5 Personal motives by firm size
(row percentages)

Number of employees	No choice	Family trad'n	Indep.	Create security	Make money	Total (100%)
1 – 4	9	2	54	8	16	595
5 – 9	5	6	52	8	15	324
10 – 14	4	7	51	9	20	124
15 – 49	3	11	40	10	25	233
50 – 99	0	14	44	4	34	50
100+	0	13	31	6	37	16
Total No:	80	71	678	111	251	1349
%	6	5	50	8	19	100

uses. The 9 per cent of the smallest firms that reported they had no alternative are likely to be recent startups who have chosen self-employment as the only alternative to unemployment. Although these Tables represent only the initial analysis, the cross-tabulation in Table 13.6 of personal motives by business objectives provides some interesting clues to the existence of distinct types of small business – entrepreneurial, traditional, avoiders, and so on.

Most of these results have an intuitive face validity. For instance, it is not surprising that 40 per cent of respondents (or twice the average 21 per cent) motivated to make money have the growth of profits as their business objective or that 38 per cent (or three times the average) of those concerned to create security should aim at building protection for the future. Nor is it strange that respondents motivated by family tradition are five times more likely than most other respondents to aim for an accumulation of assets (for their successors). However, the non-entrepreneurial nature of many of those pushed into self-employment by, amongst other things, fear of unemployment (see Gray 1989a), is reflected in the relatively low importance they place on growth of profits and the strong importance that achieving a reasonable standard of living (status) holds for them.

In fact, the responses from those who felt they had no choice other than to turn to self-employment is not only indicative of high external locus of control but also reflects the importance of basic needs such as achieving a certain minimum standard of living, among small businesses and the self-employed. Having as a business goal the preservation of a certain lifestyle could reflect a variety of needs though not necessarily any likely to lead to business success. This lends added interest to the replies from the half of the total sample who reported that attaining independence was their main motivation for running their own business. The 40 per cent whose main business objective is the supporting of a preferred life-style is the largest sub-group, followed by the profit-maximizers (19 per cent) as a smaller but, presumably, more dynamic sub-group exhibiting high internal locus of control. These differences are highlighted in Table 13.7 where the business objectives of the entrepreneurial growers (those who reported increases in both sales turnover and employment over the past year) are contrasted with those respondents whose businesses actually declined over the past year.

The importance of profits and, to a lesser extent, sales turnover to their business success is clearly understood by the growers, who represented one in five of the total sample. The relative unimportance of supporting a lifestyle was also a feature of the growers. The declining firms were also aware of the need to boost profits (though less so than the growers) and comparatively more interested in setting business objectives aimed at attaining a certain standard of living

Table 13.6 Personal motivation by business objectives
(column percentages)

Motive> Objective	No choice	Family trad'n	Indep.	Create security	Make money	Total % number	
Sales growth	6	4	7	5	9	7	88
Profit growth	15	24	19	11	40	21	289
Staff growth	0	0	1	5	1	2	30
Status	35	16	16	15	14	16	209
Protect future	10	18	10	38	11	12	164
Assets growth	8	16	3	4	4	4	50
Lifestyle	18	17	40	19	19	30	409
Total No:	80	71	678	111	251		1349
%	100	100	100	100	100	100	

Table 13.7 Business objectives by growth
(row percentages)

Performance	Sales growth	Profit growth	Staff growth	Status	Protect assets	Future growth	Lifestyle	Total (100%)
Growers	9	28	4	16	10	3	26	313
Decliners	4	24	0	19	10	4	32	115
Neutral	6	19	2	15	13	4	32	921
Total No:	88	289	30	209	164	50	409	1349
%	7	21	2	16	12	4	30	100

(status) and supporting a lifestyle. Indeed, more than half the declining businesses (51 per cent) had these rather non-business goals as their objectives compared with only 42 per cent of the growers. These differences suggest that the more active firms may have a different outlook on business and a different set of priorities than the less active or more reactive firms.

DISCUSSION

Clearly, these initial results confirm the heterogeneous nature of the small business sector in terms of background, personal and occupational objectives, business behaviour and so on. There is strong evidence of a separate sub-group of active, entrepreneurial small business owners. Entrepreneurial small business owners seem to have a different approach to business. They are more profit oriented. They differ in their personal motivations for being in business. They are more interested in making money and less in independence. Apparently they differ substantially from most other small business owners and are certainly different from the vast majority of self-employed. However, this may reflect the fact that most self-employed and many small business owners appear motivated by non-business or non-growth goals.

One of the distinguishing features of expanding businesses is their identification of growth in profits as a business objective and the pursuit of money, followed by independence, as a personal objective of the owner. More focused research that would compare entrepreneurial with other serious but non-entrepreneurial small business owners is required to understand fully both of these findings. Money can be sought as a means of satisfying basic-level material needs or, at a higher level, as an objective measure of achievement. As mentioned above, it has been claimed that entrepreneurs seek money for its symbolic value as a sign of success. It may be that the 40 per cent of those motivated to make money (see Table 13.6) who are also profit-oriented fall into this category, and the 11 per cent who seek money to achieve a certain standard of living fall into the first category, but the 19 per cent seeking money to support a lifestyle are less easy to categorize as entrepreneurs.

If one of the main aims of industrial policy is to encourage the emergence of more genuine entrepreneurs, policy makers need to know more about the significance of money to small business owners. The main question is whether, after the requirements for working capital have been met, growth-minded small business owners value money as a source of material rewards, intrinsic satisfaction, power, social acceptance or as a measure of achievement. If it is mainly as a source of material reward, then policies such as soft loans, capital allowances, and reduced rates of taxation, policies that allow a rapid accumulation of money, should be successful. If it is instrumental in opening the doors to power or social acceptance then the avenues from business success to public recognition vested in awards, membership on public bodies, and appointments to advisory committees, have to be broadened.

However, if, as seems likely for nearly half (48 per cent) of profit-seekers personally motivated to seek independence, money is mainly seen as the measure of achievement, its value can be enhanced only by challenge. Provided the goal is attainable and valued, the motivation of entrepreneurs with high n-Ach is directly related to the challenge of achieving that goal. Basically, this means that genuine entrepreneurs need outlets for pitting their judgement and abilities against other entrepreneurs. In terms of industrial policy, this implies that policies should be aimed at creating, via infrastructural investments, improved information services, investment in public housing and transport to allow real labour mobility, an economic fabric that, in satisfying most basic-level needs nationally, channels business ingenuity and entrepreneurial talent towards satisfying higher level social transactional and personal development needs thereby promoting imagination, opportunities and challenge.

Also, because of its central importance as a self-reported motivator, the significance of independence as a goal and its relation with internal locus of control have to be fully explored. If a large segment of entrepreneurs reach their desired level of satisfaction at perceiving they have achieved a certain degree of independence (say, at realizing that they do indeed take all important decisions themselves) then it follows that few entrepreneurial firms will grow into more professionally managed active enterprises. Such growth inevitably implies an increase in delegated decision making and there is strong evidence suggesting that such a 'personal independence-loss' barrier to growth does exist around the 20 employee mark (Doyle and Gallagher, 1986). Policy-makers need to turn their attention to encouraging the belief that a more robust form of independence is only attainable beyond that barrier. Alternatively, new systems allowing the 'direct control' entrepreneurs to sell their successful firms to professional managers for a reasonable financial gain need to be developed, so that the entrepreneurs receive not only public and appropriate (money as reward) recognition for their past achievements but also sufficient capital to address new challenges by starting new businesses.

On the less attractive aspects of independence, if a large segment of the self-employed and a smaller segement of small business owners are experiencing a fear of social exposure or a fear of dominance, then the underlying causes need to be identified and alternative support structures developed for these types of non-entrepreneurs. Certainly, more focused research is needed to analyse these various concepts of independence and to determine just where self-actualization, personal autonomy, social inadequacy, alienation, freedom, non-dependence and other similar phenomena overlap and where they represent separate states. How these various aspects of independence relate to occupational behaviour in general and to small business behaviour in particular also needs more investigation. Indeed, the whole field of career theory in relation to the self-employed and small businesses is an under-researched area.

Finally, moving back from these social issues to the more specific topic of entrepreneurial motivation, the survey reported in this chapter has cleared the broad territory, but future research is needed to take a closer look at whether entrepreneurs attach stronger valences to existing small business objectives and are just more motivated and better focused than most other small business managers, or whether they have significantly different needs and objectives. What this chapter has demonstrated is that questions about entrepreneurial motivation are valid and that small businesses are the most appropriate contexts for addressing these issues.

REFERENCES

Atkinson, J. (1957). Motivational determinants in risk-taking behaviour. *Psychological Review*, **64**, 359-372.

Atkinson, J. & Feather, N. (1966). *A theory of achievement motivation.* New York: John Wiley.

Bannock, G. & Stanworth, J. (1990). *The making of entrepreneurs.* SBRT Monograph. Milton Keynes: Small Business Research Trust.

Binks, M. & Jennings, A. (1986). Small firms as a source of economic rejuvenation. In J. Curran, J. Stanworth & D. Watkins. *The survival of the small firm.* London: Gower.

Bolton, J. (1971). *Small firms – Report of the committee of inquiry on small firms.* Cmnd 4811. London: HMSO.

Brockhaus, R. (1980). Risk taking propensity of entrepreneurs. *Academy of Management Journal*, **23**(3), 509-520

Brockhaus, R. & Horwitz, P. (1986). The psychology of the entrepreneur. In Sexton & Smilor *The art and science of entrepreneurship.* Cambridge MA: Ballinger.

Carswell, M. (1987). Management training needs of small firms: A study of the engineering and clothing and textile industries. Paper presented to the 10th UK Small Firms Policy and Research Conference. Milton Keynes.

Cassidy, T. & Lynn, R. (1989). A multifactorial approach to achievement motivation: The development of a comprehensive measure. *Journal of Occupational Psychology*, **62**, 301-312.

Chell, E. (1985). The entrepreneurial personality: A few ghosts laid to rest? *International Small Business Journal*, **3**(3), 43-54.

Creigh, S., Roberts, C., Gorman, A. & Sawyer, P. (1986). Self-employment in Britain: Results from the Labour Force Surveys 1981-84. *Employment Gazette.* London: Department of Employment.

Curran, J. (1987). Bolton fifteen years on: A review and analysis of small business research and analysis in Britain 1971-86. London: Small Business Research Trust.

Curran, J. & Burrows, R. (1988). Enterprise in Britain: A national profile of small business owners and the self-employed. London: Small Business Research Trust.

Curran, J. & Stanworth, J. (1981). A new look at job satisfaction in the small firm. *Human Relations*, **34**(5), 343-365.

Curwen, P. (1976). *The theory of the firm.* London: Macmillan.

Davidsson, P. (1989). *Continued entrepreneurship and small firm growth.* Stockholm: Economic Research Institute.

Department of Employment (1989). *Small firms in Britain.* London: HMSO.

Doyle, J. & Gallagher, C. (1986). *The size-distribution, potential for growth and contribution to job-generation of firms in the UK, 1982-84. Research report 7.* Newcastle-upon-Tyne: University of Newcastle.

Gray, C. (1988). Entrepreneurs perceptions of business problems as key indicators of success. Paper presented to the 13th International Association of Researchers in Economic Psychology Colloquium in Leuven, Belgium.

Gray, C. (1989a) From unemployment to self-employment: A manageable change? Paper presented to the 4th West European Congress of the Psychology of Work and Organisation at Robinson College, Cambridge, England.

Gray, C. (1989b). The entrepreneur's self-concept and economic theory. Paper presented to the 14th International Association of Researchers in Economic Psychology Colloquium in Kazimierz Dolny, Poland.

Gray, C. & Bannock, G. (1988). The growing small businesses of Britain: Trends in quarterly profiles of growing small firms 1984-88. Paper presented to the 12th National Small Business Research and Policy Conference, Cardiff.

Gray, C. & Stanworth, J. (1986). Allowing for enterprise: A qualitative assessment of the enterprise allowance scheme. London: SBRT.

Hakim, C. (1988). Self-employment in Britain: Recent trends and current issues. *Work, Employment and Society*, **2**(4), 421-450.

Institute of Employment Research (1987). *Review of the economy and employment.* Coventry: University of Warwick.

Keeble, D. (1987). Entrepreneurship, high-technology industry and regional development in the United Kingdom: The case of the Cambridge phenomenon. Paper presented to the seminar on Technology and Territory at the Istituto Universitario Orientale, University of Naples, Italy.

Kets de Vries, M. (1980). *Organisational paradoxes.* London: Tavistock Publications.

Labour Market Quarterly Report (1988). Sheffield: Manpower Services Commission.

London Business School (1987). *A study to determine the reasons for failure of small businesses in the UK.* London: Stoy Hayward.

Maslow, A. (1954). *Motivation and personality.* New York: Harper and Row.

McClelland, D. (1961). *The achieving society.* New York: Van Nostrand.

McClelland, D. & Winter, D. (1971). *Motivation and work behaviour.* New York: Free Press.

Marris, R. (1964). *The economic theory of 'managerial capitalism'.* London: Macmillan.

Murray, H. (1938). *Explorations in personality.* New York: Oxford University Press.

National Economic Development Office (NEDO) (1986). *External capital for small firms: A review of recent developments*. NEDC: London.

Osipow, S. (1983). *Theories of career development*. New Jersey: Prentice Hall.

Rotter, J. (1966). Generalised expectancies for internal versus external control of reinforcement. *Psychological Monographs*, **80**. No. 609, whole.

Schein, E. (1981). *Occupational psychology*. New York: McGraw Hill.

Schumpeter, J. (1934). *The theory of economic development*. Cambridge, MA: Harvard University Press.

Small Business Research Trust. (1985-90). *The quarterly survey of small business in Britain. Volumes 1-6*. London: SBRT.

Stanworth, J. & Curran, J. (1973). *Management motivation in the smaller business*. Aldershot: Gower.

Stewart, V. & Stewart, A. (1981). *Business applications of repertory grid*. London: McGraw Hill.

Super, D. (1980). A life-span approach to career development. *Journal of Vocational Behavior*, **16**, 282-298.

Timmons, J., Smollen, L. & Dingee, A. (1977). *New venture creation*. Illinois: Irwin Homewood.

Vroom, V. (1964). *Work and motivation*. New York: Wiley.

14. The wife's employment family fit

Simon James, Bill Jordan and Marcus Redley
University of Exeter

INTRODUCTION

The subject of this chapter is the reported experiences of wives in low income households in relation to their labour market decisions. These responses will be used to develop a model of married women's labour market decisions referred to as the 'Wives' Employment Family Fit' or the WEFF. This work forms part of a larger study of 'Labour Market Decisions in Low Income Households' and originated from speculation as to whether enough was known about the factors which influence such decisions, particularly in low income families. The study also set out to investigate how members of low income households arrived at these decisions and how, if at all, any potential conflicts were reconciled. The respondents consisted of 36 couples with children and a further group of lone parents were interviewed for comparative purposes. For the main project the interviews were conducted with each partner individually followed by a joint interview. This chapter draws on the wives' interviews. A more detailed account of the findings of the study as a whole will be published in 1991 and this survey is being followed by a similar one into labour market decisions in higher income households.

An enormous amount of research has already been undertaken into work and labour markets by investigators with a wide variety of academic and other backgrounds. The approach adopted by economists (summarized, for example, by James & Nobes, 1988, Chapter 4) is usually based on the analysis of the income and substitution effects of taxation. The income effect arises from changes in work caused by the changes taxation has on an individual's real income. It is generally supposed that, by reducing real incomes, taxes may encourage individuals to increase their earnings. In contrast, the substitution effect describes the fact that higher taxes reduce the return to paid employment relative to other activities and may therefore induce a fall in the willingness to work. As these two effects work in opposite directions the empirical evidence is particularly important and this is discussed, for example, in Brown (1983) and Hausman (1985).

Other possible influences on labour supply have been considered by economists though few studies have attempted to examine the decision-making process from the viewpoint of the individuals concerned. Brown and Dawson (1969) have pointed out that misconceptions of the tax system may influence work incentives and it seems clear that the peculiar way in which the UK income tax is administered means that British taxpayers are unusually ignorant of their tax system (James, Lewis & Allison, 1987). Musgrave (1959, p. 240) suggested there might be a spite effect of taxation, especially for taxes which are considered to be unfair. It has also been recognized by economists, for example Kay (1990), that the way taxation influences the decisions of earners may not only be through finely balanced decisions about the amount of labour supplied and net pecuniary returns. Attitudes to work more generally and therefore career choices and so on may also be important. Furthermore life-cycle considerations, and in particular children, have been recognized as having an important influence on female labour supply (Goldin, 1989 and Even, 1987) as has the importance of social norms (Romme and Georges, 1990).

In both the relevant econometric surveys and the American negative income tax experiments, one of the main findings was that married women's 'component earnings' in such households were far more sensitive to the disincentive effects of the tax and benefit systems than were their male partners' main earnings (SRI International, 1983). In addition the UK benefit system has particularly severe disincentives for women married to unemployed men, as Kell and Wright (1990) demonstrate and which we confirm.

Nevertheless, it is clear that women's earnings are crucial for the living standards of poor households. Furthermore, married women have been a growing element in the employed labour force. In 1921 only 9 per cent of married women were 'economically active'. By 1951 the percentage was 24.8. It had grown to 34.2 per cent by 1961 and 48.9 per cent by 1971. In 1981 the figure was 56.8 per cent. For such reasons the position of married women requires closer inspection. This is especially relevant in the light of survey evidence that the wives of unemployed men are far less likely to be in paid work than are the wives of employed men – 27 per cent of the former compared with 61 per cent of the latter (General Household Survey, 1984, Table 6.18). Indeed between 1973 and 1984, the number of couples with two earners rose by 6 per cent, but those with no earners by 7 per cent; this has led to suggestions of an increased polarization between multi-earner and no-earner households, widening the gap between a relatively affluent majority, and an impoverished minority (Pahl, 1984).

These findings are reinforced by a few small scale qualitative studies. Bell and McKee (1985, p. 393) noted that in Kidderminster only wives with well-paid or long established jobs maintained them after their husbands became unemployed. In contrast, women doing temporary, casual, or informal work withdrew from it, or postponed further employment. Similarly, Morris (1985, p. 404) found that in South Wales, wives of redundant steel workers frequently experienced redundancy soon after their husbands. In both studies, the response of a wife taking a full-time job following her husband's loss of his job was very rare.

Both statistical and qualitative studies suggest that these findings are related to the conditions for receiving benefits. This was illustrated particularly in a study by Daniel (1981), who found that while only 2 per cent of wives moved out of paid work within a month of their husband becoming unemployed, a larger shift occurred when unemployment benefit ran out. This was because of the more generous disregard of wives' earnings in unemployment than in supplementary benefits (as they then were). Similarly, Moylan *et al.* (1984) concluded that 'some of the changes in wives' employment status seem to be systematically related to the type of benefit the family was receiving in respect of the man's unemployment. The main result is the high proportion of wives in the families receiving Supplementary Allowance who left employment' (pp.131–2).

Yet these analyses do not clearly locate the wives' decisions in an overall context of labour market decision making. Taken in isolation, they could be read as suggesting that married women's decisions are more economistic (concerned with optimizing their work-income equation to rather refined calculations) than are the men's. This seems paradoxical, in view of other findings about women's attitudes towards employment. Our aim here is to analyse the women's accounts of their experiences with a view to locating their responses to tax and benefits disincentives in an overall context of how women construct and legitimate their choice of paid work, and its relation to unpaid work in the household.

Our method of analysing the accounts proceeds from the position that description is a social activity (Cicourel, 1968; Potter & Wetherell, 1987) and thus the women routinely construct their particular versions of the world with reference to contextual expectations and contraints. In our case, the respondents account for their actions to a social enquirer rather than, say, an official from the Department of Social Security or a social worker. In constructing their accounts the wives draw upon a shared and public understanding of accepted norms and roles (Cuff, 1980). Aware that their accounts are open to critical judgement by the hearer, the wives 'produce and manage' their descriptive activity so as to accomplish a morally adequate account, that is, an account that presents the teller as a competent and reliable speaker. In terms of the analysis this allows us, as social enquirers, to read the transcribed accounts as simultaneously the artful practices of individuals and also as a display of the culturally shared roles and expectations of a wife in a low income household.

In line with this interpretive procedure, our accounts were collected using unstructured, open-ended interviews. The interview data were collected from low income couples with dependent children, living on the same estate. The respondents thus had approximately equal geographical access to employment opportunities and transport. The families of which the wives are members are not a homogeneous group as Table 14.1 shows. 'Unemployment' in Table 14.1 refers to someone without formal paid employment or self-employment. Table 14.2 indicates the type of employment taken by the wives. The interviews were conducted in the respondents' homes, tape recorded and later transcribed. To preserve confidentiality the names of all interviewees referred to in the chapter have been changed to names of rivers.

In constructing their accounts of their labour market decisions the women situated themselves as mothers, with the attendant responsibility of childcare. Allied to this are the requirements of being a wife. This is a role that demands that a woman normally curtail her employment potential to meet the need to fit in with her husband's hours of employment, such that she is able to take on the bulk of the childcare responsibility.

We refer to these features of the woman's labour market decisions as the WEFF, which is represented in Figure 14.1.

Specifically, to satisfy the requirements of the WEFF a wife must have:

1. A positive attitude towards her job, that is, sufficient reasons to get and keep her job.
2. She must be able to provide childcare for the time she is at work.
3. Her hours of employment must fit in with her husband's hours such that it is she rather than her husband who provides the bulk of the childcare.

Table 14.1 The families' employment status

Husband and wife both employed	18
Husband and wife both unemployed	10
Husband employed, wife unemployed	7
Husband unemployed, wife employed	1

Table 14.2 The wives' employment

Housewife	17	Machinist	2
Cleaner	6	Warehouse manager	1
Caterer	3	Factory supervisor	1
Shop assistant	2	Chambermaid	1
Shelf-filler	2	Care assistant	1

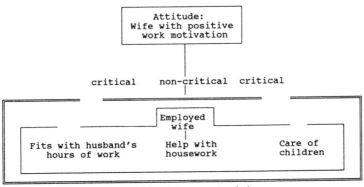

Figure 14.1 The wives' employment family fit (WEFF) model

4. She is dependent on the available job opportunities in the labour market for a job which satisfies the above requirements.

Below are some illustrations. The first extract is from a wife without paid employment who had hoped to take a weekend job; however, the husband's job also entailed weekend work:

> Well when he started working for [Company X] they told him he had to work Saturdays and Sundays so of course I had to tell the . . . you know the person at the Job Centre that I wouldn't be able to go for the interview because my husband would be working weekends and nobody'd be able to watch them [the children]. (Mrs Ryton, 11)

In the following example both partners are working full-time, their daughter is minded by her maternal grandmother. Asked if she expects to be working in six months time, the wife replies:

> No, shouldn't think so . . . no. On account of this I'm not gonna be able to rely on my mother for much longer, I mean she is nearly seventy. I'm not gonna be able to rely on her, she's not gonna be able to handle her [the child] once she's running around everywhere, you know . . . so . . . No I can't . . . I can't visualize me being there [at work] much longer. (Mrs Cherwell, 29)

Even in cases where both husband and wife are unemployed the idea of 'the fit' comes into play. Asked if she would take a job the wife replied:

> Yeah I suppose I could really. The trouble is you see he [the husband] . . . I can't always depend that he will be here to look after them [the children] like he hates staying in the house. (Mrs Cam, 9)

Clearly in such a situation the wife does not have to fit in with her husband's job but she acknowledges the need to fit in with his need to be out of the house.

THE WIVES' EMPLOYMENT FAMILY FIT

The WEFF is common to all the accounts – except for what we identify as deviant cases. But its particular articulation is dependent on each household's accounted for circumstances and resources. This chapter will initially examine the WEFF variables: motivation, fitting in with the husband's hours of work, childcare and job opportunities of working wives and husbands. The chapter will then examine households with different employment patterns and describe the deviant cases.

Motivation

The following reasons were given for taking paid employment:

> Um . . . I think really the only thing really was the money. That's all. I mean, we were struggling weren't we?

. . . and a little later

But I thought, well just that little bit of independence. (Mrs Avon, 4)

Another wife said:

I went back out to work, just to get a little bit of independence. (Mrs Hodder, 12)

Another:

Yeah, I looks forward to going out [to work] . . . you know . . . gives me a break from . . . the little one. 'Cause he's a handful. (Mrs Rother, 7)

Another works at night:

We [workmates] get on really well and really it's like a night out with the girls really more than anything. 'Cause you go out, have a yap and everything. (Mrs Parrett, 16/17)

The opportunity to work means various things to these women, extra income, independence, a break from caring for the children and a social event. However, not only is there a requirement for a positive motivation to take and keep a job, there is also the need to satisfy the requirements of the WEFF – such that the wife is responsible for the bulk of the childcare.

Childcare

All the women had spent some time out of the labour market due to childbirth. None of the working women currently employed a childminder. Two of the women had previously employed a childminder but both thought it too expensive:

It worked out I was sort of paying more than I was earning. Yeah. (Mrs Plym, 17)

Cost was one reason given by the women, but for both the employed and unemployed women childminding was seen in a very negative way:

I just wouldn't. I don't . . . No I don't think, I don't think it's right; it's like if my, if my mother . . . I mean [my mother-in-law] says that you know . . . that she would look after her . . . I mean I've got a lot of people that would look after her but I don't believe in Tom, Dick and Harry looking after them you know. (Mrs Cherwell, 30)

> I still miss it [work] now but uh . . . we're finding it a struggle financially without another wage coming in but still . . . I still don't think it's right when you got little ones to dump them on someone else which is what it is literally. (Mrs Severn, 4)

Four alternative strategies were identified by which mothers were able to arrange care for their children. The first is having a job that fits in with the husband's hours of work.

> I asked if I could be transferred to [name of workplace] because it was half past five to half past seven which meant I didn't have to get a baby sitter 'cause my husband was there [at home] which made things a lot easier for us. I mean it was less hours, less pay but you know, didn't have to pay a baby sitter which saved in the long run anyway. (Mrs Wear, 2)

Second, there may be a neighbour or relative who is able to look after the children.

> Four days a week I've got to get my children up at six o'clock in the morning and I've got to sort myself . . . well they go up my sister's at quarter past seven; that's a shame on them but then again . . . we need the money. (Mrs Derwent, 2)

Third, young children can be left under the supervision of an older sibling.

> I decided that um . . . well you got to trust 'em at some point or other and Claire is sixteen this year and Mark's three years younger than her . . . but um they always come home together like. So trusted them. (Mrs Nene, 8)

Fourth, school, for those old enough to attend, provides 'childcare' facilities as illustrated by this woman who might have to give up her job during the school holidays:

> In the holidays when they got six weeks holiday, because if John's [husband is in casual employment] working then and . . . there won't be nobody to look after 'em. (Mrs Hodder, 26)

Of course a child could always be left to fend for itself but no 'mother' will admit to this, though one husband did.

Husband and children

The reality of the WEFF is that the wife usually has to fit her job and childcare responsibilities around her husband's working hours. This was most clearly expressed when overtime was discussed:

Sometimes I do [overtime], like I say, at three until half past four, but I've got to be home by five to let [my husband] go to work. (Mrs Derwent, 9)

Yes. As long as I could fit it in round the children. And I don't have to get anyone to look after them. (Mrs Wear, 5)

But occasionally I might. Do an odd couple of hours or . . . but not very often. 'Cause even with him working a split shift it makes it harder anyway and we . . . I mean baby sitters are dear. (Mrs Clyde, 3)

Labour market

None of the women said that there were no jobs available, indeed some women thought it was easier for them to obtain employment than it was for their husbands.

Like women always seem to get a job quicker than ah men. So that's whys went out and got a job. (Mrs Humber, 5)

So I thought well I could get a job easier than what [my husband] could you know so I went to work as well. (Mrs Itchen, 10)

Housework

A key expectation of a wife is that she does the housework though some wives had more help from their husbands and older children than others had. No wife claimed that such help was critical to her keeping her job.

I mean he's ever so good, I mean, if I said [husband's name] the bedroom needs doing, he'd go and do the bedroom. It don't worry him if I, you know, although he don't like ironing when he's on a day off, but if I was stood here with an ironing board he'd say 'well you know you do yours and [name of daughter]'s and I'll do the boys' and mine'. (Mrs Derwent, 9)

Again:

When we were married, he just . . . helped, you know. Sunday mornings when I hoovered, he ironed, or vice versa, and we thought it was totally natural and we always have done. And then when the children came along . . . um . . . he drew the line at disgusting nappies, but apart from that he's helped with the children. (Mrs Calder, 11)

One wife received help with the housework once she started work:

Before I went to work . . . before I went back to work like you know, when I was at home with the kids then I did it. (Mrs Nene, 11/12)

Also, among the respondents two wives had husbands who changed their working hours to enable a WEFF to be made easier. Mr Nene changed his hours so that he could drive his wife to work:

> His [the husband's] hours is supposed to be 9 to 6 but he actually changed them to do 8 to 5 so that he could, that he would drop us off. But they [employer] didn't mind actually because it meant the garage was open an hour earlier. (Mrs Nene 13)

Mr Cherwell changed his work pattern from shift work to night work at the place where both he and his wife work:

> If she [the daughter] won't go to bed he's got more patience. Whereas I can't have her running around at 9, 10 o'clock at night; it gets on my nerves . . . you know . . . whereas he doesn't mind you see, so I decided that I would be out of it evenings and be home in the morning. (Mrs Cherwell 26)

The ability of a woman to maintain a WEFF is a precarious accomplishment. All the women had periods of unemployment related to the factors shown in Figure 14.1. The reasons given for leaving a job involved one or more of the WEFF variables.

Unemployed wives of working husbands

The WEFF is also applicable to unemployed wives of working husbands and there were seven such families in our group.

Mrs Ryton has a positive attitude towards work:

> When I've finished all my housework and that and . . . you've got absolutely nothing else to do and she's [her daughter] asleep and [the other child is] playing, I think, you know I, I wish I was back at work again like I used to be. (Mrs Ryton, 4)

In addition to her positive attitude to work there was also potential support from her husband in relation to childcare.

> If I see something come up again like that probably apply for it . . . 'cause I'll know they're safe, in safe hands with their Dad and I won't have to pay him so it'll be ideal for me. (Mrs Ryton, 12)

With both a positive attitude towards work and potential childcare from her husband, all Mrs Ryton needed was a job that would fit in with her husband's hours of work.

Mrs Severn gave up her job owing to the birth of her child who is now two years old. Asked if she had looked for another job she replied:

Well I've got . . . always glance through the papers you know in case there's anything which would fit in with something I could do, maybe evenings or during the day. I've done a bit of child minding for a friend when she went to work. Looked after a little girl for a few hours a week. Once she starts going to play school then maybe I can find something else. (Mrs Severn, 4)

Mrs Ribble expressed a similar opinion:

When I'm, when he's five I might go back to work then . . . you know because [indistinct] you know, when he starts school I won't have nothing home here . . . you know, but 'cause to me five years is too much of an age gap to have another child. (Mrs Ribble, 7)

It can be seen that the labour market decisions of unemployed wives also follow the WEFF but at least one of the criteria of attitude, childcare, job opportunities and fitting in with the husband is not fulfilled.

Both adults unemployed

Wives of unemployed husbands do not, of course, have to fit in with their husband's working patterns. The WEFF applies to some of these families but not to all. Mrs Cam believed there was work available but her husband did not like the idea of her taking full-time employment and she was also worried about childcare:

You know now Christmas is coming I can always get a job somewhere around you know. As long as, as long as there was someone here to look after the children and I don't have the worry of who was going to pick them up. I, I, would go out to work full time [indistinct] we can't because he doesn't want me to have to go out you know, he feels that I shouldn't have to go out to work you know. (Mrs Cam, 9)

Not only was Mrs Cam's husband against her going out to work, she does not feel she can leave the children in his care:

The trouble is you see, he, he's I can't always depend that he will be here to look after them you see, like he hates staying in the house. (Mrs Cam, 9)

Mrs Cam's chances of gaining employment seemed slim, but she had a plan:

Hoping to get a job addressing envelopes, something that I can do at home, you know just to sort of bring up the income a bit. (Mrs Cam, 1)

By proposing to be employed addressing envelopes Mrs Cam would be fitting in with her husband's expectation that she does not go out to work and because she is at home she will be able to mind the children. Mrs Cam, in this way, would then have satisfied the requirements of the Wives' Employment Family Fit.

A similar case to Mrs Cam's is that of Mrs Frome, but she is against the idea of fitting in with normal working requirements.

> I wouldn't want to go to work again. The thought of having to start work at half past eight or nine o'clock in the morning and finish at five and trudge home does not appeal at all. You know I've got no desire to do that whatsoever. (Mrs Frome, 9)

However, Mrs Frome would consider typing at home and gives the following reasons:

> But that's the only thing I'd really like to do so, so that I'm not away from home [indistinct] much more my own boss; I can do it in my time and . . . I like doing it. (Mrs Frome, 8)

Also:

> It was all right at first [working]. It was okay until I suppose . . . he [the child] started becoming interesting then I found I was missing out on rather a lot and [indistinct] sort of found it very difficult to reconcile the two [work and children]. (Mrs Frome, 4)

Mrs Frome's view can be seen to be compatible with the WEFF, but she has an ambiguous attitude towards work and childcare.

It is however among the families where both adults are unemployed that there are cases which deviate from the WEFF. The reason:

> Well if I was gonna go out to work then I wouldn't go out part-time. I'd go out full time. Because part-time it's just a waste of money because . . . it's just a waste of time because they're just gonna . . . whatever I earn they'll take off [my husband's] dole money see. So really it won't be worth it in the long run. (Mrs Itchen, 12)

Another wife of an unemployed man was asked if she had considered taking a job:

> Yeah I would . . . cafe work and things like that, it's hard work innit?
> Q. Yeah.
> They're low pay aren't they? I keep saying I'll get a job but . . . like say work in the hospital or something like that . . . but time you've paid the rent, you would have to pay the rent bit extra on the rent and . . . um . . . have to pay for, what else would I have to pay for . . . ah bus fares and thing like that I suppose and . .

Q. So what you think you'd be?
I'm just as bad off as I am I suppose really . . . yeah. (Mrs Dovey, 5)

Mrs Parrett recalls a period when her husband was unemployed and she had to give up her job:

Yeah I had to stop because they said that I was only allowed to earn £4. I think I was earning something like £50 and they would let me keep £8 of it. I thought no not that much of a mug. (Mrs Parrett, 13)

In response to the unemployment trap Mrs Derwent recalls taking a job which she did not declare.

This was just in a pub. I done a couple of nights and they paid me like cash in hand.

When the husband's situation changed then Mrs Derwent began working legitimately:

He started his job in February and I got a job in April, like, you know, once he was back in employed then I went and got one [a job]. A proper one. (Mrs Derwent, 10)

These women are in a situation where it does not make economic sense to them to take employment. There may be jobs available, their husbands may be supportive and there may be childcare available but these women do not see it worth their while to take a job which they have to declare because their wages would not compensate for their loss of income from the state. The women are caught in the unemployment trap. The trap exists because the amount of one partner's earnings disregarded for income support is £5; anything above that is deducted from the family's weekly benefit. This is a major disincentive for married women, because most of them take part-time rather than full-time work. Hence their earnings are enough to reduce the amount of benefit the family receives, but not enough to get the family off benefits. This trap is a product of the benefit system, and changes in the availability of part-time work, or even of childcare provision, would not remove it.

A working wife of an unemployed husband

Given the disincentives involved it is not surprising the respondents included only one working wife married to an unemployed husband (although some others had undeclared earnings). Mrs Wye, as a full-time warehouse manager earns enough to support the family and Mr Wye, who has been unemployed for three years, does not claim benefit. He is also happy looking after the children and Mrs Wye has a positive attitude to her employment:

> It's the money innit? You, I couldn't live, we couldn't live on the dole money; it was a struggle; we were borrowing every other week sort of thing, 'cause you could only get paid fortnightly, so it wasn't lasting the full fortnight . . . like I said to 'em no way I am going back on dole money. (Mrs Wye, 17)

Mrs Wye's husband has taken responsibility for childcare.

> Kids seem happy enough; they're not wanting, they're not crying when I go off to work in the morning, say oh don't want you to go this morning. If they started doing that then I would have said right enough you'll [the husband] have to go and find a job and I'll stay home. But . . . they'm quite happy with Dad home. (Mrs Wye, 16)

Mrs Wye does not have any problems fitting in with her husband when she does occasional overtime:

> Um . . . it's . . . not very often I turn it [overtime] down, 'cause it's always handy, little bit extra money. (Mrs Wye, 17)

Under the terms of the WEFF Mr and Mrs Wye have effected a role substitution.

Taxation

Among the families 14 of the 19 employed women worked part-time. As is well known, the growth in part-time work by married women is related to employers' attempts to reduce non-wage costs; many such jobs are constructed to fall just below the thresholds for income tax and National Insurance contributions. Although there was evidence from women interviewed in our study that they were aware of this, it provoked little comment, perhaps because part-time work was seen as compatible with the WEFF.

No woman claimed that income tax affected her motivation to take employment but among those women taxpayers there was a greater or lesser degree of economic calculation. Mrs Wye and Mrs Parrett apparently had the greatest understanding of their tax liability. In particular Mrs Wye took advantage of the fact that, before the introduction in April 1990 of independent taxation for married couples, where only one spouse went out to work the man could claim only the married man's allowance, whereas if it were the woman who worked they could take advantage of both the married man's allowance and the wife's earned income allowance.

Well, because [my husband's] not working I'm claiming his tax allowance so I only pay . . . a very small amount. (Mrs Wye, 19)

Mrs Parrett actually changed her working hours after calculating her taxable income:

There was a lot of us together, we worked it out that um if you worked two nights or four nights it was just right. But if you did like the third night or fifth night that was when you got collared for it. (Mrs Parrett, 9)

Other women do not appear to be discouraged from doing overtime by tax considerations:

Not really, no I know you're not so well off 'cause of paying tax but you still got that extra couple pound whatever. (Mrs Plym, 15)

Other responses to the issue of taxation were a need 'to work it out', to ignore it or there was simply a failure to understand how it is calculated. Mrs Rother has two part-time jobs and is in the process of sorting her tax affairs out:

Well I'm in the middle of trying to get it but . . . I've been in about it 'cause I does two jobs. And I've seen me supervisor; she sent off the number I had to go, but I'm still waiting. (Mrs Rother, 6)

Mrs Nene does not appear to be influenced by tax considerations:

I don't really take a lot of note about that [tax]. I just look at what hours I did and what overtime and that's it. I generally think, well that must be right so . . . yeah. (Mrs Nene, 6)

Mrs Hodder, asked if her tax is always the same replied:

No . . . tax and insurance is different. Some weeks it's three pounds seven pence, some weeks it's two pounds ninety-seven and I can't never make that out. Why is it always different? (Mrs Hodder, 23)

Although there were a variety of responses to questions about income tax and although for some it seemed to have some effect upon overtime, it did not appear to discourage wives from taking employment.

The WEFF with its features of motivation, childcare, fitting in with the husband's hours of work and labour market opportunities, illustrates the wives' presentation through their interview accounts of culturally accepted norms and roles. The 'wife' is a woman who tailors her life to the requirements of her children. The route to the satisfaction of her own needs via paid employment is subjected to the constraints of the labour market, the benefit system and her husband's work patterns.

Our study puts women's responses to tax and benefits disincentives in a context – the WEFF. Women's sensitivity to tax and benefits constraints must be seen alongside their sensitivity to other, in many instances more influential, factors which affect their labour supply behaviour. Employment must above all fit with the wives' perceptions of themselves as well as with immediate pecuniary considerations.

ACKNOWLEDGEMENTS

The authors gratefully acknowledge the support of the Economic and Social Research Council in undertaking this work (award number G00 23 2446).

REFERENCES

Bell, C. & McKee, L. (1985). Marital and family relations in times of male unemployment. In B. Roberts, R. Finnegan & D. Gallie (eds), *New approaches to economic life*. Manchester: Manchester University Press.

Brown, C. V. (1983). *Taxation and the incentive to work, 2nd Edition*. Oxford: Oxford University Press.

Brown, C. V. & Dawson, D. A. (1969). *Personal taxation incentives and tax reform*. London: PEP Broadsheet, No. 506.

Cicourel, A. V. (1968). *The social organisation of juvenile justice*. New York: John Wiley.

Cuff, E. C. (1980). *Some issues in studying the problem of versions in everyday situations*. Manchester: Department of Sociology, Manchester University Occasional Paper No. 3.

Daniel, W. (1981) *The unemployed flow interim report*. Policy Studies Institute.

Even, W. E. (1987). Career interruptions following childbirth. *Journal of Labor Economics*, **5**, 255-277.

General Household Survey (1984). London: HMSO.

Goldin, C. (1989). Life-cycle labor-force participation of married women: Historical evidence and implications. *Journal of Labor Economics*, **7**, 20-47.

Hausman, J. A. (1985). Labour supply. In A. J. Auerbach & M. S. Feldstein (eds), *Handbook of public economics*. North Holland.

James, S., Lewis, A., & Allison, F. (1987). *The comprehensibility of taxation: A Study of taxation and communications*. Aldershot: Gower.

James, S. & Nobes, C. (1988). *The economics of taxation, 3rd Edition*. Philip Allan/ Prentice Hall.

Kay, J. A. (1990). Tax policy: A survey. *Economic Journal*, **100**, 18-75.

Kell, M. & Wright, J. (1990). Benefits and the labour supply of women married to unemployed men. *Economic Journal*, **100**, 119-126.

Morris, L. (1985). Renegotiation of the domestic division of labour. In B. Roberts, R. Finnegan & D. Gallie (eds), *New approaches to economic life*. Manchester: Manchester University Press.

Moylan, S., Millar S. & Davis, R. (1984). For richer for poorer? *DHSS study of unemployed Men*. London: HMSO.

Musgrave, R. A. (1959). *The theory of public finance: A study in public economy*. New York: McGraw-Hill.

Pahl, R. E. (1984). *Divisions of labour*. Oxford: Blackwell.

Potter, J. & Wetherell, M. (1987). *Discourse and social psychology*. London: Sage.

Romme, A. & Georges, L. (1990). Projecting female labour supply: The relevance of social norm change. *Journal of Economic Psychology*, **11**, 85-99.

SRI International (1983). *Final report of the Seattle Denver income maintenance experiment. Volume 1: Design and results.*

15. A model of negotiations for the sale of a house

Gerrit Antonides
Erasmus University, Rotterdam

INTRODUCTION

Negotiations are usually studied from two different points of view. Many studies look at the behaviour of negotiators in a given setting and include the number of parties involved in a conflict and the type of conflicting interests (cf. Nash, 1950, 1953; Raiffa, 1982; Fisher and Ury, 1981). Typically, the number of parties is limited in these studies and the consequence of not reaching an agreement coincides with the status quo. The study of coalition bargaining (Komorita, 1984; Murnighan, 1978) has a wider scope since it deals with the issue of who negotiates with whom and with the terms of agreement. However, neither the tactics nor the environment of negotiating (for example, the effect of a third party) is studied in coalition bargaining. In this chapter we study the negotiations taking place in a market, in particular the housing market. A characteristic of a market is that many opportunities for a business relationship are available. In other words, many coalitions may form. Whether or a the coalition is formed does not depend only on a match with the right partner but also on the result of negotiations with that partner. (An experimental study of these aspects regarding the job market has been conducted by Sondak and Bazerman, 1989). In other words, the allocation of the coalition's payoffs over the members of the coalition determines whether the coalition will form.

Several rules for the division of the payoffs exist. For example, there is division according to the Shapley value (Shapley, 1953) or the pivotal power of the parties (Shapley and Shubik, 1954). There are the weighted probability and the equal excess models (Komorita, 1984). The division of payoffs is frequently based on equity considerations (cf. Adams, 1965; Festinger, 1954) in that it is proportional to the relative power associated with the bargaining positions of the parties.

This study deals with both aspects of negotiations in a market. It considers the relative power of buyers and sellers on the market as the perceived probability that a bid is acceptable to the other party. The perceived probabilities may be influenced by the market environment. In this chapter, we first develop a theoretic framework of the negotiations in a market. We conducted a survey on negotiations regarding the sale of a house and this is described and our results are reported. Finally, our conclusions are discussed.

THEORY

The theories mentioned in the Introduction usually do not deal with the perception of the bargaining position. Yet, it is known that the perception of objective variables such as probabilities and prices influences behaviour in a different way from economic or game theoretic predictions (see Antonides, forthcoming).

The bargaining position of a seller is determined by the supply and the demand for a commodity on the market. In the case of the housing market, this concerns the number of people able and willing to sell or to buy a particular type of house. If there are many people moving away from an area, supply will be high and the bargaining position of sellers is weak. In other words, the probability that buyers are willing to pay a high price in such an area is relatively low. However, the perception of this probability may differ across sellers. In Figure 15.1(a), a seller's perceived probability density function, $l(P)$, concerning the feasibility of a particular selling price is shown. The associated cumulative distribution function of prices, $L(P)$, indicates the seller's perception of the buyer's willingness to pay a particular asking price or the perceived probability that a buyer will consider this price acceptable. (See Figure 15.1[b]). Conversely, the buyer's perceived probability density function, $h(P)$, concerning the price which is acceptable for a seller is shown in Figure 15.1(a). The cumulative distribution function, $H(P)$ in Figure 15.1(b), indicates the buyer's perception of the seller's willingness to accept a particular bid. The functions $L(P)$ and $H(P)$ resemble the functions in Gabor and Granger (1966) regarding the probability that a price is considered too high or too low by consumers. Our approach with respect to these functions is fundamentally different since they do not represent the actual proportion of people judging a price too high or too low but the perception of these proportions by a market agent. In

(a)

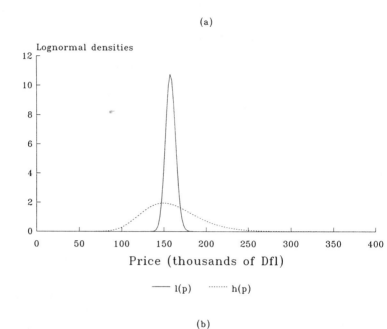

(b)

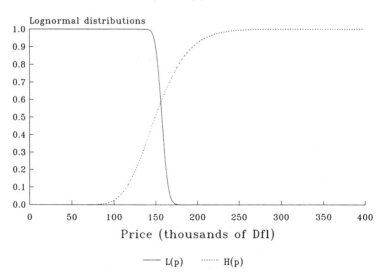

Figure 15.1 Buyer's and seller's perceived probabilities that a price is acceptable to the other party

their research on consumer prices, they find strong indications that $l(P)$ and $h(P)$ are lognormal density functions.

The assumption of lognormal probability functions appears to be reasonable because the price range is naturally bounded on one side and people's opinions concerning innumerable issues have been found to follow the normal probability distribution. We shall apply the assumption of lognormal perception functions as a working hypothesis. The location and the shape of these perception functions are interesting in themselves because they convey information about psychological variables at work in the market. Furthermore, these functions are assumed to play a part in the formation of the negotiated price. Gabor and Granger (1966) consider the so-called buy-response curve, $1-L(P)-H(P)$, representing the likelihood that a given price is within the acceptable range. The analogue of this curve concerning the negotiated price represents the likelihood that a given price is acceptable to both the buyer and the seller. As Gabor and Granger (1966) and Granger (1988) note, the buy-response curve is not a probability density function. However, it can be transformed to a probability density function under certain conditions (see Appendix 1). The expectation of this function equals the negotiated price. Several contextual variables are assumed to influence the perceived bargaining position and the result of negotiations. As most buyers and sellers of houses infrequently act as such, their experience and information may be quite different. As a result, their perceived bargaining position (represented by the perception functions considered above) may be different. There are several contextual variables and some of them are described below.

First, the presence or absence of a third party, such as a real estate agent does not unequivocally increase the bargaining power of the party with whom he or she is associated. Frequently, commission has to be paid which might force up the negotiated price. Second, we can consider information, differentially available to the parties, as in the appraised value of a house. Obviously, the possession of information is an advantage. Lack of information on the buyer's (seller's) side is likely to increase (decrease) the negotiated price. Third, there are indications of market misperception, such as the number of rejected candidates. According to the law of large numbers, the right partner in negotiations will show up if one's perception of the market is correct. If it is not correct, behaviour in negotiations will be too demanding, which decreases the probability of an agreement and increases the number of rejected options. Fourth, time pressure, for example, whether or not the buyer has sold his former house and whether or not the seller has already purchased another house, should be considered. Time pressure can be directly related to the price. To satisfy the time constraint, the probability of an agreement should be increased. Buyers (sellers) can accomplish this by increasing (decreasing) the bid price. Finally, price limits, either self-imposed or imposed by the environment, as in a mortgage, must be taken into account. This pertains to the reservation price which is the buyer's (seller's) highest (lowest) price which he is able to pay (accept). The higher (lower) the buyer's (sellers) reserve price the higher (lower) the negotiated price will be. The effect of contextual variables on the perceived bargaining position is investigated later.

SURVEY DATA

In June 1988, Ronald Kornaat and Willy Schiebel sent a questionnaire to about 1000 potential buyers or sellers of a house. The sample was selected from advertisements in local newspapers and from real estate information guides in the Netherlands. After two months, 220 questionnaires had been returned, 134 of which yielded complete responses regarding the variables of interest to this chapter. In 26 cases the response indicated that negotiations were still continuing. There were 31 subjects who reported the purchase of a house, 41 subjects reported the sale of a house, and 36 subjects reported both the sale and the purchase of a house. This response is substantial given the fuss associated with buying, selling and moving. The sellers gave information about the number and the heights of subsequent bids during the negotiations and about the contextual variables mentioned above. The buyers gave the same type of information supplemented with a good deal of information regarding their opinions and evaluations of the attributes of the house. Regarding the sale of a particular house the response contained either the buyer's information or the seller's information considered above. It was too cumbersome to collect the information from both parties involved in the negotiations. The questions presented in Appendix 2 are of special relevance to this study.

RESULTS

First, the sample information regarding the variables of interest in this study are presented. Next, the estimation of the perceived probability functions and the influence of the contextual variables on them are dealt with. Finally, the effects of the perceived probabilities on the negotiated price are considered. Table 15.1 contains summary information regarding the survey questions shown in Appendix 2 and regarding the contextual variables.

Table 15.1 Sample information regarding perceived probabilities and contextual variables

	Sellers		Buyers		
P_1	184 826	(1 024)	P_4	200 164	(1 627)
$L(P_1)$	0.414	(0.040)	$H(P_4)$	0.554	(0.044)
P_2	172 513	(979)	P_5	217 381	(1 707)
P_3	169 052	(961)	P_6	215 843	(1 740)
$L(P_3)$	0.908	(0.015)	$H(P_6)$	0.859	(0.026)
P	181 196	(1 223)	P	210 358	(1 716)
Real estate agent (in %)	78			39	
Appraisal value obtained (in %)	45			40	
Number of rejected options	1.54			7.42	
Duration of negotiations (months)	1.63			2.46	
Number of observations	77			67	

Notes: Prices are in Dutch Florins.
    Standard errors in parentheses.

The price statistics in Table 15.1 indicate that on average the buyers spend more on the purchase of their house than the sellers get from their sales. This reflects the fact that some of the sellers are moving into a more expensive house. Furthermore, the average negotiated price (P) lies in between the first bid (P_1 and P_4, respectively) and the reservation price (P_3 and P_6, respectively), which is according to expectations. However, on average the negotiated price is higher than the seller's expectation, but lower than the buyer's expectation. This is clearly not to be expected with well-informed agents in a market. The perceived probability that the first bid would be accepted by the other party is on average 40 to 60 per cent; for the limiting bids it is 85 to 90 per cent.

Sellers obtain the assistance of a real estate agent twice as often as buyers do. Each party has obtained an appraisal value of the house in

40 to 45 per cent of the cases. It appears that the search for a suitable house takes more effort than the search for the right buyer of a house. Sellers on average reject only one or two potential candidates whereas buyers on average reject more than seven options before they succeed. The average duration of the negotiations is about two months. It appears that buyers' and sellers' price expectations are different relative to the negotiated price. If this effect is reliable it should be reflected in the respective perceived probability functions. The perceived probability functions of buyers and sellers are estimated from the equations shown in Table 15.2. These equations are based on the assumption of lognormal perception functions regarding the probability that a price will be accepted by the other party. The location and the shape parameters of these functions are found by minimizing the residual sum of squares of the equations. It appeared that many people gave the same probability estimate for the first bid and for the limiting bid. Since the estimation process did not converge for these observations, they were removed from the analyses. For this reason, the number of observations in Table 15.2 is less than in Table 15.1. The parameters of the perceived probability functions can be estimated fairly accurately from the three data points given in response to the questionnaire. The average price is assumed

Table 15.2 Equations and average estimated parameters of the perceived probability functions

Sellers	Buyers
$\ln P_1 = \mu_1 + \sigma_1 N^{-1}\{1-L(P_1);0,1\}$	$\ln P_4 = \mu_2 + \sigma_2 N^{-1}\{H(P_4);0,1\}$
$\ln P_2 = \mu_1 + 0.5\sigma_1^2$	$\ln P_5 = \mu_2 + 0.5\sigma_2^2$
$\ln P3 = \mu_1 + \sigma_1 N^{-1} \{1-L(P_3);0,1\}$	$\ln P6 = \mu_2 + \sigma_2 N^{-1} \{H(P_6);0,1\}$
μ_1 11.966 (0.071)	μ_2 11.914 (0.167)
σ_1 0.037 (0.003)	σ_2 0.205 (0.096)
μ_2^* 11.914 (0.072)	μ_1^* 12.311 (0.158)
$\ln P$ 11.940 (0.071)	$\ln P$ 12.112 (0.111)
N 64	N 40

Notes: Standard errors of the parameters in parentheses.
      N = number of observations

to correspond to the expectation of the lognormal distribution, $\mu + 0.5\sigma^2$ (cf. Aitchison and Brown, 1960). In contrast to the results above, it appears from Table 15.2 that the average negotiated log-price is lower than the log-price that is expected by the sellers to be acceptable for the buyers ($\mu_1 + 0.5\sigma_1^2$). Also, the average negotiated

Table 15.3 The effects of contextual variables on the location of the perceived probability function

	Sellers μ_1	Buyers μ_2
Constant	0.308 (0.120)**	0.313 (0.730)
Log-price	0.983 (0.010)**	1.025 (0.064)**
Real estate agent	-0.017 (0.012)	-0.169 (0.083)**
Appraisal value obtained	-0.003 (0.011)	-0.152 (0.091)
Number of rejected options	-0.015 (0.011)	-0.026 (0.003)**
Duration of negotiations (months)	-0.025 (0.010)**	-0.036 (0.092)
$\bar{R}^2$	0.995	0.924
Number of observations	64	40

Notes: Standard errors of the parameters in parentheses.
       ** Significant at the 5% level.

log-price is higher than the log-price that buyers expect to be acceptable for the sellers ($\mu_2 + 0.5\sigma_2^2$). The difference with the result regarding the expected prices in Table 15.1 can be explained as follows. Because the price distribution is skewed, the log-price shows a more normal distribution than the raw price. In addition, the information in Table 15.2 is based on three data points giving a more reliable view of the perception functions.

The effect of contextual variables on the perceived probability functions will be dealt with by regressions of μ_1, μ_2, σ_1 and σ_2 on these variables. Although the negotiated price is considered a result of perceived probabilities, it is included in the regression as a proxy of the type and the quality of the house. The effect of this is that the regressions show the effects of contextual variables on perceptions, controlled for the effect of the type and the quality of the house. The parameters, estimated from the regressions of the location parameters are shown in Table 15.3. In both regressions, the log-price has a significant effect on the location of the perceived probability functions. This indicates that the higher the quality of the house the more to the right the function is located on the price axis. The other variables have a negative effect on the location parameters. It appears that the real estate agent has a significantly negative effect on μ_2, thus increasing the buyer's perceived probability that a given price will be accepted by the seller. According to the theory, this has a moderating effect on the negotiated price.

The number of rejected options has a significantly negative effect on μ_2. This indicates an increasing buyer's confidence in negotiations, probably resulting from a better knowledge of the market due to experience.

The duration of negotiations has a negative effect on μ_1, reflecting a shift in the seller's perception function. This results in a price

Table 15.4 The effects of contextual variables on the shape of the perceived probability function

	Sellers σ_1	Buyers σ_2
Constant	0.347 (0.075)**	0.279 (0.913)
Log-price	-0.024 (0.006)**	-0.042 (0.080)
Real estate agent	-0.002 (0.008)	0.207 (0.104)*
Appraisal value obtained	-0.001 (0.007)	0.215 (0.114)*
Number of rejected options	-0.009 (0.007)	0.026 (0.004)**
Duration of negotiations (months)	-0.002 (0.006)	0.078 (0.116)
$\bar{R}^2$	0.197	0.576
Number of observations	64	40

Notes: Standard errors of the parameters in parentheses.
** Significant at the 5% level. * Significant at the 10% level.

decrease in order to be accepted by the buyer. The presence of a real estate agent does not have a significant effect on the seller's perception.

The regression results regarding the shape parameters σ_1 and σ_2 are reported in Table 15.4. The results indicate that the buyers' perceived probability functions have a flatter shape if they use a real estate agent, if they have obtained an appraisal value of the house and if they have rejected more options (because σ_2 is smaller in these cases). Since these factors increase the information about the market, this result is important because it indicates that more information leads to a wider range of prices that are perceived as acceptable to the sellers, thus increasing the likelihood of agreement. The seller's perceived probability function appears to be steeper with a lower price of the house, indicating a greater sensitivity regarding the acceptability to the buyer of a certain price. Although we have information from only one of the negotiation parties, the other party's perception function follows from the assumptions regarding the negotiated price. The buyer's missing value of μ_2 (to be denoted by $\mu_2{}^*$) and the seller's missing value of μ_1 (to be denoted by $\mu_1{}^*$) can be computed directly from $\ln P = (\mu_1 + \mu_1)/2$ (see Appendix 1; the values are shown in Table 15.2). This result has been derived from several assumptions regarding the perceived probability distributions of buyers and sellers. If the result is correct, μ_1 should equal $\mu_1{}^*$ (and μ_2 should equal $\mu_2{}^*$), conditional on the type and the quality of the house. In addition, σ_1 should equal σ_2. This has been investigated by considering the regressions of μ_1 (which equals μ_1 for sellers and $\mu_1{}^*$ for buyers) and log-σ (log-σ_1 resp. log-σ_2) on a dummy variable indicating a seller (dummy equals 1) or a buyer (dummy equals 0) and on the negotiated log-price. The results of these regressions are shown in Table 15.5. (The results regarding μ_2 and $\mu_2{}^*$ are not reported in Table 15.5 since they are equivalent to those regarding μ_1 and $\mu_1{}^*$). It appears from Table 15.5 that both μ and σ differ significantly between buyers and sellers. This indicates that the negotiation party of a seller in the survey does not have the same perception function as a buyer in the survey. This is not expected, given the assumptions in Appendix 1. A conclusion is that the assumptions of equal variances of the perception functions and of a negotiated price at the mean of μ_1 and μ_2 are of doubtful validity.

Alternatively, we consider the joint probability density function (p.d.f.) regarding the negotiated price. It is assumed that the negotiated log-prices correspond to the maximum joint probability density. The joint p.d.f. implies the following likelihood function of the negotiated log-prices:

$$L = \prod_{i=1}^{N} n(\ln P_i \; ; \mu_1, \sigma_1) \, n(\ln P_i \; ; \mu_2, \sigma_2)$$

with $n(.)$ the normal density function. Maximizing L with respect to its parameters results in the following estimator of the negotiated log-price:

$$\ln P = (\sigma_1^2 \mu_2 + \sigma_2^2 \mu_1) / (\sigma_1^2 + \sigma_2^2)$$

This maximum likelihood (*ML*) estimator does not require equality of σ_1 and σ_2. However, if σ_1 equals σ_2, the *ML* estimator equals the expression obtained by using the buy-response curve. Since for each observation in the survey we have information about the perceived probability function of only one of the negotiators, the negotiated log-price cannot be predicted directly. It is possible, however, to estimate the mean values of μ_2^* and σ_2^* for the sellers and the mean values of μ_1^* and σ_1^* for the buyers by using the *ML* estimator. This amounts to running the following regressions:

sellers: $\ln P = \mu_2^* + \sigma_2^{*2}(\mu_1 - \ln P)/\sigma_1^2$

buyers: $\ln P = \mu_1^* + \sigma_1^{*2}(\mu_2 - \ln P)/\sigma_2^2$

where μ and σ denote the estimated values in Table 15.2. The estimated values of these parameters are shown in Table 15.6. The μ parameters in Table 15.6 are slightly different from those in Table 15.2, whereas the σ parameters are much smaller.

Table 15.5 A test of equality of μ_1 and μ_1^* and of σ_1 and σ_2

	μ	$\ln\sigma$
Constant	0.601 (0.903)	2.664 (2.055)
Log-price	0.967 (0.074)**	-0.483 (0.169)**
Dummy (seller/buyer)	-0.178 (0.095)*	-0.498 (0.217)**
R^2	0.637	0.087
Number of observations	104	104

Notes: Standard errors of the parameters in parentheses.
    ** Significant at the 5% level. * Significant at the 10% level.

Regarding μ, the analysis in Table 15.5 is repeated in Table 15.7. Regarding σ, it is not significant to repeat the analysis because the parameters are too different. It appears that μ_1 (for sellers) is not significantly different from μ_1^* (for buyers) and μ_2 (for buyers) is not significantly different from μ_2^* (for sellers) since the dummy variables in Table 15.7 are not statistically significant.

Table 15.6 Maximum likelihood estimators of μ_1^*, σ_1^*, μ_2^* and σ_2^*

	Sellers	Buyers
μ_2^*	11.932 (0.073)	
σ_2^*	0.007 (0.005)	
μ_1^*		12.117 (0.116)
σ_1^*		0.011 (0.013)

Note: Standard errors of the parameters in parentheses.

Table 15.7 A test of equality of μ_1 and μ_1^* (ML estimators)

	μ_1	μ_2
Constant	5.939 (0.605)**	5.660 (0.614)**
Log-price	0.510 (0.050)**	0.518 (0.050)**
Dummy (seller/buyer)	-0.063 (0.064)	0.072 (0.065)
R^2	0.514	0.501
Number of observations	104	104

Notes: Standard errors of the parameters in parentheses.
　　　** Significant at the 5% level.

CONCLUSIONS

The economic-psychological approach in this chapter has been substantiated by survey data regarding actual negotiations on the sale of a house. The market power of buyers and sellers has been estimated by the perceived probability functions regarding the acceptability of a price to the other party. The result of negotiations on average is as expected from these perception functions. Several contextual variables influence the location and the shape parameters of the perception functions. The influence of a real estate agent on the location of the buyer's perception function is to increase the perceived probability that a given price will be accepted by the seller. This has a moderating effect on the negotiated price. The seller's perception function is not influenced by the use of a real estate agent. According to the theory, the bargaining power of sellers is not increased by the

Gerrit Antonides

use of real estate agents. The duration of the negotiations has a negative influence on the seller's perceived probability that a price will be accepted by the buyer. This influences their bargaining position. The location of the buyer's perception function is also influenced by the number of rejected options. The more houses that have been considered the greater the perceived probability that a price will be accepted by the seller. This will have a moderating effect on the negotiated price, too. The buyer's use of a real estate agent, the availability of an appraisal value and the number of rejected options also tend to increase the perceived range of prices that are acceptable to the seller.

Since these factors increase the buyer's knowledge of the market, this result indicates that market information tends to increase the likelihood of a sale. A conclusion is that buyers will benefit from the use of a real estate agent, from deliberate choice including the rejection of a number of options and from the availability of an appraisal value of the house. As a general result, it appears that the higher the price of a house, the lower the probability that a given bid price will be accepted. Furthermore, the higher the price the smaller the seller's perceived range of prices that are acceptable to the buyer. According to the theory, this tends to decrease the likelihood of a sale.

Gabor and Granger's theory about the acceptability of consumer prices (1966) has been applied to the acceptability of a given price to both parties involved in the sale of a house. The assumptions implied by this theory turn out to be unwarranted in the case of two negotiation parties each with a different shape of the perceived probability function regarding the acceptability to the other party of a given price. Alternatively, a maximum likelihood estimator of the negotiated price has been derived based on the perceived probability functions. This estimator does not include the strong assumptions made by Gabor and Granger (1966). Since information from only one negotiation party is available in the survey, only partial support for the validity of the maximum likelihood estimator has been obtained.

ACKNOWLEDGEMENTS

Grateful acknowledgements are due to Ronald Kornaat and Willy Schiebel for creating the dataset. The author thanks Susanne Wollin and Wim Niesing for their comments on an earlier draft of this chapter.

REFERENCES

Adams, J. S. (1965). Inequity in social exchange. In L. Berkowitz (ed.), *Advances in experimental psychology. Volume 2.* New York: Academic Press. Pp.267-299.

Aitchison, J. & Brown, J. A. C. (1960). *The lognormal distribution.* London: Cambridge University Press.

Antonides, G. (forthcoming). *Psychology for economists.*

Festinger, L. (1954). A theory of social comparison processes. *Human Relations,* **7**, 117-140.

Fisher, R. & Ury, W. (1981). *Getting to yes: Negotiating agreement without giving in.* Boston: Houghton Mifflin.

Gabor, A. & Granger, C. W. J. (1966). Price as an indicator of quality: Report on an enquiry. *Economica,* **46**, 43-70.

Granger, C. W. J. (1988). Appendix. In A. Gabor, *Pricing.* Cambridge: Cambridge University Press.

Komorita, S. S. (1984). Coalition bargaining. In L. Berkowitz (ed.), *Advances in experimental social psychology. Volume 18.* New York: Academic Press. Pp.183-245.

Murnighan, J. K. (1978). Models of coalition behavior: Game theoretic, social psychological and political perspectives. *Psychological Bulletin,* **85**, 1130-1153.

Nash, J. F. (1950). The bargaining problem. *Econometrica,* **18**, 155-162.

Nash, J. F. (1953). Two-person cooperative games. *Econometrica,* **21**, 128-140.

Raiffa, H. (1982). *The art and science of negotiation.* Cambridge, MA: Harvard University Press.

Shapley, L. S. (1953). A value for n-person games. In H. W. Kuhn & A. W. Tucker (Eds), *Contributions to the theory of games. Volume 2.* Princeton NJ: Princeton University Press.

Shapley, L. S. & Shubik, M. (1954). Method for evaluating the distribution of power in a committee system. *American Political Science Review,* **48**, 787-792.

Sondak, H. & Bazerman, M. H. (1989). Matching and negotiation processes in quasi-markets. *Organizational Behavior and Human Decision Processes,* **44**, 261-280.

APPENDIX 1

Derivation of the price expectation from the buy-response curve

$L(P)$ denotes the seller's perception of the probability that the buyer will accept the price. $H(p)$ denotes the buyer's perception of the probability that the seller will accept the price. These probability functions are assumed to be lognormal. $L(P) = 1-N(\ln P; \mu_1, \sigma_1)$, $H(P) = N(\ln P; \mu_2, \sigma_2)$.

The function $B(P) = 1-L(P)-H(P)$ is not a probability density function, since it may take negative values and integration over $(-\infty,\infty)$ does not yield the value one. It can be shown that, if μ_1 is not equal to μ_2 and $\sigma_1=\sigma_2=\sigma$, $b(P) = B(P)/(\mu_2-\mu_1)$ is a probability density function with expectation $(\mu_1+\mu_2)/2$ and variance $\sigma^2+(\mu_2-\mu_1)^2/12$. (The variance derived in Gabor & Granger, 1966 and Granger, 1988 contains a small error.) Apparently, the expected log-price is the mean of the location parameters of buyer's and seller's perceived probability distributions.

APPENDIX 2

Survey questions (The variable names correspond with those in Table 15.1.)

Questions for sellers	Answer	Variable
'Please state your original asking price'.	Dfl.....	P1
'What did you think about the probability that you can/could sell your house for this price? (100% = almost sure, 0% = absolutely uncertain)'	.....%	L(P1)
'What do you think is the average price one would pay for the house?'	Dfl.....	P2

'What is the lowest price at which you would have sold/would sell the house?'	Dfl.....	P3
'What did you think about the probability that you can/could sell your house for this minimum price?'	.....%	L(P3)
'Please state the selling-price.'	Dfl.....	P

Questions for buyers	Answer	Variable
'Please state your original (first) bid.'	Dfl.....	P4
'What did you think about the probability that you can/could buy the house for this price? (100% = almost sure, 0% = absolutely uncertain)'	.....%	H(P4)
'What do you think is the average price one would pay for the house?'	Dfl.....	P5
'What is the highest price at which you would have purchased/would purchase the house?'	Dfl.....	P6
'What did you think about the probability that you can/could buy the house for this maximum price?'	.....%	H(P6)
'Please state the selling-price.'	Dfl.....	P

Author Index

Subject Index